Hezekiah Butterworth

A Zigzag Journey in the Sunny South

Hezekiah Butterworth

A Zigzag Journey in the Sunny South

ISBN/EAN: 9783744799072

Printed in Europe, USA, Canada, Australia, Japan

Cover: Foto ©Andreas Hilbeck / pixelio.de

More available books at **www.hansebooks.com**

IN THE

SUNNY SOUTH;

OR,

WONDER TALES OF EARLY AMERICAN HISTORY.

BY

HEZEKIAH BUTTERWORTH.

A VISIT TO THE SCENES AND ASSOCIATIONS OF THE EARLY AMERICAN SETTLEMENTS IN THE SOUTHERN STATES AND THE WEST INDIES.

FULLY ILLUSTRATED.

BOSTON:
ESTES AND LAURIAT
301-305 WASHINGTON STREET.
1887.

Copyright, 1886,
BY ESTES AND LAURIAT.

All Rights Reserved.

PREFACE.

HIS *mélange* of historical and dialect stories is intended to direct the attention of young people to the romances of the South, and to suggest literary and historic studies relating to the Gulf States and the Islands of the Southern Cross. The narrative takes one to Florida and the islands first visited by Columbus.

The writer is indebted to his friends for several interpolated sketches and stories, — among them, to Mrs. HARRIET PRESCOTT SPOFFORD, Mr. JAMES PARTON, PAUL H. HAYNE, Mrs. MARIE B. WILLIAMS, Mrs. MARY E. C. WYETH, and the late "SHERWOOD BONNER."

The volume has grown out of courses of reading which the writer took to prepare him for a winter excursion to Jacksonville, Tampa, and Havana, and follows the course of the other Zigzag books in picturing countries by stories.

H. B.

28 WORCESTER STREET, BOSTON

CONTENTS.

Chapter		Page
I.	Strange Stories	15
II.	How to visit Cuba. — A Romance of North Carolina	56
III.	The Old Red Settle and an Evening of Merry Provincial Stories	82
IV.	Some Strange Historic Stories	106
V.	The Old Red Settle goes South	144
VI.	Charleston, and the Stories of William Gilmore Simms	170
VII.	Beautiful Savannah, and Southward	180
VIII.	Story-telling at St. Augustine	206
IX.	Funny Tales of the Negro Cabins. — The St. John's River	233
X.	The Isle of June	253
XI.	Old Hispaniola	278
XII.	Columbus's own Stories of New Spain	290
XIII.	At the Tomb of Colon. — The Mississippi	306

ILLUSTRATIONS.

	PAGE		PAGE
Old Times in St. Augustine . .	*Frontispiece*	Washington's House at Mount Vernon .	166
In the Heart of Florida	17	Washington's Grave at Mount Vernon .	167
Jesuit Mission in Florida	21	Charleston	171
Indians in Flight	29	Sumter	173
Admiral Gaspard de Coligny	39	Marion	175
Massacre of the Huguenots at Fort Caroline	43	Pickens	178
		Oglethorpe with the Indians .	181
The French discovering the Remains of the Ribaut Expedition	47	Savannah Harbor	183
		Fountain in Forsyth Park, Savannah .	184
Landing of Columbus	52	View of Jacksonville Harbor	186
Statue of Columbus	54	Natural Forest	187
Havana	57	Water-carrier	191
George II	61	In the Everglades	199
Charles Edward	69	Scene on the St. John's River	203
The Emigrant's House in the Clearing .	72	The Auction	209
Arrest of Charles Edward . . .	73	The Boy Promises	214
"Us Chilluns"	80	Scene in Martinique	218
The Old Red Settle	83	In the Heart of Georgia	227
The Scarecrow	90	Ancient Negro Burial-places . .	229
The Barn Theatricals	97	Mouth of the St. John's	235
Look Aloft	98	"She done clomb up de chimney!" .	239
English and Dutch Quarrels	101	"I found tree geese"	241
Fight between a Settler and Indian Chief	109	Negro Village in Georgia . . .	248
Indian Attack on Settlers	115	Ascending the River	249
Alexander carried a Prisoner to Plymouth	119	Nassau	254
Destruction of Pequots	125	Royal Victoria Hotel, Nassau	256
Mrs. Rowlandson and her Captors .	129	The Natives	257
Philip's Head brought to Plymouth . .	133	A Planter's House	261
Treaty of Peace with Indians . . .	139	Columbus nearing the Islands	267
Capitol at Washington	145	Friendly Indians dealing with the Voyagers	271
George Washington	149	
Governor Spotswood on the Blue Ridge	157	Avenue of Palms	279
Wives for the Settlers	163	Santiago de Cuba	282

ILLUSTRATIONS.

	PAGE		PAGE
View of Cienfuegos	286	Settling in the New Land	303
The Young Women waving Palm Branches	288	Cathedral of Havana	307
		A Negro Family	309
Scene in San Domingo	291	Jesuit Mission	313
Exploring the Islands	299	Murder of La Salle	317

A ZIGZAG JOURNEY

IN THE

SUNNY SOUTH.

A ZIGZAG JOURNEY

IN THE

SUNNY SOUTH.

―――•―――

CHAPTER I.

STRANGE STORIES.

"HE romance of North American history lies largely in the South."

The remark was made by Mr. Charles Laurens to Charlie Leland on the piazza of an old New England tavern at Lakeville, Mass. Mr. Laurens was a native of St. Augustine, Fla., a gentleman of means and fine historic tastes. He and his wife and son were spending the summer in Massachusetts, at the old historic towns of Plymouth, Duxbury, and Middleborough.

Lakeville is a part of Old Middleborough. Mr. Laurens had been led hither by the Indian associations and traditions of Assawamsett Lake, a calm expanse of water that lay directly in front of the hotel. On the shores of this lake is the old Winslow Reservation; and here live the descendants of Massasoit, the good sachem who protected the infant colony of Plymouth for nearly forty years.

Mr. Laurens had brought with him, on this visit to the North, his son Henry, a lad of about sixteen years, hoping to stimulate his historic taste. There were a number of summer boarders at the hotel. Among these were Mr. Leland and his own son Charlie, a lad of whom some account has been given in a former volume of this series. Mr. Leland was a Boston gentleman and a representative business man, as Mr. Laurens was a worthy representative of the culture of the South. The two gentlemen became friendly, and their sons, Charlie Leland and Henry Laurens, intimate.

"I supposed it was the North that was the fuller of stories and legends," said Charlie Leland to Mr. Laurens.

"Not of the picturesque and romantic kind," said Mr. Leland.

"Who are some of the heroes of the Southern romances?" asked Charlie.

"Well, first, Columbus."

"But Columbus did not visit our shores."

"No; but the Antilles, the scene of the most romantic voyage ever foreseen by faith and made by man, are in America and in the Sea of the South. The bones of Columbus lie in Havana."

"They ought to find their last resting-place beneath the rotunda of our National Capitol," said Mr. Leland.

"I could not now more than begin to enumerate the Southern romances," continued Mr. Laurens: "as, for example, the Spanish voyages of discovery; the search for the Seven Cities of Gold and the Fountain of Youth; Ponce de Leon; De Soto; La Salle; the Huguenots; the Spanish legends of St. Augustine and Mobilea; the poetic episodes of Sir Walter Raleigh; Bienville; Iberville; Oglethorpe; Flora Macdonald; Pulaski; Lord Fairfax and the boyhood of Washington; grand Lord Baltimore; Marion and his men; Greene in South Carolina; Moultrie; Tarleton; Cornwallis; Balfour; John and Charles Wesley's visit; the preaching of Whitefield. Pardon me; only a few of the old romances come to my mind now. The South has found no true historian; and with the exception of William Gilmore Simms, no one who has written in sympathy her

IN THE HEART OF FLORIDA.

picturesque eras and heroic people. Southern history is a long poetic procession, going on for more than three hundred years."

"I never dreamed that the South was associated with such names," said Charlie. "I knew it as mere history lesson, but I never so pictured it in my mind before."

"There are two sections of our country," said Mr. Leland, "that the true historian and the poet have but half touched. One is the vast empire of the Southern States, and the other is Rhode Island."

"Little Rhode Island?" asked Charlie, incredulously.

"Yes."

"But why, father?"

"I will give you a few points after the manner of my good friend Mr. Laurens: the Northmen; Verrazano; Bishop Berkeley; Massasoit; Roger Williams under the protection of Massasoit at Mount Hope; King ·Philip; Anne Hutchinson; Sir Henry Vane and Williams; the Antinomians; the first Baptists; the proclamation of liberty of the conscience and freedom of the soul, — a principle that has made America what she is, and that has revolutionized Europe, and has just been promulgated in India; the Revolutionary romances; Greene; Barton; Prescott; — but I, too, will stop. It is a tremendous history for so small a territory; there ought to be a history of Rhode Island written in the spirit and coloring of Hawthorne's 'Twice Told Tales.'"

"The tales of the Massachusetts Bay Colony and of Plymouth have been twice told, and many times told," said Mr. Laurens. "The world knows them, while the equally noble stories of other colonies and parts of the country have scarcely been told at all. History is dumb until it finds a poet, or what is the same thing, a poetic historian. The whole world knows Germany, because her heroes, her lakes, rivers, and mountains, her trades and occupations, have all found a poet. It is the land of song."

"I wish," said Charlie Leland to Mr. Laurens, "that you would tell us some of the old tales of the South that are not generally known."

"I think," said Henry, "that the most delightful stories of the South for boys and girls are those that are never printed at all, — the half-fairy tales and stories of old family history as related in the old negro cabins."

Charlie Leland looked surprised.

"The negroes are the natural story-tellers of the South," said Mr. Laurens. "A story, to fill the imagination of the young, must have a flavor of superstition and mystery. The negro is superstitious to such a degree as to lend a lively coloring to the most homely romance."

"When I was a little boy," said Henry, "I always used to go to the negro cabins for my stories. Father never could interest me; but old Moxon, the revivalist preacher, could."

"I used to belong to a society at school called the Zigzag Club," said Charlie Leland. "It had for its object the telling of legendary and historic stories, and afterward the visiting of the places associated with these stories. Why could not we form a little society, for the few days that we are to be together, for the telling of stories, — strange stories of the North and South, stories but little known out of the sections where they occurred?"

"Provincialisms," said Mr. Laurens.

"Would you not oblige us by telling some of the stories of the South that you have suggested?"

"Thank you for the compliment. My son has just said that I could never interest him in telling a story; but I will agree to tell a story of Southern life, historical or social, or even of the old negro cabins, for every story that you tell me of your own delightful region. How will that do?"

"I think, perhaps, that father should answer that question for me."

"I will do my best," said Mr. Leland.

JESUIT MISSION IN FLORIDA.

" And you, Henry ? "

" I will relate as many stories of the South as you will of the North, as many of St. Augustine as you of the region about the Middleborough lakes, even if I have to resort to old Moxon's bugaboos, as father used to call them."

" Let us call ourselves the Assawamsett Club, and begin our story-telling this evening. Could we not meet on the piazza for story-telling every evening, immediately after supper ? "

Mr. Laurens smiled approvingly; and thus began on the piazza of the old tavern some agreeable story-telling which ended in a journey which it is the purpose of this book to describe, — a journey from Plymouth to the tomb of Colon at Havana, by the way of the Southern seaboard cities, and the St. John's River through Florida.

It was June, the time of the most delightful days of the Northern climate. The daylight does not fade out of the crimson sky until nearly nine o'clock in the evening. The hours of the lingering light are full of long shadows, and comfortably cool; they are the pleasantest hours that can be spent on the piazza of a Northern hotel.

Great orchards shaded the landscape around the Lakeville inn. The lake was surrounded with woods. It was full of sunshine in the long June days; and when the full moon rose upon it, it seemed a mirror. The ospreys wheeled over it and screamed in the noonday sunshine, and the night-hawks or whippoorwills made sad the groves with their notes through half the nights.

The road in front of the inn was old, protected by gray stone walls, and followed provincial curves and zigzags. In the evening the quiet old country town seemed like dreamland; for here perished the Indian tribes of old, and their graves are here, and the shells of their feasts and the arrows of their warfare fill the soil.

The first meeting of the Assawamsett Club found an audience that filled the piazza. The club was organized with seven members, — Mr. and Mrs. Laurens and their son, Mr. Leland and Charlie, a stately old lady named Endicott, and an old Middleborough farmer named Felix; both the latter had the reputation of being "antiquarians" and good story-tellers. Their membership had been suggested by the people of the hotel.

The purpose of the club was announced to be "The Telling of Provincial Stories, North and South."

There was but one article to the Club's verbal constitution, "*That only stories that are strange shall be told.*"

This article was Charlie Leland's suggestion. By "strange" he meant, we suppose, such stories as are generally unfamiliar, that have not been the subjects of romances, poems, and boys' books, and that have an original stamp and coloring.

The Club was ready for a story.

Who should begin?

Mr. Leland suggested Mr. Laurens, but he was not quite prepared.

Mr. Laurens suggested Mr. Leland.

"Not prepared."

They both suggested Mr. Felix.

"Not quite ready."

Then Mrs. Laurens suggested Mrs. Endicott, — "the Widder Endicott," she was called in Middleborough.

The Widow Endicott raised her gold-bowed spectacles in a very self-possessed way.

"A strange story?" said she.

"Yes," — "yes," — "yes."

"Well, you good Southern people have come to the right region for strange stories. This place was first all full of Indians, then of witches and ghosts, and then of patriots. But I have n't any story to tell."

"Tell the one about the Powder-Candle," said Felix.

"Well, Felix, as all the rest seem to have backed down at the very start, and as somebody must begin, else where will the Club end, I will do the best I can. Strange that you should fix upon me!"

The widow gave her gold-bowed spectacles another push, and said:

MY GRANDMOTHER'S GRANDMOTHER'S CHRISTMAS CANDLE.

There were no Christmas celebrations in my old Puritan home in Swansea, such as we have in all New England homes to-day. No church bells rung out in the darkening December air; there were no children's carols learned in Sunday-schools; no presents, and not even a sprig of box, ivy, or pine in any window. Yet there was one curious custom in the old town that made Christmas Eve in many homes the merriest in the year.

It was the burning of the Christmas candle; and of this old, forgotten custom of provincial towns I have an odd story to tell.

The Christmas candle? You may never have heard of it. You may fancy that it was some beautiful image in wax or like an altar-light. This was not the case. It was a candle containing a quill filled with gunpowder, and its burning excited an intense interest while we waited for the expected explosion.

I well remember Dipping-Candle Day; it was a very interesting day to me in my girlhood, because it was then that the Christmas candle was dipped.

It usually came in the fall, in the short, lonesome days of November, just before the new schoolmaster opened the winter term of the school.

My grandmother brought down from the garret her candle-rods and poles. The candle-rods were light sticks of elder, some fifty in number, and the poles were long pine bars. These poles were tied two each to two chairs; and the rods, after they had been wicked, were laid upon them at short distances apart.

"Wicking the candle-rods" is a phrase of which few people to-day know the meaning. Every country-store in old times contained a large supply of balls of cotton candle-wick. This wick was to be cut, put upon the candle-rods, twisted, and tallowed or waxed, so as to be convenient for dipping.

How many times have I seen my grandmother, on the long November evenings, wicking her candle-rods! She used to do the work, sitting in her easy-chair before the great open fire. One side of the fireplace was usually hung with strings of dried or partly dried apples, and the other with strings of red peppers. Over the fireplace were a gun and the almanac; and on the hearth there were usually, in the evening, a few sweet apples roasting; and at one end of it was the dog, and at the other the cat.

Dipping candles would seem a comical sight to-day. My grandmother used to sit over a great iron kettle of melted tallow, and patiently dip the wicks on the rods into it, until they grew to the size of candles. Each rod contained about five wicks, and these were dipped together. The process was repeated perhaps fifty or more times.

A quill of powder was tied to the wick of the Christmas candle before dipping, and the wick was so divided at the lower end that the candle should have three legs. The young people took a great interest in the dipping as well as the burning of the Christmas candle.

My grandmother's candle-rods had belonged to her grandmother, who had lived in the early days of the Plymouth Colony. They had been used since the days of King Philip's War.

There was a story of the dark times of the Indian war that my grandmother used to relate on the night that we burned our Christmas candle, — a story that my grandmother told of her grandmother, and of the fortunate and timely explosion of one of that old lady's Christmas candles in the last days of Philip's War, when the sight of a hostile Indian was a terror to the unarmed colonist.

"It was well that candle went off when it did," my grandmother used to say. "If it had not, I don't know where any of us would have been to-night; not here, telling riddles and roasting apples and enjoying ourselves, I imagine. I have dipped a powder-candle every season since, not that I believe much in keeping holidays, but because a powder-candle once saved the family."

She continued her story: —

"My grandmother was a widow in her last years. She had two children, Benjamin and my mother, Mary. She lived at Pocasset, and the old house overlooked Mount Hope and the bay. Pocasset was an Indian province then, and its Indian queen was named Wetamoo.

"My grandmother was a great-hearted woman. She had a fair amount of property, and she used it for the good of her less fortunate neighbors. She had kept several poor old people from the town-house by giving them a home with her. Her good deeds caused her to be respected by every one.

"The Indians were friendly to her. She had done them so many acts of kindness that even the haughty Wetamoo had once called to see her and made her a present. The old house was near an easy landing-place for boats on the bay; and the Indians, as they came from their canoes, passed through the yard, and often stopped to drink from the well. It was no uncommon thing, on a hot summer's day, to find an Indian asleep in the street or under the dooryard trees.

"Among the great men of the tribe was an Indian named Squammaney; Warmmesley he was sometimes called, also Warnmesley-Squammaney. He was a giant in form, but his greatness among his people arose from his supposed magical power and his vigorous voice. It was believed that he could whoop and bellow so loud and long as to frighten away evil spirits from the sick, so that the patient would recover. All the Indians regarded old Squammaney with fear and awe, and he was very proud of his influence over them.

"When an Indian fell sick, Warmmesley-Squammaney was called to the bedside. If old Warmmesley could not drive the evil spirits away, the patient believed that he must die.

"Squammaney did his supposed duty in such cases. He was a faithful doctor. He covered himself with dried skins, shells, and feathers, and approached the hut of the patient with as mysterious and lofty an air as one of the old-time physicians of the gig and saddle-bags. As he drew near the hut, he would rattle the dried skins, and howl. He would look cautiously into the hut, then run away from it a little distance, leap into the air, and howl. Then he would cautiously return; and if the case were a bad one, he would again run away, leap into the air, and howl. At last he would enter the hut, examine the sick man or woman, and utter mysterious cries. He would fix the mind of the sufferer entirely upon himself by a kind of mesmeric influence; then he would begin to move in a circle around the patient, shaking the dried skins and beads, bobbing his plumes, and chanting an Indian ditty. Gradually his movements would become more swift; he would howl and leap, his voice rising higher at every bound; he would continue this performance until he fell down all in a heap, like a tent of dried skins. But by this time the mind of the patient was usually so withdrawn from his sufferings as to quite forget them; and consequently it often happened that the invalid and old Warmmesley-Squammaney rose up together, and indulged in hand-shaking, thus concluding an exhibition of some of the remarkable effects of mesmeric influence, which were possible in those old times as well as now.

"In his peculiar way old Warmmesley once cured of rheumatism a Puritan deacon who rewarded him by calling him a 'pagan.' The deacon had been confined to his room for weeks. Some Indians called to see him, and pitying his condition, set off in great haste for Warmmesley. The latter came, in his dried skins, with his head bristling with horns and feathers. The astonished deacon forgot his infirmities at the first sight of the terrible object; and as soon as Warmmesley began to leap and howl, and shake his beads, shells, and dried skins, the white man leaped from his bed, and running to the barn, knelt down and began to pray. There his wife found him.

"'It is old Warmmesley,' said she.

"'The old pagan!' said he, rising up. 'What was it, Ruth, that was the matter with me?'

"My grandmother had caught the spirit of Eliot, the Indian Apostle, and she used to hold in the old kitchen a religious meeting, each week, for the instruction of the 'praying Indians' of the town. The Indians who became Christians were called 'praying Indians' by their own people, and came to be so called by the English. Among the Indians who came out of curiosity was the beautiful Princess Amie, the youngest daughter of the great chief Massasoit, who protected Plymouth Colony for nearly forty years.

"Warmmesley came once to my grandmother's meetings, and tried to sing. He wished to out-sing the rest, and he did, repeating over and over again, —

"'He lub poor Indian in de wood,
An' me lub God, and dat be good;
I'll praise him two times mo'!'

"Just before the beginning of the Indian war, my grandmother offended Warmmesley. The English had taught him bad habits, and he had become a cider-drinker. He used to wander about the country, going from farm-house to farm-house, begging for 'hard' cider, as old cider was called.

"One day my grandmother found him lying intoxicated under a tree in the yard, and she forbade the giving of Warmmesley any more cider from the cellar. A few days afterward, he landed from his canoe in front of the grounds, and came to the workmen for cider. The workmen sent him to my grandmother.

"'No, Warmmesley, no more,' said she, firmly. 'Steal your wits. Wicked!'

"Warmmesley begged for one porringer, — just one.

"'Me sick,' he pleaded.

"'No, Warmmesley. Never. Wrong.'

"'Me pay you!' said he, with an evil look in his eye. 'Me pay you!'

"Just then a flock of crows flew past. Warmmesley pointed to them and said, —

"'It's coming — fight — look up there! Ugh, ugh!' — pointing to the crows. 'Fight English. Look over' — pointing to the bay — 'fight, fight — me pay you! Ugh! Ugh!'

INDIANS IN FLIGHT.

"My grandmother pointed up to the blue sky, as much as to say that her trust was in a higher power than man's.

"Warmmesley turned away reluctantly, looking back with a half-threatening, half-questioning look, and saying, 'Ugh! Ugh!' He evidently hoped that my grandmother would call him back, but she was firm.

"The upper windows of the old house overlooked the bay.

"It was fall. The maples flamed, and the oak leaves turned to gold and dust; the flocks of birds gathered, and went their unknown way. The evenings were long. It was harvest time. The full moon rose in the twilight, and the harvesters continued their labors into the night.

"Philip, or Pometacom, was now at Mount Hope, and Wetamoo had taken up her residence on the high shores of Pocasset. The hills of Pocasset were in full view of Mount Hope; and between lay the quiet, sheltered waters of the bay. Philip had cherished a strong friendship for Wetamoo, who was the widow of his brother Alexander.

"Night after night the harvesters had noticed canoes crossing and recrossing the bay, moving like shadows silently to and fro. The moon waned; the nights became dark and cloudy; the movement across the water went on; the boats carried torches now, and the dark bay became picturesque as the mysterious lines of light were drawn across it.

"From time to time a great fire would blaze up near the high rocks at Mount Hope, burn a few hours, and then fade.

"It was whispered about among the English that Philip was holding war-dances, and that Wetamoo and her warriors were attending them; yet Philip had just concluded a treaty of peace with the English, and Wetamoo professed to be a friend to the Colony.

"War came on the following summer, stealthily at first. Englishmen were found murdered mysteriously in the towns near Mount Hope. Then came the killing of the people in Swansea as they were going home from church, about which all the histories of the Colonies tell; then the open war.

"Philip flashed like a meteor from place to place, murdering the people and burning their houses. No one could tell where he would next appear, or who would be his next victim. Every colonist during the year 1675, wherever he might be, lived in terror of lurking foes. There were dreadful cruelties everywhere, and towns and farm-houses vanished in smoke.

"Wetamoo joined Philip. She had some six hundred warriors. Philip had made her believe that the English had poisoned her husband Alexander, who was also his brother, and who had succeeded the good Massasoit. Alexander had died suddenly while returning from Plymouth on the Taunton River. The mysterious lights on the bay were now explained.

"Before Wetamoo joined Philip, one of her captains had sent word to my grandmother that as she had been a friend to the Indians, she should be protected.

"'I have only one fear,' said my grandmother often, during that year of terror, — 'Warmmesley.'

"Warmmesley-Squammaney had gone away with Philip's braves under Wetamoo. He was one of Wetamoo's captains. Wetamoo herself had joined Philip, like a true warrior-queen.

"The sultry August of 1676 brought a sense of relief to the Colonies. The warriors of Philip were defeated on every hand. His wife and son were captured; and broken-hearted he returned to Mount Hope — the burial-ground of his race for unknown generations — to die. Wetamoo, too, became a fugitive, and was drowned in attempting to cross to the lovely hills of Pocasset on a raft.

"The war ended. Where was Warmmesley-Squammaney? No one knew. Annawon, Philip's great captain, had been captured, and nearly all the principal leaders of the war were executed; but old Squammaney had mysteriously disappeared.

"Peace came. October flamed, as Octobers flame, and November faded, as Novembers fade, and the snows of December fell. The Colonies were full of joy and thanksgivings.

"'I am thankful for one thing more than all others,' said my grandmother on Thanksgiving Day; 'and that is that I am now sure that old Squammaney is gone where he will never trouble us again. I shall never forget his evil eye as he said, "I will pay you!" It has troubled me night and day.'

"That fall, when my grandmother was dipping candles, she chanced to recall the old custom of the English town from which she had come, of making a powder-candle for Christmas. The spirit of merry-making was abroad upon the return of peace; and she prepared one of these curious candles, and told her family that they might invite the neighbors' children on Christmas Eve to see it burn and explode. The village schoolmaster, Silas Sloan, was living at the old house; and he took the liberty to invite the school, which consisted of some ten boys and girls.

"Christmas Eve came, — a clear, still night, with a white earth and shining sky. Some twenty or more people, young and old, gathered in the great kitchen to see the Christmas candle 'go off.' During the early part of the evening 'Si'

Sloan entertained the company with riddles. Then my grandmother brought in the Christmas candle, an odd-looking object, and set it down on its three legs. She lighted it, blew out the other candles, and asked Silas to tell a story.

"Silas was glad of the opportunity to entertain such an audience. The story that he selected for this novel occasion was awful in the extreme, such as was usually told in those times before the great kitchen fires.

"Silas — 'Si,' as he was called — was relating an account of a so-called haunted house, where, according to his silly narrative, the ghost of an Indian used to appear at the foot of an old woman's bed; and some superstitious people declared that the old lady one night, on awaking and finding the ghostly Indian present, put out her foot to push him away, and pushed her foot directly *through him*. What a brave old lady she must have been, and how uncomfortable it must have been for the ghost! — But at this point of Silas's foolish story, the dog suddenly started up and began to howl.

"The children, who were so highly excited over Si's narrative that they hardly dared to breathe, clung to one another with trembling hands as the dog sent up his piercing cry. Even Si himself started. The dog seemed listening.

"The candle was burning well. The children now watched it in dead silence.

"A half-hour passed. The candle was burning within an inch of the quill, and all eyes were bent upon it. If the candle 'sputtered,' the excitement became intense. 'I think it will go off in ten minutes now,' said my grandmother.

"There was a noise in the yard. All heard it distinctly. The dog dashed round the room, howled, and stopped to listen at the door.

"People who relate so-called ghost stories are often cowardly, and it is usually a cowardly nature that seeks to frighten children. Si Sloan was no exception to the rule.

"The excitement of the dog at once affected Silas. His tall, thin form moved about the room cautiously and mysteriously. He had a way of spreading apart his fingers when he was frightened, and his fingers were well apart now.

"A noise in the yard at night was not an uncommon thing, but the peculiar cry of the dog and the excited state of the company caused this to be noticed. My grandmother arose at last, and amid dead silence opened the shutter.

"'I think that there is some one in the cider-mill,' said she.

"She looked toward the candle, and, feeling confident that some minutes would elapse before the explosion, she left the room, and went upstairs, and there looked from the window.

"From the window she could see in the moonlight Mount Hope, where Philip had so recently been killed, and also the arm of the bay, where Wetamoo had perished. She could see the bay itself, and must have remembered the lights that a year before had so often danced over it at night. She lingered there a moment. Then she called,—

"'Silas — Silas Sloan!'

"Silas hurried up the stairs.

"They both came down in a few minutes. Silas's face was as white as the snow.

"'What is it?' the children whispered.

"There was another painful silence. Grandmother seemed to have forgotten the candle. All eyes were turned to her face.

"Then followed a sound that sent the blood from every face. It was as if a log had been dashed against the door. The door flew open, and in stalked two Indians. One of them was Warmmesley-Squammaney.

"'Ugh!' said Warmmesley.

"'What do you want?' demanded my grandmother.

"'Me pay you now!— Old Squammaney pay you. Cider!'

"He sat down by the fire, close to the candle. The other Indian stood by his chair, as though awaiting his orders. The young children began to cry, and Silas shook like a man with the palsy.

"'Me pay you!— Me remember! Ugh!' said Squammaney. 'Braves all gone. Me have revenge— Old Squammaney die hard. Ugh! Ugh!'

"The door was still partly open, and the wind blew into the room. It caused the candle to flare up and to burn rapidly.

"Squammaney warmed his hands. Occasionally he would turn his head slowly, with an evil look in his black eye, as it swept the company.

"The candle was forgotten. The only thought of each one was what Squammaney intended to do.

"All the tragedies of the war just ended were recalled by the older members of the company. Were there other Indians outside?

"No one dared rise to close the door or to attempt to escape.

"Suddenly Squammaney turned to my grandmother.

"'White squaw get cider. Go — Go!'

"The Indians threw open their blankets. They were armed.

"The sight of these armed warriors caused Silas to shake in a strange manner, and his fear and agitation became so contagious that the children began to tremble and sob. When the sound of distress became violent, Squammaney would sweep the company with his dark eyes, and awe it into a brief silence.

"My grandmother alone was calm.

"She rose, and walked around the room, followed by the eyes of the two Indians.

"As soon as the attention of the Indians, attracted for a moment by the falling of a burnt stick on the hearth, was diverted from her, she whispered to Silas,—

"'Go call the men.'

"The attitude of Silas on receiving this direction, as she recalled it afterward, was comical indeed. His hands were spread out by his side, and his eyes grew white and wild. He attempted to reply in a whisper, but he could only say,—

"'Ba–b–b–ba!'

"Squammaney's eyes again swept the room. Then he bent forward to push back some coals that had rolled out upon the floor.

"'Go call the men,' again whispered my grandmother to Silas; this time sharply.

"'Ba–b–b–b–ba!' His mouth looked like a sheep's. His hands again opened, and his eyes fairly protruded. His form was tall and thin, and he really looked like one of the imaginary spectres about whom he delighted to tell stories on less perilous occasions.

"Squammaney heard Grandmother's whisper, and became suspicious. He rose, his dark form towering in the light of the fire. He put his hand on the table where burned the candle. He turned, and faced my grandmother with an expression of hate and scorn.

"What he intended to do was never known, for just at that moment there was a fearful explosion. It was the powder-candle.

"A stream of fire shot up to the ceiling. Then the room was filled with the smoke of gunpowder. The candle went out; the room was dark.

"'White man come! Run!' my grandmother heard one of the Indians say. There was a sound of scuffling feet; then the door closed with a bang. As the smoke lifted, the light of the fire gradually revealed that the Indians had gone. They evidently thought that they had been discovered, pursued, and that the house was surrounded by soldiers.

"At last my grandmother took a candle from the shelf and lighted it. Silas, too, was gone. Whither? Had the Indians carried him away?

"Late in the evening the neighbors began to come for their children, and were told what had happened. The men of the town were soon under arms. But old Warmmesley-Squammaney was never seen in that neighborhood again, nor was his fate ever known to the towns-people. That was the last fright of the Indian war.

"Silas returned to the school-room the next day, but he never visited the old house again. Whatever may have been his real belief in regard to people of the air, he had resolved never again to put himself under a roof where he would be likely to meet Warmmesley-Squammaney.

"After this strange event two generations of grandmothers continued to burn, on each Christmas Eve, the old powder-candle."

The story of the Powder-Candle suggested stories to other members of the Club. It proved a good illustration of the kind of story the Club might properly seek in this little-visited but very historic region.

"I wish that you would make some plan for us to visit the historic places so near to us," said Mrs. Laurens,— "the places associated with Massasoit and his family, with Roger Williams, and with the pioneers of religious liberty."

"It would give me pleasure not only to show you how to visit such places," said Mr. Leland, "but to accompany you and your family to them, if you will accept the service. This is a good place to begin to study the beginnings of our history."

"We would like to accept your offer," said Mr. Laurens, "but we could do so only on one condition."

"What is that, may I ask?" said Mr. Leland.

"That you will spend a winter with us in Florida, and allow us to accompany you to some of the places of romance and history in the South. Florida is a good place to study the beginnings of history."

"That is an invitation that I would be glad to accept," said Mr. Leland. "I thank you."

"And I," said Charlie, — "I could think of nothing that I would so much like."

"I would take you on a canoe trip on the St. John's," said Henry. "We would there visit the scenes of the Spanish occupation where occurred the massacre of the Huguenots."

"I never heard of the massacre of the Huguenots," said Charlie.

"Then I have a story that I will relate to you," said Mr. Laurens.

"DERNIER VOYAGE AUX INDIES."

A TALE OF FLORIDA.

To me the most interesting stream in Florida is the River St. John. You see on either side the orange groves descending to the water's edge, the strange tropical growths, birds like living flame, butterflies of the intense blue of the sky overhead, — a region so full of light and color, so beautiful both by nature and cultivation, that it is only by an effort you remember the banks of this lovely stream were once stained by a terrible tragedy. I do not know that the chronicle of Captain Jean Ribaut and his companions has ever been translated, but it is from it I draw these incidents.

The French Huguenots, under their leader, Gaspard de Coligny, Admiral of France, fitted out an expedition to found an empire in New France, as the Floridas were then called.

On the 18th of February, 1562, two ships, commanded by Captain Jean Ribaut and Réné Laudonnière, distinguished French officers of marine, set sail from Dieppe. After a tempestuous voyage they reached the coast of Florida, which had been discovered before by Verrazano in 1523.

They entered the St. John, which they called the River of May, from having discovered it on the first of that month. As usual with the explorers of that day, they set up a column at the mouth of the river, engraved with the arms of France, in token that they took formal possession of the country in the name of the French sovereign. They built Fort Charles at Port Royal, and then returned to France.

On the 22d of April, 1564, Laudonnière returned to Florida, with three vessels containing emigrants, provisions, and arms for the little colony, and built Fort Caroline, near the mouth of the St. John. The following year Ribaut also returned to Florida, with a large fleet, to relieve Laudonnière of his command. It is the story of that last disastrous voyage I wish to tell you.

Captain Ribaut, in the obsolete French of that day, tells of the voyage and the high hopes of the emigrants who were going out. They believed that everything which could delight the soul of man was to be found in that favored clime. The country was neither frozen in winter nor parched by summer suns. It was rich in gold mines, fertile plains, and lofty mountains, and the trees distilled precious gums.

"In fact," says the worthy captain, "every man was sure that what he most desired was to be found in that new country. I had not seen these great things when I was there; but I said nothing, for I knew too little myself of the country."

On the 14th of August, 1565, the vessels arrived off the coast of Florida, and meeting some Indians there, asked them where the new colony, Fort Caroline, was situated. They told him they had heard there were white men fifty miles toward the north. The vessels sailed until they reached the St. John, and taking two of the smallest ships, Captain Ribaut followed the stream until they reached Fort Caroline.

Laudonnière met them at the bank.

"At last, God be praised!" he cried. "We thought you had abandoned us, and we are starving, — yes, actually starving. The Indians will not bring us food, and we were too few to venture in those hostile woods to seek it. I will return to France immediately. I can bear a great deal, but the limit has been reached."

"But," asked Captain Ribaut, "we found the Indians friendly and obliging when we first came. Why do they now refuse to bring provisions?"

Laudonnière shrugged his shoulders.

"Ah, well, you see, our men have made enemies; you see, they were hard to control. They made forays, brought prisoners to the fort, and, to speak frankly, acted like fools, and worse. If you had not come when you did, you would not have found us here, and our scalps would have decorated the wigwams."

Captain Ribaut shook his head. He knew well the danger of awakening the hostility of the savages.

"It is bad," he said, "for we shall have two enemies. Philip of Spain is sending out a fleet under Don Pedro Menendez de Aviles, to drive us from Florida if he can. We are ordered to resist him to the death."

ADMIRAL GASPARD DE COLIGNY.

Menendez reached the coast of Florida, his fleet badly storm-beaten. Ribaut demanded his business. He was told that war was declared between Spain and France, and that they were there as enemies.

The French considered it more prudent to retreat a short distance, until their preparations could be made, and the Spaniards only pursued them to the mouth of the river they called Dauphin. Jean Ribaut, returning to Fort Caroline, took on board nearly all the able-bodied men, much against the will of Laudonnière, who was left with invalids, women, and a small number of troops. Ribaut intended attacking the Spaniards, and in one decisive engagement to drive them from Florida.

But Menendez, who had gained a foothold, and commenced building Fort Marion, had his spies among the Indians, and knew that Captain Ribaut had taken all the available forces from Fort Caroline. Now was the time to surprise the fort. To get possession of it, with the Indians as allies, would be to control the country. Taking Indian guides, with a strong force he made his way through marsh and morass, and in the midst of a terrible storm swooped down on the fort, and took it after a short resistance.

Said one of the survivors, in a narrative written in 1568, as nearly as I can recall it, —

"I escaped, God knows how, and ran to the thick woods. I stopped at some little distance, and hiding behind the trees, looked down at the inner court of the fort, where the massacre was going on. It was so horrible that I covered my eyes with my hands, and ran on headlong, knowing not and caring not where I was going, if I could only get away from that spot. The thorns tore my flesh, the great vines hanging from tree to tree tripped me up, but I felt nothing. Suddenly in front of me I heard groans and cries, and came upon some of our men who had also escaped. We knelt down and prayed God to help us. But Monsieur Lebeau said, —

"'My friends, we can go no farther in this wilderness. We do not know what course to take, and the forest is full of wild beasts and hostile savages, who would kill us with horrible tortures. Let us return to the fort, and give ourselves up to the Spaniards. They may spare us, but death is certain here.'

"Then I cried out, and asked if it was not better to trust God than those butchers, whose hands were even then red with the blood of our friends.

"But some said no, it would be better to return; and six decided to do so. We all returned with them to the edge of the woods, watched them enter the fort; and before they had time to cry for mercy, they were barbarously murdered, and their dead bodies dragged to the bank of the river, and piled up in a mound with the rest of our slaughtered friends. Some of the bodies were suspended from trees.

"We heard afterward that Captain Jean Ribaut in his vessel 'The Pearl,' had anchored in front of the fort while the butchery was going on, and some of our men escaped and swam to it. Don Pedro Menendez called to Captain Ribaut to surrender. He refused; and the Spaniards tore the eyes out of the dead Frenchmen and cast them, with dreadful curses, toward the vessel.

"As for us poor wretches, in that trackless forest, we travelled through dreadful places, hearing the bellow of the crocodiles, and the hiss of immense snakes as our steps disturbed them. We chewed the bark of trees, and found some fruit to satisfy our hunger. We did not know that it was poisonous, for it had a strange, sweetish taste, and was yellow and oblong (probably the pawpaw), but we would have eaten it all the same. We were making for the seacoast as well as we could shape our course. We came across rivers which we crossed, sometimes by swimming, sometimes by the aid of fallen trees. At last, when exhausted and ready to lie down and die, we came to a vast seamarsh; and one of our men, climbing a high tree, saw, a short distance off, not only the sea, but the vessel of Captain Maillard, which he signalled, and they sent boats after us.

"More dead than alive, we were taken on board, and there we found the Sieur Laudonnière, who had also escaped. Shortly afterward 'The Pearl' sailed up to us, and Captain Jean Ribaut told how his vessels had been dispersed and wrecked by the hurricane, during which the fort had been taken; but he said he would never leave the coast while there was a chance of any of our men escaping,—that it was his duty to stay and give them aid. But Captain Maïllard sailed for France, taking us with him."

This is a brief summary of the "dernier voyage aux Indes," as the narrative is called which I have imperfectly given; and any one who will master the old French dialect in which it is written will find it most interesting.

It only remains to tell of the fate of the heroic Huguenot, Captain Ribaut, who would not desert his post of duty.

He was again tempest-tossed, and his remaining vessels driven ashore. The French wandered about, half-starving, and knowing well that the Indians, whom the soldiers at the fort had angered, would take the first chance to revenge themselves.

A body of Spaniards came upon them. They were too weak to resist, and gave up their arms, upon a solemn promise from Vallemande, the commanding officer, that they should be treated as prisoners of war.

MASSACRE OF THE HUGUENOTS AT FORT CAROLINE.

Ribaut, honorable and truthful himself, believed the treacherous Spaniard. They were marched on; and had he not been in front, he would have seen that his thirty men had their hands tied behind their backs.

As they entered the fort, the massacre began.

Captain Ribaut himself was first to fall.

One by one they entered the fatal gate, their hands tied behind them. One by one grew the pile of dead bodies.

With what emotions must each have first made the awful discovery of his fate!

All were stricken down, one by one; nine hundred Huguenots were murdered on the banks of the St. John.

It was on St. Matthew's Day the fort was taken,—a second St. Bartholomew. There have been few such scenes in American history, and the tragedy has been but little noted. The lovely Floridian river retains no token of this massacre. While we remember the treachery and bloodshed of that fatal day, we do not forget the heroic self-sacrifice of brave Jean Ribaut, who literally gave up his life upon the bare chance of saving some fugitive from the cruel Spaniards.

"I never knew before that such a tragedy took place on our shores," said Charlie.

"That shows," said Mr. Leland, "how unequal is the knowledge of historic stories. Those incidents that find historians, story-writers, and poets, are the most famous. A poet will make a minor event of history seem great. The historical stories of Massachusetts are famous because they have found Hawthornes, Longfellows, and Whittiers to tell them. Rhode Island stories are little known because they have found no voice of genius to give them life. So with the South, as we have already remarked."

"If you will come to Florida in the winter, there is one excursion that I would be glad to make with you, that I know would give you pleasure," said Mr. Laurens.

"Where?" asked Mr. Leland.

"To Havana in a steam yacht from Tampa Bay, to visit the tomb of Columbus. It can be made in a few days, going and returning.

The water of the Gulf is warm and smooth at that season, and the nights on the sea are tropical splendors. You could never forget them." He added: "I might be able to secure a steam yacht, and take you over the very course of the first voyage of Columbus."

"That would be an historic excursion indeed," said Charlie. "I shall never stop thinking of it until I have made it. I would rather stand before the tomb of Columbus than before the tomb of any other man who ever lived."

"I have the same feeling that Charlie has about such an excursion," said Mr. Leland. "I accept your invitation most cordially, and if my health and business will allow, you may find us at St. Augustine another winter; if not then, some other winter."

"I have visited the tomb of Columbus," said Mr. Laurens. "The subject brings to my mind some incidents associated with his voyage that are not commonly known; and as comparatively unfamiliar stories are to be told in our Club, I will give them. The incidents relate to the devotions of Columbus on approaching land."

THE HYMN AND PRAYER OF COLUMBUS.

A STORY OF THE BAHAMAS.

There is a little book (one of the numerous publications of the late Mr. Bohn) which I always regard with peculiar interest, because it was the book which led to the discovery of America. I mean the "Travels of Marco Polo," who went all over Asia about the year 1300, and wrote this brief, fascinating account of what he heard, saw, and did.

Wonderful things did Columbus — a map-maker plying his trade in Lisbon — read in this book, and it is no wonder that he was fascinated by them.

He read in it of lands where rubies, diamonds, emeralds, and pearls were in the greatest profusion; of a country where all the money consisted of plain gold rods, cut into lengths; of an island where gold was so abundant that the king's palace was roofed with it, and some of the furniture made of it; of a

THE FRENCH DISCOVERING THE REMAINS OF THE RIBAUT EXPEDITION.

region where spices and drugs, then worth their weight in silver all over Europe, were so cheap that the poorest people had them; of a seaport from which sailed every year a hundred ships laden with spices.

Moreover he had previously discovered that these rich countries, filling the eastern parts of the round world, could be reached by sailing to the *west!*

He found something else in his Marco Polo which, as a Roman Catholic, he was bound to consider of far more importance than worldly wealth. It was that the great Khan of Tartary, who was long the most powerful monarch of Asia, had expressed the strongest possible desire to know more concerning the Christian religion.

Such was the Khan's interest in the matter that he had despatched a special embassy to the Pope, asking his Holiness to send him a hundred Christians thoroughly acquainted with the principles of their religion, and qualified to prove its truth by fair argument to the learned men of Tartary. The Khan said that if the Tartar gods were false he wished to know it, and to turn his subjects from their worship.

It was further asserted in this book that the embassy had reached the Pope, who had actually sent, not indeed one hundred Christians, but two learned friars, charged with presents to the Khan and authorized to instruct the Tartars in the Christian faith; and not only that, but to consecrate bishops, arrange dioceses, and do all things in Tartary which the Pope himself could do if he were present there.

The two friars had started on their mission, but after proceeding some distance had turned back, discouraged by the perils of the way, and returned to Rome.

Two centuries had passed; the Khan had died long ago, as well as his son and his grandson; but the mission had never been renewed, and that vast unknown continent of Asia remained "in heathen darkness."

All this, besides deeply impressing the imaginative and religious mind of Columbus, furnished him with an irresistible argument when he asked the assistance of Queen Isabella of Spain.

When he spoke to King Ferdinand on the subject, no doubt he dwelt upon the spices, the rubies, and the gold, and of the king whose palace-roof was made of the precious metal; but when he spoke to the queen, a devoted and enthusiastic Catholic, we may be sure that he laid the greatest stress upon the story in Marco Polo, of the great emperor who had asked the Pope to send him a hundred Christian priests. We may be quite certain that this was the argument which induced the queen to favor the expedition and sell her jewels to promote it.

I do not doubt that Columbus himself fully appreciated the rubies and the gold described by Marco Polo. At the same time the avowed object of the expedition was to convey a knowledge of the Christian religion to the "Prince who is called the Grand Khan, who sent to Rome to entreat for doctors of our Holy Faith!"

This was the object stated by Columbus himself in the first pages of his diary, which began thus:—

"In nomine D. N. Jesu Christi!" ("In the name of our Lord Jesus Christ").

The expedition, therefore, had a religious character; and Columbus regarded himself in the light, not of a missionary indeed, but as the forerunner of missionaries, and the preparer of the way for them. I wonder he did not have a priest with him. He did not, however, although he carried a notary to take possession of any lands he might discover, in the name of the King and Queen of Spain.

All who have read the fascinating narrative of Washington Irving remember that the Admiral offered a reward to whomsoever should first discover land. On the nineteenth day of the voyage a voice from one of the vessels, the "Pinta," was heard crying,—

"Land! Land, Señor! I claim my reward!"

It was Martin Alonzo Pinzon who uttered the joyful cry, pointing at the same time towards the southwest, at a low-lying bank of mist which had deceived him.

Columbus, too, was deceived, and threw himself upon his knees to offer thanks. All the crew of the two vessels in advance knelt also, while Pinzon, the sailors, and the Admiral united in chanting,—

"Gloria in excelsis Deo; et in terra pax hominibus bonæ voluntatis. Laudamus te; glorificamus te," etc.

The anxious voyagers soon discovered their mistake, and their spirits sank within them. A second time they were cheered by signs of land. Besides a quantity of fresh weeds they saw fish which they recognized to be of a kind that live near rocky ledges. They saw also a branch of thorn with berries on it, and picked up a reed, a small board, and, most thrilling of all, a carved staff.

Again the crew broke into joyous thanksgiving; and when the evening came the crews of all the ships sang with peculiar fervor the vesper hymn to the Virgin,— an act which they never omitted during the whole voyage. The translation of this hymn, now in use in Catholic churches, begins thus:—

> "Gentle star of ocean!
> Portal of the sky!
> Ever Virgin Mother
> Of the Lord most high."

It ends with stanzas peculiarly appropriate to their situation : —

> " Still, as on we journey,
> Help our weak endeavor,
> Till with thee and Jesus
> We rejoice forever.
>
> " Through the highest heaven
> To the Almighty Three,
> Father, Son, and Spirit
> One same glory be ! "

When this hymn had been sung with feelings which we can but faintly imagine, the Admiral stood forth and preached a brief but impressive thanksgiving sermon. The official history of the expedition mentions that he dwelt particularly upon the circumstance that they had been continually cheered with fresh signs of land, which had increased in frequency and significance the farther they had gone, and the more they needed solace and encouragement.

He thought it probable that they would make land that very night, and promised to whomsoever should see it first a velvet doublet in addition to the pension promised by their king and queen.

That very evening, soon after twilight had darkened into the tropical night, Columbus himself saw a light glimmering afar off, and at two o'clock the next morning a gun from the " Pinta " announced that land had been descried.

On Friday morning, Oct. 12, 1492, Columbus saw before him at a distance of a mile a beautiful level island, covered with trees like an orchard, and full of people, who were seen running out of the woods down to the shore, all naked, gazing at the ships in wonder.

Soon the boats were manned, armed, and made ready. The Admiral, clad in scarlet and holding the royal standard of Spain, stepped into his own boat and led the way to the shore, followed by a boat from each of the other vessels, all showing a special banner emblazoned with a green cross, and having on either side the initials of the Spanish sovereigns.

The chronicle of the discovery informs us that as the voyagers approached the shores of the New World, they were all charmed with the purity of the air and the beauty of the scene. As soon as Columbus landed, he sank upon his knees, and kissed the soil, shedding tears of joy.

As the crews of the other boats came on shore, they all knelt beside and behind the Admiral, and joined him in a Latin prayer, which, it appears, had been previously composed for the occasion, and which, by order of Ferdinand

and Isabella, was adopted as the form of thanksgiving for all future discoverers. It was used by Pizarro, Cortez, and Balboa: —

"Lord God, eternal and omnipotent! By thy sacred word thou didst create heaven, earth, and sea. Blessed and glorified be thy name; thy majesty be

LANDING OF COLUMBUS.

praised! Grant aid to thine humble servant, that thy sacred name may be known and lauded in this other part of the world."

Having recited this prayer, Columbus rose to his feet, and all the company gathered round him. He drew his sword, and unfolded the royal standard to the breeze. Then, in the immediate presence of the captains of the vessels and the notary of the expedition, the sailors who had landed standing near, he took formal possession of the new-found land and gave it the name of San Salvador. When this had been done, he required all present to take the oath of obedience to him as representing the sovereigns and wielding their power.

During these ceremonies the great crowd of dusky natives stood transfixed with wonder. They were amazed at the whiteness of the Spaniards, at their shining armor, their gorgeous banners, their splendid garments, and particularly the scarlet dress of their chief and his majestic demeanor. They little thought that the coming of these strange men meant misery, bondage, and swift extinction to all their race.

Columbus, on his part, never knew that the land he had found was no part of the regions described by Marco Polo. He had discovered a continent, and died without suspecting it.

THE GRAVE OF COLON.

The genius of Columbus was so universal, and his fame is so world-wide, that it seems almost strange to hear him spoken of as Colón, and find his grave in a Catholic church in Havana. An American is so accustomed to think of Columbus as the grand discoverer of the New World — his world — that for a moment he feels quite like resenting the exclusive claim of that not over clean and badly governed city to the custody of his ashes.

Columbus — or Christobal Colon, as we must say at Havana, if we wish to be understood — died at Santo Domingo; but his remains were subsequently removed to Havana and interred in the cathedral, where they now repose beneath a pillar within the altar; and properly proud are the Havanese-Spanish families of their great fellow-countryman by adoption, whose last resting-place is with them.

Beneath a rather doubtful bust of the great discoverer is a marble tablet set in the pillar, and inscribed with the following characteristic Spanish epitaph in the old-time tongue of Castile: —

STATUE OF COLUMBUS.

"O, RESTOS Y YMAGEN DEL
GRANDE COLON! MIL SIGLOS
DURAD GUARDADO EN LA URNA
Y EN LA REMEMBRANZA DE NU-
ESTRA NACION."

"O remains and likeness of great Columbus! Let a thousand centuries hold thee, guarded sacredly in thy urn and in the memory of our nation."

More correct to life, it is asserted, is the statue of Columbus in the *patio* of the Captain-General's palace, a few squares below the cathedral. This statue is also of marble, life-size, with the right hand pointing to a globe set by the left foot,—that globe which he was persecuted for believing to be round and not flat. The head and face are those of a man forty-five or fifty years of age; and the countenance indicates a certain pathetic faith and purpose, half buried, and struggling beneath tides on tides of trouble.

No one can for a moment look upon that face and believe that the life of this man was a happy one; rather that he suffered and was weighed down by anxiety from first to last,—from the day he first set forth to raise funds for his ridiculed expedition, to that last hour in Santo Domingo, where his noble life expired under ingratitude and malice.

Such a face is a silent and lasting reproach to the age which it looked down upon.

To visit the tomb of Columbus was a worthy aspiration for an American boy, and the route suggested for such a journey would tend to show the greatness and results of the inspired Italian's discovery.

CHAPTER II.

HOW TO VISIT CUBA. — A ROMANCE OF NORTH CAROLINA.

"I MIGHT be able to secure a steam yacht and take you over the very course of the first voyage of Columbus."

The plan of making an excursion to Havana to visit the tomb of Columbus, going by the way of St. Augustine and the St. John's River, began to haunt Charlie Leland's mind more vividly than ever, and especially the words "St. Salvador Day!"

The words dropped from Mr. Laurens's lips in the hearing of Charlie, and his imagination was at once excited.

"What day did you say?" he asked.

"St. Salvador Day. I was remarking that it ought to be made a national holiday."

He continued: —

"I was saying to your father that the claim is made that the nation needs more holidays. In some States local holidays are made to supply the want. Thus, in certain States of the West, Arbor Day, a festival day of tree-planting, furnishes a delightful holiday in the most inspiring month of the year. Massachusetts has Bunker Hill Day; New York, New Year's Day. Lincoln's Day is more or less observed locally. Easter Sunday is becoming a church holiday among all

HAVANA.

denominations of Christians. The observance of Watch Night as a religious service is becoming every year more common. If more national or local holidays are needed, we certainly have grand historic events to inspire them. Spain recalls her mediæval glory and maritime triumphs by celebrating St. Salvador Day, or the day when Columbus beheld the New World (October 12). As we are reaping the fruits of the great discovery, the celebration of this day better befits us than the land that has lost the provinces of her once great empire; the praise of Columbus might be well transferred from the South of Europe to the Western World."

" St. Salvador Day sounds poetic," said Charlie.

" The four hundredth anniversary of the discovery of Columbus (1492-1892) is near; and the event will invite splendid ceremonies in Spain, Portugal, and Italy, and will fix upon the date the attention of the Western World. The celebration in Cuba and the islands of the Antilles will doubtless be splendid and inspiring."

" What are the best ways of visiting Cuba?" asked Charlie.

HOW TO VISIT CUBA.

". The most delightful route from the North is by sea by the way of the Bahama Islands, and by land by the ports of Florida. It is well to combine the two routes in the journey.

" The Ward line of palace steamers — and there are few more delightful boats on the ocean — sail from New York for Havana weekly, and every other week to Nassau, Bahama, and to Cienfuegos, Cuba. From Cienfuegos there is a short route to Havana by rail.

" One of this splendid fleet of steamers calls at St. Augustine for Havana weekly, and from Havana weekly, thus offering one the short and quick sea voyages to and from that port."

" What is the expense of such a trip?" asked Charlie.

" About $95 to Nassau and return, by steamer from New York

to New York, and about $100 to Cienfuegos, Cuba, from New York to New York. These rates are for sea routes.

"One of the best routes to Cuba is the following, offered by the World Travel Company, for about $106.75 : By Ward line to Havana (including meals and berth), Morgan line to Key West and Tampa, rail and boat to Jacksonville, rail or boat to Savannah or Charleston, and steamer back to New York (including meals and berth). Tickets good to stop over.

"Cook's ticket rates are about $50 to Havana by steamer, and $90 to Havana and return by sea.

"The World Travel Company offers a great number of routes to Jacksonville and return at a uniform rate of about $50. It is but a short distance from Jacksonville to St. Augustine, and it is easy to make a connection from Jacksonville with Tampa Bay, by the way of the beautiful St. John's River. A most delightful winter trip can be made from Florida by the Ward line of steamers, by going from St. Augustine to Havana, thence by rail across the island of Cuba, by rail by the way of Matanzas to Cienfuegos, and thence returning to New York by the way of Nassau. The fare from Florida by this route is about $116.

"Among the World Travel Company routes from St. Augustine are the following, with rates at the present, which might vary in the future, but not greatly: —

"By Ward line direct to Havana (including meals and berths), and return the same way to St. Augustine, $55.

"By Ward line direct to Havana, and return by direct steamer to New York (including meals and berth), $75.

"By Ward line direct to Havana, thence Morgan line by the way of Key West and Tampa to New Orleans (including meals and berth on all steamers), $65.

"By Ward line direct to Havana, thence Morgan line by the way of Key West and Tampa to New Orleans, and direct rail-route

GEORGE II.

or steamer to New York (including meals and berth on all steamers), rail tickets from New Orleans, limited, $100.

" By Ward line direct to Havana, thence Morgan line by the way of Key West and Tampa to New Orleans, Mississippi River steamer to St. Louis and direct rail-route to New York (including meals and berth on all steamers), rail tickets from St. Louis, limited, $105.

" A very satisfactory excursion could be made to Cuba, including the Bahamas by one route and the St. John's River by another, with hotel fares and all expenses, for about $200. An economical person who would stop at the respectable low-rate hotels might make the trip for $175 or $150.

" Cook offers a very safe and picturesque route from Boston which he calls the " Land-locked Route to Havana," with fast trains, elegant equipment, by the way of the New York and New England Railroad, Atlantic Coast Line, and Tampa, fifty-two hours rail, and thirty hours on the placid waters of the Gulf of Mexico, leaving Boston at 6.30 P.M. Wednesday, arriving at Havana, Monday morning. Fare from Boston to Havana, $55.75."

The story-telling on the next evening turned towards the South. Mrs. Laurens was the leading entertainer. Her first story related to Flora Macdonald, who aided Prince Charles to escape from his enemies, he taking the dress of a woman and the guise of a servant. Flora lived in the Scottish Isles, or Hebrides, and she conducted the prince from the Highlands to the Isle of Skye. She had not been friendly to the prince's cause until she met him. The fate of the prince was at one time in her keeping. She did not meet the fate recorded in Scott's novel, but married and came to America.

A ROMANCE OF NORTH CAROLINA.

When I was a young girl, and quite wild over the " Waverley Novels," you can fancy my delight at my dear little grandmother's looking up, with her bright brown eyes, and saying, " I knew her, — your beautiful Flora ! "

"You knew her?"

"I have sat on her knee, and she once kissed me," said Grandma.

"Then it was true about her?"

"In a measure," said Grandma, taking up her knitting again. "The idea of her was true. You might say she sat for the portrait. Her real name, you know, was Flora Macdonald."

"Oh, was she like the story?"

"That I can't quite say. I was so young, I can hardly remember how she looked," said Grandma. "I kept only the sensation that she was something beautiful and grand. I heard them talking about her, and I trembled when she touched me."

"Was she tall and dark and pale, with drooping curls and proud glances? And did she sing about Highland heroes, and adore Prince Charlie?"

"A gentleman who was entertained by her in Scotland says she was a little woman, mild and well-bred. The legend of her in North Carolina, where she went to live, is that she was dignified and handsome. As for the rest of your questions, I rather think that at that time she talked of seasickness and the weather during her voyage; and if she adored anybody, I suppose she adored her husband."

"Her husband? Why, Flora went into a convent!"

"In the story. In real life she married an officer, and went to live in North Carolina, as I told you before. But she stopped in Nova Scotia, either going or coming; for it was there she visited my uncle, good old Judge Des Champs, and there I sat upon her knee."

"And what was the truth about her, Grandma?" I asked in woful disappointment. "Was n't *any* of the story true? Tell us, can't you? Tell us, please now, just how it was."

"Well," said Grandma, "you have read about Charles Edward the Pretender?"

"Oh, yes, of course. He is the prince in the story."

"The prince in the story, and the prince in history. For all that is known of him then, I have no doubt that at that time he was as lovely a gentleman as the prince in the story. His mother was a Sobieski, you know,— an heroic race, long descended from heroes in old Poland ; and he was one of the Stuarts, who had a way of taking all men's hearts.

"Gallant and gentle and noble, self-forgetting, dauntless, beautiful, in those early days a superb fellow, people felt that they could die for him,— and die they did. Just think what a career he had in his youth! In Venice he was received with royal honors. When France was going to invade England at a time when England was half unprotected, he was sent for to take command of the army.

"He embarked with Marshal Saxe, the greatest soldier of his day; and the throne of his grandfather was just within his reach, when a furious tempest rose, and raged a week, and sank the vessels, full of troops, to the bottom, and threw him back upon the coast. The French would not try again; and it was all his friends could do to prevent the prince from setting sail for Scotland alone in a fishing-boat.

"When, after a while, he did arrive with his seven friends in Scotland, the clans flocked about him, and he had at first some splendid successes. He 'drew his sword' and 'threw away the scabbard,' as he said, and prepared to invade England.

"But at last," said Grandma, after a little pause, "there came an end to all his efforts in the disaster at Culloden, where the field was lost through the sullen pride of the Macdonalds."

"Why, how could that be?"

"The Macdonalds, you know, were an immense clan; and it happened that they had been placed on the left of the army, but they had claimed it as their right, ever since the service they had done at the battle of Bannockburn, that they should charge on the right; and so they refused to charge at all, and lost the prince the day.

"The poor Chevalier! What must his wrath and despair have been when he saw so great a cause ruined by so petty a whim? But at that, he and his adherents fled for their lives; for they had been defeated, and defeat made them guilty of high-treason, and their lives were the forfeit if they should be captured.

"A hundred and fifty thousand dollars was the price set upon the head of the prince by the British Government. Five months he wandered in the wild passes of the Highlands, hiding in caverns, under crags, among the gorse and heather, slipping in a skiff from island to island, starving, perishing with cold, in rags, hunted everywhere, and every pass guarded by the Duke of Cumberland's troops!

"It was only the love of the people, of the common people, which saved him. How they used to sing songs about him! And, a generation later, how I used to sing them myself!

"That kiss of Flora Macdonald's made me espouse the cause of the Jacobites, as the supporters of the house of Stuart were called. 'Charlie is my darling, the young Chevalier,' and 'What's a' the steer, Kimmer?" and 'Come o'er the stream, Charlie,' and 'Wha'll be king but Charlie?' and 'Flora Macdonald's Lament,' and all the rest."

The Lament of Flora Macdonald.

The moorcock that crows on the brows o' Ben-Connal.
 He kens o' his bed in a sweet mossy hame:
The eagle that soars o'er the cliffs o' Clan-Ronald,
 Unawed and unhunted his eyrie can claim;
The solan can sleep on the shelve of the shores,
 The cormorant roost on his rock of the sea,
But, ah, there is one whose hard fate I deplore,
 Nor house, ha', nor hame in his country has he;
The conflict is past, and our name is no more,
 There's nought left but sorrow for Scotland an' me!

The target is torn from the arm of the just,
 The helmet is cleft on the brow of the brave,
The claymore forever in darkness must rust,
 But red is the sword of the stranger and slave;
The hoof of the horse and the foot of the proud
 Have trode o'er the plumes on the bonnet of blue.
Why slept the red bolt in the breast of the cloud
 When tyranny revell'd in blood of the true?
Farewcel, my young hero, the gallant and good!
 The crown of thy fathers is torn from thy brow.

"I will sing you one of these old songs," said Mrs. Laurens. "It may help to give interest to the story."

"That song stirs my old blood now," continued Grandma.

"Well, it happened that Flora was on a visit in the neighborhood of one of his hiding-places. It was proposed, all other ways having failed, that the prince should put on the clothes of some woman, and be passed off as her waiting-maid, — he had already played the part of servant to Malcolm McLeod.

"It was a daring undertaking, with all the scrutiny the British watch-dogs never dropped a minute. The officer from whom Flora had to obtain a passport was Flora's father-in-law. He had no idea what he was doing when he gave her a safe conveyance for herself, her young escort, Neil Macdonald, Betty Bourke, a stout Irishwoman, and some others.

"Betty Bourke was the prince; and it must have been a great trial to a modest and timid young girl to carry out such an imposition, but she was rewarded by the love of a whole people. They sailed for the Isle of Skye one bright June day.

"When they landed, they went to the house of the Laird of Sleite, which was full of hostile soldiers eager in the search for the royal prize; and Flora told her secret to the kind lady of the house, who straightway helped her along on her way home to Kingsburg.

"And she at last saw the prince safely through; and his last words to her were: 'Farewell, gentle, faithful maiden! May we meet again in the Palace Royal!'

"Young Neil Macdonald followed him to France, and his son became by and by one of Napoleon's marshals. But great was the anger of the British Government when it was found that Charles Edward had escaped.

"They knew the thing could only have been managed by a woman; suspicion fell on Flora, and she was arrested, together with Malcolm McLeod and others, carried on board of a man-of-war, and changed from one vessel to another, until she had been nearly a year on shipboard, before being taken to London and thrown into prison to stand a trial for high-treason.

"How cruel for the brave, sweet girl! But her youth, her beauty, her courage, began to create what you might call a reaction in her favor, especially as she had not previously been on the prince's side, either in respect to his claims to the throne or his religion.

"The king himself — it was George II. — asked her how she dared save the enemy of his crown and kingdom, and she replied, —

"'I only did what I would do for your Majesty in the same condition, — I relieved distress.'

"And it all ended by their sending her home with Malcolm McLeod. It

CHARLES EDWARD.

was about four years afterward that she married Allan Macdonald. It seems, when you hear her story, as if half the people of Scotland were Macdonalds.

"In 1775, being in some trouble for money, and hearing how well his country-people who had emigrated were getting along there, Allan Macdonald followed them to North Carolina; and there he settled with his wife at Fayetteville, where the ruins of their house may yet be seen, I believe, unless recently removed.

"The vast difference between the chills and mists of the Scotch Highlands and the balmy air in which she found herself, I should think must have been very striking to Flora; she must have enjoyed the wonderful fruits and flowers at what seemed to her untimely seasons, and in the coldest months the great wood-fires furnished by the pitchy forests, — that still seem inexhaustible, I am told.

"They only lived a little while in Fayetteville, before they moved to Cameron Hill, twenty miles distant. They had no sooner established themselves there than the Revolution began. It must have seemed to Flora as if a state of rebellion and warfare were the natural state of man, or as if she were fated never to escape it.

"The chief of the Macdonald clan among the North Carolina emigrants had been given, whether through policy or not, a commission as general in the British King's army. The Stuart struggle being over and done with, there probably appeared to him no reason why he should not take it. He summoned all loyal Highlanders to meet under his standard, and march with him to join General Clinton.

"They did so, fifteen hundred strong, but were met by the rebels against King George, — and in no State was the feeling that led to our independence more ardent than in North Carolina, — and Caswell and Moore routed them in a desperate fight; and among those taken prisoners was Flora's husband.

"When Captain Macdonald was at last released, his land was confiscated, his property gone, his hopes shattered; and he took his wife and shipped for Scotland. It was on the way home, in this British ship, that they encountered a French frigate; and of course there was a sea-fight.

"But Flora Macdonald did not go below then, and spend her time between screaming and praying, as some women might have done. She stayed on deck through the whole action, binding up wounds, encouraging and helping, and presently she had her arm broken for her pains.

"'I have hazarded my life,' she said, 'for the House of Stuart and for the House of Hanover; and I do not see that I am a great gainer by either of them.'

"But she was satisfied in having the French frigate beaten, and she reached Scotland at length in safety. She must have been a woman of iron nerves, I think. She had five sons, all of whom were soldiers. And when she died at last, her shroud was made of the sheets in which the Prince Charles Edward had slept at Kingsburg.

"You see, if you have your story of Lady Arabella Johnson here, they have quite as good a one of their Flora Macdonald down in the old North State, which, perhaps you may not know, claims to be the first of the thirteen on whose shores the English landed, and the first in which the old Colonists threw off the British yoke."

THE EMIGRANT'S HOUSE IN THE CLEARING.

"You spoke," said Charlie Leland to Mr. Laurens, "of the stories of the old slave cabins. I have read 'Uncle Remus' and the 'Dialect Stories' by Sherwood Bronson. Could we not have a story of that class?"

"I am not prepared to-night, or such a story does not now occur to

ARREST OF CHARLES EDWARD.

me. Perhaps Mrs. Laurens may have some such incidents in mind. I will try to recall some of the cabin tales for some other occasion."

"I recall one of my experiences on making a change of residence in the South," said Mrs. Laurens. "It happened in my girlhood. It might give you a characteristic picture of the negro mind and habits before the war. Father had moved into a new district on the Mississippi, and up to that period I and my sister Del had seen little of the colored people of the country, but only the servants of the best New Orleans families."

"DUN COME TO SEE Y' ALLS."

For the first week or two we got on very well. Papa and the boys were planting our little garden and tinkering up things generally. After that they went off every morning to the outskirts of the claim, and worked at clearing up the boundary lines and felling trees for fence rails. And so day after day, and week after week, we were left alone all day long in the silence. "Oh, that silence!" exclaimed Del. Indeed, it was almost beyond endurance.

The sun shone silently in the far-off sky; the clouds floated silently above us; the grass grew silently at our feet; all around us the tall trees stood in solemn silence. A sense of unutterable loneliness pervaded the air. Nothing we could do seemed to disenchant the terrible solitude.

We busied ourselves with our household duties; we read, and practised our music lessons, — papa had sent out a melodeon for us from Little Rock, — and we fed the cow and pigs and chickens and dogs until it was a wonder they did n't burst; but for all our efforts the days seemed to have the length of weeks, and the insupportable loneliness only increased with each succeeding week.

Neighbors we had none. We were just surrounded by miles and miles of forest in every direction.

Of course, papa and the boys made things a bit lively for us in the evenings and early mornings, but somehow the days only seemed more desolate and the silence more intolerable after they were gone. Sometimes I wonder Del and I did n't turn into wooden girls or raving maniacs.

But one day when we had exhausted every resource of occupation, we concluded to drown our sorrows in forgetfulness, if possible; and although it was nearly five o'clock, and pretty nearly time to prepare supper, we lay ourselves down and deliberately went to sleep.

I was awakened by Del shaking me, and whispering in a frightened voice that there was a knocking at the door.

Sure enough, there was a steady knock, knock, knock!

I sprang to my feet, bolted the door, and called out, "Who's there?"

"'T ain't no pusson jis' 'cep' us chilluns," came the quick response, in unmistakable accent. "Us chilluns dun come to see y' alls."

Del just danced up and down. "For mercy sake, Dodo," she said, "do open that door some time to-day, and let them in!"

You can't think how excited we were. The bare idea of company, no matter of what sort, so it was friendly, made the blood bound in our veins; and I could feel my heart beat as I slid back the bolt to welcome our unexpected guests.

"Where in the world did you come from?" cried Del, as soon as the open door revealed "us chilluns" to our view.

"Ki, missy!" giggled the largest of the five, "us chilluns dun bin gwine a-nuttin' an' a-'simmonin', an' we's *dat* fur f'm home der ain't no use in ebber studyin' 'bout gittin' back dar dis day. We dun heerd y' alls bin libbin' hyah, so we jis' goed fur to come fer to see ye."

"Well, do come in," said Del, delightedly, taking the girl by the hand and drawing her into the room. "Come in, children. Are n't you tired? Where do you live? Who *are* you?"

"Laws, missy!" answered the girl, who seemed to be about fifteen years old. "We lib wid Uncle Ben an' mammy down to de Fawks, jis' apast de Brainch. 'Corse we 'se tired, dun trabbled dat fur dis yer day. We 'se jis' us chilluns. We dun heerd 'bout y' alls. My laws! Ain't dis yer fine?"

She stood wide-eyed and wide-mouthed, gazing around the room. Del gave the children seats, and asked them if they were hungry. This aroused the big girl, and she turned on the children, —

"No, yo' is n't hungry. Yo' *dar* say yo'se hungry. Yo' Meriky! Yo' Moffy Jane! Yo' Usly Ann! Yo' Pinky Boodle! Yo' jis' *dar* say yo'se hungry!"

"Dell law! Bobry, yo'se hungry yo'se'f," retorted the one whom she had designated as Meriky. "Yo' dun say yo'se'f, jis' outside de do', as how yo' specs dem white folks —"

"Yo' shet yo' sassy mouf, yo' Meriky," interrupted Bobry, charging upon Meriky, who dodged behind Moffy Jane, upsetting her and Pinky Boodle, who in her turn set up a lusty howl, having bumped her nose against the sharp corner of a cricket.

"Now, looky heah, Bobry," put in Usly, — she of the solemn countenance, — "yo' don' go for to upsotting de chilluns dat ar way when yo' go for to see white pussons. Jis' yo' take a cheer an' sot down, jis' like missy tole yo'."

Del just acted like a crazy girl. She kept saying, " O Dodo! is n't it too funny? Did you ever see anything so charming? Don't let them go away. Let's keep them, every one."

I picked up Moffy Jane from her tangle of chairs, comforted Pinky Boodle, and gave them all the promise of a good supper. Then while Del went to the pantry to open a can of peaches, I questioned the children a bit more leisurely.

Bobry subsided sufficiently to inform me that "mammy dun lib in de cabin down to de Fawks; an' Uncle Ben, he's pap, he dun bushin' in de clarin'," by which felicitous phrase she meant to convey the fact of her father's employment at fencing in with brush his bit of cleared land.

"We'se dun got heap o' crop dis year, we is; and us chilluns dun gwine fotch y'alls some sweet-tater squashes nex' time we comes. *Is* yo' got heap o' 'simmons?"

"Not many," I answered, explaining that the persimmon trees grew at some distance from our house, and that we did not often go into the woods.

"*Is* you got *pee*-cons?" was her next inquiry.

I told her we had very few.

"*Pee*-con trees on de Brainch, — heaps ob 'em. Us chilluns gwine fotch yo' some dem, too," she said. After a moment she inquired, —

"What *is* yo' got?"

By this time I began to comprehend that Bobry's proffered generosity ought to meet with some return, so I hastened to answer, —

" Oh, we have some raisins. I'll give you some to eat with your pecans."

"Dell law!" exlaimed Bobry, "Meriky, Usly, yo' heah dat? Missy dun got *ressuns!*" And the five grinned in unison.

Just then Del came in with saucers and spoons, and dished out the canned peaches, adding a huge slice of currant cake to each saucer of fruit. Every one of those young ones said, "Tankee, missy," in one and the same breath, and then fell to devouring the cake and peaches, while Del sat and looked on as pleased as any two-year-old baby with five new dolls.

"You can't go home to-night, children," said Del; "the Branch is ten miles from this place."

"Dell law!" cried Bobry. "Dat's sho! 'Clar' I fought it was hunnerd miles, Pinky Boodle poke 'long wuss 'n a pole-cat. *Is* yo' got any co'n meal for make de good hoe cake for y' alls an' us chilluns?"

"Oh, yes, indeed," said Del, "and flour too, and lots of nice things you never get. Oh, you shall have the best kind of a supper. Now tell us what you can do. Sing? Dance? Do something, if you can."

At this the grave and severe Usly rose to her feet, and took a position in the middle of the room. Rolling her eyes in a wonderful manner, she began to sing, hopping first on one foot, then on the other, in a jerky fashion, keeping time, however, to her tune, which she sang to words like these, —

> "Nigger gwine fer to eat good grease,.
> Hoo-dah! hoodah!
> Possum fat, hog liver, chicken-foot grease,
> Hoo-dah! hoodah! hoo!
>
> "Kink up de wool, nigger, fling out de toe,
> Shuffle up de pigeon-wing — cut, jis' so!
> Hoodah! hoodah! hoodah! hoodah!
> Hoo-dah! hoo!"

Nothing more comical could well be imagined than this preternaturally solemn-faced young one, cutting around that cabin floor in such grotesque manner. In the middle of this song Papa and the boys came home to supper.

"Heigh-ho!" said Papa, "what is all this? Where did you raise your minstrel troupe?"

He looked astonished enough, too; and the boys, — well, they took the whole thing in at a glance, and how they did laugh at us!

Well, I never could tell you of the rare fun we had that evening, cooking and serving the supper.

But the most curious exhibition came after supper, when Bobry gave us her experience. We had family worship immediately after the supper-things were disposed of, and the room tidied; and I hope you won't misunderstand me when I confess that my enjoyment of that domestic service exceeded anything I had ever experienced.

It differed in kind more than in degree, perhaps; for at the end of every petition, as my father prayed, Meriky uttered a dismal groan, and Usly and Moffy Jane both cried out, "Ya-as, dat's sho." And every now and again Bobry would pipe out in the shrillest voice, "Amen! Oh, glory!"

I assure you that although this was the shortest prayer I ever knew Papa to offer, yet certainly it was the one that met with the heartiest response from those who worshipped with him.

When Papa and the boys went out to look after the cattle, Bobry volunteered her experience, and I tell it because it shows a common phase of religious life among the negroes. Said she, talking through her nose in a most unnatural twang, —

"Sistering, ef yo' dun say de wuhd, I gibs yo' my 'sperience."

"What's that?" said Del.

"Dat my 'sperience, missy. Dat de way I dun got dat 'ligion."

"Do tell us about it." And thus she began : —

"Ye see I'se sich a pow'ful sinnah! I dun seek 'ligion, an' seek 'ligion. Cain't find him nowhars. Folks say, ' Yo' go down in de valleys, yo' Bobry, — go down dem deep valleys, — dar yo' gets shet dem sins, — dar yo' gets 'ligion, po' sinnah.'

"Dell law! I dat wickid I could n't fin' dem valleys.

"Den one night I wake up, an' I rise out de bed in de middle ob it, an' I mawches out in de wile woods, kase I ain't gwine cum back no mo' tell I finds dem valleys whar dey gits 'ligion, I says.

"O missy, I mawched straight to dem valleys, an' dar I see big white angel a-standin'.

"'What yo' want, yo' Bobry?' he say.

"'Oh, good golly! Marse angel,' I say, 'I'se dat onregenrit I'se dun bin seekin' 'ligion.'

"'Yo' see dat pit ob fiah, Bobry?' he say.

"Den fo' I cotch my bref he dun grab po' Bobry by de froat an' hole her ober de pit.

"Ki! how de flames roll up an' de smoke po' out! 'Yo' see dat smoke?' de angel say.

"Den he jis' chuck po' Bobry up an' down, up an' down, in dat smoke an' ober dem flames. Den de angel say, —

"'Dis yer torment waiting for all sich as yo' is. Yo' g' 'long an' git dat 'ligion now, fo' sho. None o' yo' foolin'. G' 'long an' find dem feastin' tables ef yo' don't want be drap *in* dis torment.'

"O missy, I *dat* skeered! I prayed de Lawd, 'O Lawdy Mussy, O Mussy, Mussy, Lawd,' all de way up dem valleys; an' sho's yo' baun, all on a sudden dar peared dem feastin' tables way high up in de a'r.

"Bobry dun feasted on glory! Bobry dun eat an' drink he'self chock plum full ob dat 'ligion! Oh, what I gwine keep my mouf shet fo'? When de Lawd sot me free, yo' spose he sot me free fo' be a dumb chile? Oh, I'se free, I'se free, an' I ain't no dumb chile."

"I should think not," said Del, who was half shocked at the strange exhibition.

At that moment Papa returned.

"There is a wagon of some kind coming down the road," said Papa. "I should n't wonder if these children's people were in search of them."

Sure enough, the sound of creaking wheels could be heard, and the dogs set up a fearful barking, and in the midst of the din we heard a man's voice shouting, —

"US CHILLUNS."

"Hallo! Mostah!"

Papa opened the door; and there, perched up on the front seat of the funniest little old cart, drawn by a skinny mule, sat the queerest-looking pair, — Uncle Ben and Mammy, we knew at a glance.

"Good eben, mostah," squeaked the man. "Is you dun seed dem chilluns?"

"Dar dey is," screamed the woman, who caught a glimpse of them through the open door. "Yo' Bobry! ef I don't peel de hide off yo'!"

"Scuse me, mostah," spoke up Uncle Ben. "Dem's my chilluns; dey dun run away. Dey de mose onreasonin'. Ole 'oman an' me bin dribin' ebber sence fo' clock, clar frum de Brainch, arter dem chilluns."

"Here they are, all safe," said Papa; "but you can't take them home to-night, so you'd better alight and come in. We'll contrive to take care of you and your family and beast for the night, I reckon."

But Uncle Ben could n't be persuaded. He "wan't used, like, ter leavin' de cabin an' dem dogs all night by derselves."

Del began to coax the old mammy to come in and stay, and assured her that we had enjoyed the children's visit, and added, "Particularly Bobry's experience, which she has just given us."

"Now yo' 'll cotch it," said the solemn Usly, turning to Bobry.

You ought to have seen that woman as she listened to Del.

"Bobry dun gub yo' dat 'sperience? Bobry! g' 'long climb in dat kyaht. I'll bust yo' head, yo'. Dat ar ain't Bobry's 'sperience, missy; dat onregenrit nigga jis' stoled dat' sperience. Laws, missy, dat Bobry ain't got no 'ligion. Nebber did hab. Dat *my* 'sperience she dun bin gub yo'. She hyar me tole it in the 'sperience meetin', and den she pick it up an' say it her one.

"Moffy Jane, climb in dat kyaht. Meriky, *is* yo' in dar? I'se *dat* 'bleeged to y' alls, mostahs an' missys, fur keepin' dem yer sassy chilluns; an' ef ebber dey comes 'roun' a-pesterin' y' alls ag'in, I 'se be pow'ful 'bleeged to yo' ef yo' sets dem dogs onto 'em. Dat 'll fix 'em. Ain't dat so, Uncle Ben?"

Uncle Ben answered with a great haw-haw in his funny, squeaky voice, and the little mule with its comical load started off just as our clock struck ten.

I reckon they got to the Forks about breakfast-time next morning, but I don't know. We never heard of any of them again. We lived on the memory of that visit, however, for weeks.

CHAPTER III.

THE OLD RED SETTLE AND AN EVENING OF MERRY PROVINCIAL STORIES.

WHEN the Club came together on the next evening, a part of the members were much surprised at finding a quaint-looking piece of furniture on the piazza. It was old, worm-eaten, high-backed, and painted red, — an odd kind of settee, with a colonial look about it.

"This is an interesting piece of furniture, evidently," said Mr. Laurens. "What do you call it?"

"That is a settle," said the Widow Endicott, with good-humored dignity.

"It excites my curiosity," said Mrs. Laurens. "May I ask how it came here?"

"I brought it here from the garret. Every house of note used to have a red settle in colony times, and most stories in those days were told upon it."

The settle now began to be examined by the people on the piazza. The Widow continued: —

"Most of the stories of old times related to ghosts and Indians, or people who had sold their souls to the Evil One. They had no fairy stories; such stories would have been regarded as wicked.

"The old red settle used to be set before the open fire. The fireplaces were enormous. They were furnished with great back-logs and fore-sticks; and in the long evenings the fires were fed with seasoned wood. The workpeople and the children used to sit upon the settle; and the story-teller, who was sometimes an old man or an old woman, or the bachelor member of the family, or the schoolmaster, or even the minister, would take the end seat, and turning half around so as to face the others, would assume a very mysterious look,

THE OLD RED SETTLE.

and relate such horrible accounts of haunted houses as would take the wink out of the eyes of the listeners, and fix them in one stone-like stare. Sometimes the story-teller would be a sailor; if so, his tale would be like Nix's Mate, the old tar who was falsely accused and hung, and who caused the green island to die in Boston Harbor. The dead island is there yet. You need n't laugh.

"The fire would at times flame up during the telling of the narrative, and its light would fall upon the white faces and staring eyes. I do think that it was wicked to tell such stories to children. I used to go to bed after hearing them, and cover up my head with the blankets, and shake at every sound I heard in the room. One night the cat jumped upon my bed, and I came very near having a fit, for I thought that the cat was a witch. Witches were said to turn into cats, — black ones.

"I happened to see the old settle in my garret to-day among the rubbish, and I thought it would be just the article of furniture for story-telling, — kind of inspiring. Oh, the lies that have been told upon that settle!"

"But were all settles painted red?" asked Mrs. Laurens.

"Yes, they were all painted red."

"But why red?"

"I do not know, — the question is too deep for me; for the same reason, I suppose, that chimneys were painted red and blinds green."

The settle would hold seven persons comfortably, and so the whole Club were seated upon it.

The story-telling took a light turn, which was suggested by a remark by Mrs. Laurens.

"There are several things," said she, "that I have noticed about your farms that seem to me peculiar. One is the quaint scarecrows in the corn-fields; another, the open barns with their fragrant haylofts; and the last, the stone ovens for shell-fish in the orchards. The cool barns with their open doors and new hay, and the swallows flitting in and out, have a real charm that recalls the old English pastoral poetry; but the stone ovens on the ground, the shell-fish dinners in the orchards, and the quaint people who watch and tend the stone ovens with such anxious care, are incidents of life heretofore unfamiliar to me."

These remarks led Old Felix, the farmer, to relate a rather amusing tale of the summer woods and fields, — about a character that figures greatly in New England country life, but not often in story-books, poems, or fiction.

A STORY OF THE OLD NEW ENGLAND SCARECROW.

"Caw! caw! caw!"
"Whoa!" said Farmer Tolley. The team stopped. Farmer Tolley leaned on the plough-handle, and looked up to a clear space in the sky, which was as cerulean as a sea.
"Caw! caw! caw!"
There were light clouds drifting across the blue expanse, driven by the warm western winds; and between the earth and sky there was flying a dark object, — a solitary crow.
"Caw! caw! caw!"
"Yes, I hear ye," said Farmer Tolley. "Come to pull up my corn this year before it is planted. I know you of old. I dèclare it is too bad! Go 'lang!"
Not far from the field where the farmer was ploughing was a swamp. In winter, when it was frozen and "sledding" was good, the farmers worked there, cutting their summer's wood. But as soon as spring came, it was a miry bog. The great trees rise as from countless mossy islands. No one could penetrate it after April during the warm season, except when there was a drought. In this watery solitude, in the tops of the tall pines, the crows made their nests.
Farmer Tolley glanced up from the neat furrow the plough was turning, to see where the dark object was going. The black sails of the pirate of the air swept before the warm winds towards the pines in the deepest bogs of the swamp.
"I declare it is too bad!" reiterated the farmer. "Too bad! Just like your relations waitin' round fer your property before you die. Go 'lang!"
At the end of the furrow the farmer stopped his team, and went to the well-sweep in the dooryard for some water. While the well-pole was descending, his wife came to the door.
"Sophia, what do you think? I've seen *that* crow again."
"Sho! You don't say so, Pelick?" (Farmer Tolley's Christian name was Peleg.)
"Sure as you're alive, I have!"

"Do you think, Pelick, it was *the* same one?"

"Yes; he knew me, and spoke to me from the sky, just as though I had been one of the old prophets, and he'd been sent to try my patience. Blast him, it is too bad!"

'Do you think it was the same one that pulled your corn so last year, Pelick?"

"The same one, Sophia. Pulled the whole field up, so that I had to plant it all over ag'in, — when I had gone away to the Four Days' Meetin', and as a delegate too! I sha'n't go this year, if they elect me. That crow did me well-nigh on to fifty dollars' damage, — I don't know but a hundred."

Farmer Tolley tipped the bucket on the stone well-curb.

"Don't you want I should bring you out the dipper, Pelick, or a tumbler, or somethin'?"

"No, I can use the bucket just as well."

"Well, Pelick, I don't know what you'll do."

Peleg went back to his team.

The note of the bluebirds fluted through the mild air; the woodpecker tapped the trees; a flock of wild geese, honking, sailed along the sky; the fields and woods were full of pleasant sounds, that told that the season was changing; and Farmer Tolley would have been happy but for the warning voice of that terrible crow.

That evening, after milking and doing the chores, he sat down by the fire — for the evenings were yet somewhat long and cool — and took up the agricultural journal.

"Pelick," said his good wife, "what do you think I found? There's a piece in that paper about crows."

"Where, Sophia?"

"Let me take the paper, and I will find it for you. *There*, Pelick!"

Farmer Tolley adjusted his spectacles, and began to read. The cat climbed into his lap, and rubbed against the paper with a faint mew.

"You get down, puss! Let me read this. *Sophia!* Sophia, I say! It says here, Professor Solomon, one of these great professors that arranges the planets and all them things, I suppose — it says he says, Sophia, that the crow never alights *beneath* an object of which he is afraid. Just you listen a moment: 'It is a fact well known to ornithologists that a crow never alights *beneath* any object of which it is afraid. Hence scarecrows should be erected high in the air, like barrels on tall poles, etc. The New England custom of *stringing* the field is for this reason very effective.' Stands to reason that is so, Sophia. Folks are discoverin' almost everything now-a-days."

Farmer Tolley stroked the cat. He was a very guileless, tender-hearted man. It must have been a very mean kind of a crow to have pulled *his* corn, when he had "gone away to the Four Days' Meetin' as a delegate, too!"

After the bluebirds came the robins; after the robins, the martins; after the martins, the orioles; and then it was planting-time.

One day, when Farmer Tolley was industriously dropping corn and rejoicing in the sunshine, a black shadow swept across the row, like a partial eclipse, and his feet were arrested by a familiar voice,—

"Caw! caw! caw!"

"You black wretch!" said Farmer Tolley. "I'll fix you. You go along with your caw-caw-cawin'! Wait till I get up my scientific scarecrow! *That* will make your eyes stick out. You won't do as ye did last year when I set up my straw man. Kept a-comin' a little nearer and a little nearer and a little nearer, and finally, one damp day, you dropped down and lit upon his head. But I've got ye this year! There's nothin' that's like science."

The peach-boughs reddened with blossoms, the pear-trees became white as snow. Then the orchard burst into bloom, like hills of roses. There were burning bushes in all the roadsides and pastures. Then planting-time was over.

The bobolinks came, and the tender blades of corn began to form geometrical lines in the brown fields.

Just at this time, when there were damask mornings, and dewdrops on every leaf and blade of grass, and the clover was incense, and the roses were filling, as cups with wine, a wonder appeared in Bonneyville, such as the oldest inhabitant had never seen.

It was in Farmer Tolley's corn-field.

In the middle of the said field there was a rock. It was on this rock that the wonder appeared.

It consisted of the figure of a man, or rather of a giant, as though one of the champions of the aboriginal races had come back to behold the advances that science was making in the world. The effigy held in its hand a tall pole, and on the top of the pole was an *open umbrella*.

The farmer had set up this effigy one day at nightfall; it was on the evening of the first day that he discovered that his corn was beginning to break through hills.

On the morning after this gigantic apparition was made to lift up its umbrella thus high in the air, Farmer Tolley rose early, and took his milking-pails, and went out to milk his four thrifty cows. But the thought of his scarecrow, constructed after Professor Solomon's plan, so excited his curiosity that he put down his pails, and walked briskly towards the corn-field. He sat down there under a tree by the wall, and viewed with satisfaction and amazement the creation of his own hands which loomed above the sprouting field under the protecting umbrella.

The crow was also up early.

From the far-off pine-tops in the inaccessible bogs there came an exclamation of wonder.

"Caw! caw! caw!" with a flapping of glossy wings.

"Haw! haw! haw!" said the farmer, slapping his hands on his knees; "so you see it, do ye? I can take a little rest after plantin' time this year, thanks to Professor Solomon. Haw! haw! haw!"

When the neighbors saw the apparition, they also, as well as the crows, were greatly surprised. They stopped by the bars to look at it. Horses saw it from the road and were frightened. The selectmen met and talked about it. Was it safe? It might cause a skittish horse to run, or take the senses away from some nervous woman or child.

The sagacious farmer's corn came up well, and rejoiced in the sunshine of the glowing days. The farmer surveyed it with pride, and the crow with envy from afar off. When the ill-omened bird flew over that field, he flew high, as though, seized by a better inspiration, he was ascending towards the sun.

A third or fourth morning after the giant with the lofty umbrella had been placed upon the rock, Farmer Tolley again visited his field. The crow also had made a short excursion in that direction, and was contemplating the giant from a tree on the edge of the swamp.

"Caw! caw! caw!" he called, as he saw the farmer crawling through the bars of the promising field.

"You don't say so!" said the farmer. "Got along as far as you dare to, have n't ye? You see it, don't ye? How that corn is comin' up!"

The next morning brought to the farmer a further surprise. On going to the field, he found that the crow had arrived there before him, and was surveying the greenery from a tall white birch that rose from a corner in the wall.

The farmer stopped short when he first saw the black object swaying in the wind from the lithe top of the white-birch tree. He was thinking at that time of the wonderful advancement that knowledge was making in fields of discovery and in ascertaining the real relations of things, and he was rather humiliated at the suspicion that the crow also might have become a scientist and be making progress as well.

In these days of advancing knowledge the good parson called to see Peleg with an important message.

"I've been talking with the committee, Peleg, and they are unanimous that you shall go as the delegate to the June meeting this year. You had a rather hard experience last year, on account of that crow; but Deacon Holden says that he will get his little boy to watch your field this year. He thinks that he cannot go, anyhow."

"I shall not need any one to watch my field *this* year, parson. I have been studying science, and I have set up a contrivance that would terrify the boldest servant of the Prince of the power of the air — I mean, figuratively, that crow. Go out to field with me, Parson, and I will show you one of the most wonderful sights that you ever set eyes on! All the neighbors are talking about it!"

The parson and Farmer Tolley passed through the orchard towards the field. The flaky apple-blossoms drifted upon the breeze and whitened the emerald turf.

"This is a wonderful age in which we are living, Parson; steam-cars and telegraphs and balloons and pumps and things. There is one thing, Parson, that you can always trust, and — that — is — Science!"

The corn-field came into view with the colossal image erected to science under the ægis of the lofty umbrella.

"There, Parson, what do you think of that?"

"Caw! caw! caw!"

"Massy, Parson! where *did* that crow fly from? Rose right up out of the ground, like. Let's go and see if anything has touched the corn."

The geometry of the field was found to be perfect at every point.

"Peleg," said the parson, "science has many sides to it. You cannot trust a new principle of science until you know the whole of it and it is wholly proven. There are discoveries and discoveries."

"The principle of this discovery," said Peleg, "is that no crow ever alights underneath an object of which it is afraid. Now, any crow would be afraid of such an object as *that*, it stands to reason. That's so, Parson, every time. Therefore that there field is just as much protected and just as safe as though there was never a crow in all the wide world. That's what you would call logic, Parson."

"Yes, Peleg; but in these great logical questions one wants to be sure that his *premises* are correct. That crow knows more than you think he does, Peleg, and I would not leave a field of mine like that without watching at this time of year, without I was perfectly sure that my science and logic were perfectly correct. I wouldn't put any man's theory against that crow. He may have a theory of his own before you get back, Peleg. When a crow gets over being scared at an object, he becomes wonderfully tame and bold. My father once had a tame crow that would steal his shoe-strings out of his shoes when he was eating at the table. Theories are good things to work by, Peleg; but a man is accountable for the exercise of his common-sense. 'Prove all things,' the wise man said. Science is not science, and logic is not logic, unless you're sure."

Peleg and Sophia went to the June meeting. On the morning before Peleg started for this gathering of excellent, thrifty, well ordered people, which was appointed to take place in a little white church on the green of a neighboring town,

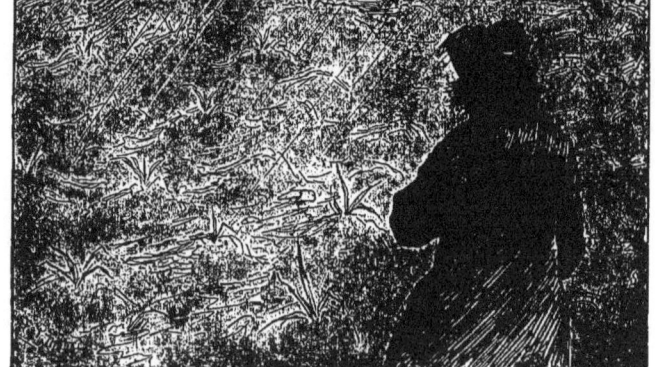

THE SCARECROW.

he walked proudly over the corn-field, which had become like a rippling sea of green. The thrushes were singing in the woods, and the robins in the orchards and dooryard trees.

"There is music everywhere," said Peleg.

A dreadful discord broke upon, or rather into, the choral harmonies of the woods and orchards and ancestral trees.

"*Young* crows, I do believe," said Peleg, — "a whole family of them; almost grown up, too. How lucky I am to have a scarecrow like *that!*"

The June meeting proved delightful to Peleg and Sophia. There was nothing selfish in Peleg's soul, and he related to several farmers who were delegates the achievements of science as illustrated by his wonderful scarecrow.

The day of his return was rainy. He remarked to Sophia that they had need of the umbrella which was protecting the giant in the corn-field. The latter certainly stood in no danger of rheumatism or catarrh.

"Never mind, Peleg," said Sophia; "it is doin' great service where it is."

Immediately on his return, Peleg visited the corn-field. He stopped at the bars. The crow did not greet him from the tree-tops, but, could it be? there was a black gulf in the sea of green. It was near the wonderful giant, who was still holding the open umbrella boldly above his head. The crow had surely been at work there.

Farmer Tolley walked slowly towards the desert in the late beautiful expanse. It was raining very hard.

As he approached the vacant space, his feet were arrested by a sound that made his lower jaw fall and his knees tremble. It came from the umbrella.

"Caw! caw! caw!"

Could it be?

Out from under the umbrella darted a dreadful object with wings like night, wildly ejaculating, "Caw! caw! caw!"

The farmer paused.

"I never!"

There was a commingling of Plutonian sounds inside of the umbrella, — a wail as from an orphan-asylum. Presently out flew a young crow.

Then another!

And another!

And a fourth!

They followed their mother, making a long, solemn procession through the windy, watery air. The poor things had lost their umbrella, but not their mother.

Farmer Tolley stood like one petrified. The collapse of science and logic and theory all in a moment, as it were, seemed to him like the blowing away of the world on which his feet of faith were planted. But he had not been gaining will power during the June meeting to fall into a passion on the very day of his return. He recalled, too, what his prudent parson had said about not being over-confident in a theory unless you are sure that all the premises are correct and well proved. He only said mildly, —

"I'll tell Sophia of that."

And he added philosophically, —

"When one plan does not work well, I've always noticed that the best way is to try another."

The next day the farmer removed the giant and the tall umbrella from the corn-field.

On the morning after the disappearance of the airy knight, a very innocent-looking scarecrow appeared upon the identical rock where science had met such a signal defeat. To the outward eye it was the figure of a man holding in his two hands a gun after the manner of a soldier presenting arms. Only Sophia knew the terrible secret contained in that immobile-looking figure.

The crow was up betimes on that morning, and beat its way through the sea of gray mist mingled with sunbeams to the lithe birch-tree in the corner of the field.

"Caw! caw! caw!"

The figure stood like a statue.

The brains of birds, like all brains, have their limitations ; and to the crow's limited philosophy that figure could not be a man. Corvus swung up and down on the tree-top in the billowy mist, and now and then added its bass notes to the sweet choruses of birds that encircled the field. Then he glided gently down on level wings into the middle of the field.

"BANG!"

Did ever a scarecrow fire a gun before?

If ever there was an astonished member of the raven family, it was that one ; astonished not only that a scarecrow should fire a gun, but that the effect should be so harmless. It took the lucky bird but a moment to recover its wings, and the way that the latter propelled a breakfastless body through space was something remarkable in the achievements of aerial velocity. The beguiled bird left the field in the dim distance before the echoes of the gun had ceased to die away among the pines. Then the scarecrow walked towards the farm-house, and had a talk with Sophia.

The summer came, and autumn powdered the autumn leaves, burned to gold. The purple swallows left the eaves ; the partridge fluttered about the walls of the corn-lands, and at last the wild geese again crossed the changing sky. The farmer raised a noble crop of corn that year.

The parson came to the husking. Peleg recited the history of the crop over the roast chickens, baked apples, and pumpkin pies.

"Parson," said he, "the premises of that last scarecrow theory were all correct, — were they not?"

"Not quite, not quite, Peleg," said the good parson. "What became of the crow?"

"He will not trouble me again next year, Parson."

Peleg was right. The crow was wise. He never again visited the philosophical farmer's fields, where scarecrows fire guns.

The story was received with applause, all clapping their hands, and a chorus of voices saying, —

"Now tell us one more, Uncle Felix?"

OUR ENTERTAINMENTS IN THE HAY-LOFT.

It happened when I was at school. One of the boys, named Brown, who was a great lover of Shakspeare, went to Boston and there became "stage-struck." When he came back he gave some performances in his room for the benefit of the class, — very remarkable performances they were, — and at last he suggested to us boys that it would be a commendable plan to get up, as he said, "some entertainments."

"We could begin with a concert, and, after some study, we could have amateur theatricals. We could at least give Othello strangling Desdemona. That would produce a thrilling effect, and would be something new in the school."

The idea of strangling Desdemona seemed to us very novel and picturesque, and we favored it.

There were quite a number in our school who enjoyed a local reputation for their declamatory abilities. We had one comic genius, and a singer or two; and with this force we hoped to achieve success. The girls of our acquaintance all promised to come, if we bought tickets for them, and pronounced the idea "splendid!"

The only difficulty was in finding a suitable place in which to give our performance.

The town-hall was out of the question, the vestries of the churches equally so, the school an impossibility; and no private house would answer, provided we could secure one.

The only available place seemed to be a spacious hay-loft over Frank Green's barn.

But, unfortunately, it would be about as well to ask Frank's mother for the use of her snapping black eyes as for her hay-loft.

Mrs. Green was one of those loud, demonstrative, hard-working women, who go stormfully through life, swift, strong, and energetic, noisy, and almost dangerous if you stood in her way.

She was the terror of all the children, although really she was a kind-hearted woman in her own way. She was always ready to do a good turn and help a neighbor in distress, but she could n't endure boys idling about her premises. She was sure they were trying to steal eggs, or fruit, or something or other belonging to her; and so she used to sally forth on them with her eyes aflame, clutching in her red right hand a most formidable cowhide.

I myself had two memorable encounters with the good lady. I once had to take a letter to a gentleman whose estate adjoined hers; and instead of going around and reaching it by the regular road, I leaped her wall and took a short cut across lots.

Just as I got about half-way, what should I behold but Mrs. Green, cowhide in hand, accompanied by two dogs, bearing down on me! To run would be utter madness, because I should be certain to have the canine fangs buried in my flesh long before I reached the opposite wall. Strategy alone could help me in this awful emergency. Politeness and very humble bearing on my part might mollify my pursuer; and these mild weapons I resolved to use, encouraged by the recollection that discretion is the better part of valor.

My plan of defence was instantly conceived.

I stood still, and began to look about me as if bewildered.

Down swept the enemy upon me.

Before she said a word — in fact, she did n't mean to speak much, except with the cowhide — I very politely asked her if she could inform me the nearest way to Mr. Anderson's. Her eyes flamed at me awhile; then, swallowing a lump in her throat, she pointed with her weapon the nearest way over the wall.

I thanked her with a bow and retreated without a glance behind, and felt extremely thankful when the stone wall was between us.

The other encounter forms the subject of this story.

Frank Green — a nice, quiet lad, like his late father — ascertained that his mother intended to go into the city soon, "for all day," at which time we might have the hay-loft for our entertainment.

"First-rate!" we shouted.

"Then we'll have your hay-loft, Frank. We'll have plenty of time to get ready!" cried Brown.

"Plenty!" we shouted.

"Tip-top!" ejaculated Brown. "And see, Frank, you can poke round up there, you know, in the mean time, and put things to rights, — get the hay tucked away and cleaned up a bit, you know. I s'pose it wouldn't do for one of us to go and help you?"

"'T wouldn't be well for mother to catch you, that's all!" said Frank, ominously.

"No! Well, all right! You'll do all that's wanted, Frank, in a quiet way, so as not to excite suspicion," said Brown. "And now, boys, you get your parts committed, and we'll have a rehearsal as soon as possible, — next Saturday afternoon, perhaps, down back of Old Smith's barn."

Brown, as I have suggested, was a forward, ambitious lad; and he took the whole management of the affair upon himself, although the suggestion was mine, in point of fact. Still I was, I confess, more apt at suggesting schemes than in carrying them into execution, and so very willingly conceded the work to my more energetic friend.

At length the memorable day arrived. It was as lovely a summer day as one could wish, — just like this. There was a brightness over everything, and our hopes were high with the pleasure we were about to enjoy and afford our friends, — especially our girl-friends, who would, no doubt, be charmed with the performance.

Mrs. Green left for the city early in the day, and was not to be home before late in the afternoon. Nearly all the school would be our audience. Everything looked in a fair way for a brilliant success.

At half-past two, the hour appointed, we began climbing the rickety ladder that led up to the hay-loft. This, of itself, made no little sport, but created some delay on account of the timidity of the girls.

In the course of time all were seated on such seats as could be improvised for the occasion. There were over twenty of us, all told, — speakers and audience. One of the boys led off with a song, in such a harsh voice that we were really glad when he broke down in the third verse and retired amid the applause of the audience.

Brown, the ambitious Brown, was dressed in a picturesque manner, and had no fewer than three pieces on the programme. His turn came next.

He stepped to the platform, — or, rather, what we called such, — made a profound bow, and just as he uttered the words "Ladies and Gentlemen," a voice from below shouting, "Who's up there?" made my hair stand on end.

There was a dead silence.

"Ladies and Gentlemen," continued Brown, "I arise to do you the honor of giving you a selection from Shakspeare. It is from 'Othello,' and I think you never saw anything like the performance that I am now about to perform."

He was right.

"I've been to Boston and have seen it done, and it brought tears to the aujunce's eyes.

"Othello, you know, was jealous of Desdemona, his wife. One day he came home and found her asleep, and determined to smother her with a bolster. This I shall now proceed to do."

The excitement was intense. Brown kicked together some loose hay, and threw his thin coat over it with the amazing declaration, —

"That is Desdemona!"

He then took a large towel he had brought, and held it up.

"That is the bolster."

In a deep voice Brown approached the supposed Desdemona on her couch, and said, —

"I will kill thee!"

"I say," said a strange, hesitating voice, not at all in the programme. It came up from below.

There was a short silence; then Brown proceeded.

"I must weep." (And he did.) "But they are cruel tears. She wakes!"

Then, in a squeaking voice, supposed to represent the waking Desdemona, he said, —

"Who's there? Othello?"

There followed an unexpected inquiry.

"I say, who's there?"

This latter question was hardly an echo. The voice seemed to come up from below. We listened with beating hearts.

But Brown was full of his subject now, and proceeded in a high voice, —

"Thou art to die!"

He then added in a changed voice supposed to be Desdemona's, —

"Heaven have mercy on me!"

Brown next bent over the bundle of hay, and proceeded to smother the helpless wife. A strange convulsive sound, as of one in mortal agony, seemed to issue from the old coat and hay. It was a thrilling moment.

Then came that other voice.

"I say, who's up there on the mow? I want to know right off now!"

It was Mrs. Green! She wasn't on the programme.

"I say, who's there?" said the voice, in such a resolute tone as caused us all to start.

THE BARN THEATRICALS.

There was profound silence.
"I hear some one up in that loft; come down, I say, at once!"
"I'm up here, mother," said Frank, with pale lips.
"Yes, and who else? It wasn't your voice I heard. Is there any one else? Tell me before I come up with the cowhide!"

LOOK ALOFT.

In the words of the poet,

"Ah, then and there was hurrying to and fro,
And gathering tears, and tremblings of distress."

Yes, it was a fearful moment, and to this day, after the lapse of thirty years, I remember my own sensations. Frank was the first to descend; and the sound of the cowhide on his jacket was by no means encouraging.

One after another we dropped to the floor, where the amiable old lady was applying the cowhide in a most vigorous style, uttering all kinds of threats and exclamations with equal force and perseverance.

At last the skirts began to make their appearance.

THE OLD RED SETTLE AND PROVINCIAL STORIES. 99

"What! Girls!"

This apparition completely bewildered her. Boys were bad enough, but girls fairly paralyzed her arm for a moment, so that the cowhide dropped at her side. But Mrs. Green was equal to the occasion, and faithfully did her duty.

"Jane, is that you?"
Whack! Whack!
"Liddy, is that you?"
Whack! Whack!
"Thankful, is that you?"
Whack! Whack!

And in this uniform manner each girl, as she descended the ladder of the improvised theatre, was met, and given an inspiration which accelerated her movements in the nearest direction towards home.

I was not forgotten in the general discipline. I had all the entertainments I cared to receive that afternoon, and I have not been to any place of amusement since. I did not even go to see " Pinafore."

The Widow Endicott related the next story. It was an experience of her girlhood, when she sung her first solo in the choir of a country church. During this maiden effort a dog got his head into a water-pitcher on the floor of the gallery, and fell over into the pews below. The story was hardly provincial or historical, but greatly amused the Laurenses.

A tale told by the intelligent old farmer Felix was more to the point.

THE SOLEMN MAN.

In an old burying-ground at the head of a smooth sheet of water known as Bullock's Cove, in what is now Seekonk, Mass., may be seen a rough stone, on which is rudely carved the following inscription : —

MDCLXXIV.
HERE LYETH THE BODY OF THE WORTHY
THOMAS WILLET, ESQ.,
WHO DIED AUGUST YE 4TH, IN YE LXIVTH
YEAR OF HIS AGE, ANNO —,
WHO WAS THE FIRST MAYOR OF NEW YORK,
AND TWICE DID SUSTAIN THE PLACE.

Thomas Willet, the successor of Miles Standish in the captaincy of the Plymouth-Colony militia, the founder of old Swansea, and the first English Mayor of New York, was born in England in 1611. He was bred a merchant, and he became acquainted with the Pilgrims at Leyden, when a mere lad, while travelling on business in Holland. He was a resolute youth, large-hearted and adventurous; and, the lofty aims of the Pilgrims having engaged his sympathies, he embarked for Plymouth in 1629, being one of the last of the Leyden company who sought a place of religious freedom in the rugged solitudes of the Western World. He was then about eighteen years of age, his mind well schooled in the duties and responsibilities of mercantile life, and polished by travel and by intercourse with the most cultivated people; his aspirations high, and his trust in God firm and pure. Soon after his arrival he was sent by the people of Plymouth to establish a trading-house at Kennebec, and to superintend their business at that place as agent. He remained there about seven years, and, though a mere youth, he bravely endured the hardships of the winter-bound forests, and fulfilled his duties with singular prudence and success.

In 1647 he succeeded Miles Standish in the command of the military of Plymouth Colony. This office was no sinecure, but one involving stern duties and grave responsibilities; and he brought to it the essential requisite of mature judgment, an unbending will, and a stout heart.

In 1651 he was elected one of the Governor's assistants in the Court at Plymouth, to which office he was annually re-elected for fourteen years.

In the winter of 1660 Captain Willet was an inhabitant of Rehoboth, Mass., having obtained permission to purchase large tracts of land in that section of country. Soon after his coming to Rehoboth he received the consent of the Court at Plymouth to purchase a tract of land of Womsitta, or Alexander, the eldest son of the friendly sachem Massasoit, which was then called the Rehoboth North Purchase, but which is now known as Attleborough, Mass., and Cumberland, R. I. He was also the original proprietor of a large tract of land known as the Taunton North Purchase, where now flourish the towns of Norton, Mansfield, and Easton, Mass., — names familiar to the traveller.

In 1664 Charles II. of England, unwilling that any but English settlers should maintain an independent government in the midst of his growing colonies, made a grant of all the territory claimed by the Dutch at Manhattan and on the North River to his brother, the Duke of York and Albany. Colonel Richard Nicholls was commissioned to take possession of these Dutch colonies, and to exercise jurisdiction over them in the name of the Crown. Colonel Nicholls, with ships-of-war and an armed force, landed at Boston in the summer of that year, and demanding and receiving reinforcements from the Massachu-

ENGLISH AND DUTCH QUARRELS.

setts and Connecticut colonies, appeared in New York Bay about the beginning of autumn.

The result of the expedition is well known,— the resolute behavior of Governor Stuyvesant, the councils at the old Stadt-house, and the easy capitulation of the town by the fat burgomasters. New Amsterdam took the name of the city from which the English duke derived his title, and the Dutch officials gave place to a new government formed in harmony with the colonial laws established by the English king.

Colonel Nicholls, after the reduction of Manhattan, turned to Captain Willet as a man of an even disposition and a well-poised mind, a professional merchant, and a fluent speaker of Dutch, to assist "in modelling and reducing the affairs of the newly acquired settlements into good English." He wrote to Governor Prince, earnestly requesting that Captain Willet might have such dispensation from his official duties in Plymouth Colony as to act as his assistant, and pointing out his especial fitness for the work.

The request was granted, and Captain Willet entered at once upon his difficult labors in New York. He was already favorably known to the Dutch, and his appointment was received by them with satisfaction.

Captain Willet encountered many difficulties in his efforts to establish pacific measures. The Dutch were hostile to the English, and the Indians were unfriendly towards the Dutch. But he succeeded so well in harmonizing the discordant elements that he won the sympathies of the new subjects, and received from them the title of peacemaker. Immediately after the organization of the government, he was elected the first English mayor of New York, which office he filled so acceptably as to secure a re-election on the following year. He afterward was chosen umpire by the Dutch to determine the disputed boundary between the New York and New Haven colonies. When the two years of his mayoralty had expired, he returned to his home in Rehoboth.

Captain Willet was a man of liberal religious views, and did not sympathize with the exclusiveness of the Colonist. He probably had connected himself in youth with the Reformed Church in Holland. Shortly before his retirement from public office he made the acquaintance of the Rev. John Miles, a Baptist clergyman who had been driven from his living in Wales by the Act of Conformity of 1662,— an acquaintanceship that ripened into warm friendship and yielded generous fruit. In 1667 Captain Willet and Mr. Miles secured from the Plymouth Court the grant of a township which they named New Swansea, from the old home of the Welsh pastor and the Sea of Swans near his home in Wales. Here they established a church, Baptist in name, but open in communion, the covenant defending in powerful language the equal rights of Christians to the table of the Lord. The mode of baptism to be administered was to be left in each case to the choice of the candidate ; and the church, free from all ecclesiastical impedimenta, went vigorously to work and soon drew to its fellowship many strong men from the Colonies. The Presbyterian adventurers from Harlem-Meer sung sweetly with the exiles from the Severn ; Baptists, Congregationalists, and Quakers worshipped under the same roof, and before the pulpit of a liberal Baptist elder.

> "We legends read of Church and State,
> Of wars in lands decaying,
> The banner of the cross in hate
> Uplifted o'er the slaying.
>
> "A better legend lingers here
> In stainless history given ;
> Sweet sung the men from Harlem-Meer
> With exiles from the Severn."

Captain Willet, shortly after the grant of the township of New Swansea, made proposals to the church and to the town concerning the admission of new settlers : —

1. That no erroneous person be admitted into the township as an inhabitant or sojourner.

2. That no man of any evil behavior, as contentious persons, be admitted.

3. That none may be admitted that may become a charge to the place.

These proposals were "ratified, confirmed, and settled as a foundation-order" by the church and the town.

It should be here stated, in justice to these worthy men, that probably this last proposal was not intended to disqualify unfortunate persons for citizenship, but to keep out the unthrifty. All well-meaning persons were welcome to the township, however poor.

Here, amid the pine groves of Swansea, near the calm waters of the Narragansett, Captain Willet passed his declining years. Respected by the expanding Colonies, revered by the church and by the inhabitants of the town he had founded, and beloved by a numerous family, the close of his life was serene and happy ; and he passed away peacefully at last, as one goes home at eventide after resting awhile on the sun-sprinkled sheaves of a bountiful harvest.

Captain Willet married Mary Brown, the daughter of John Brown the elder, at Plymouth, by whom he had thirteen children. His grandson, Francis Willet, was a prominent man in the Colony of Rhode Island. His great-grandson, Colonel Marinus Willet, served with distinguished honor in the Revolutionary

War, and was also elected Mayor of New York. The descendants of Captain Willet are numerous in New York and in other sections of the country.

His house was a fine one for colonial times, and relics of it still remain. One of the doors may be seen in an antiquarian collection in the possession of the city of New York. Rhode Island antiquarians have bricks from the chimney; and a house in South Providence, occupied by Samuel Viall, Esq., contains bricks used in building the old Willet mansion (probably imported from Holland), and two doors of like antiquity, that retain the fantastic ornamental painting of a departed age. Captain Willet's sword is in the keeping of the city of New York.

Once, in his business among the tribes of New England, certain Indians in Maine conspired to kill him.

"We are famishing," said the leader. "There is corn in the storehouse, corn from Plymouth. Willet, — let us murder him, and we will have corn."

They found Mr. Willet alone one day in his trading-house.

He was reading the Bible; and according to the thought and custom of the times, was unwilling to speak until the reading had concluded.

"Ugh!" said the leader.

Mr. Willet looked up with a solemn and severe face, but did not say a word.

"Ugh!"

Mr. Willet dropped his eyes upon the Bible, as though consulting it, and continued to read.

The Indians slowly moved back.

"He knows our plot," said the leader.

"What is he reading?" asked the others.

"The book of the Great Spirit," was suggested.

"Then he has found us out. He knows. I can see it in his face. Run!"

His grave is neglected; but antiquarians sometimes find their way to the sequestered spot, and decipher the rude inscription amid the moss and the fern. It would seem that the defender of infant colonies, the founder of flourishing churches and towns, and the first English Mayor of our great metropolis, should have a more appropriate memorial than a rough stone to mark the spot where rests his dust.

A poem by Mr. Leland, recalling scenes of the shores which often were seen on their excursions, closed the evening's entertainment.

CHAPTER IV.

SOME STRANGE HISTORIC STORIES.

THE old tavern in Lakeville is situated in a region historically interesting, and has often been the scene of story-telling. The lake that lies in front is as serene and almost as blue as the sky. In the long June days the meadows fill the air with sweetness, and the September hazes are like sun-showers of gold.

The Sassamon Reservation is not a long distance from the tavern, but is not connected with any public highway. One must go to it through private grounds; and one may have to take down and put up again many pairs of bars, before he reaches the Indian houses, of which but a few remain.

Here live the descendants of the great sachem Massasoit, in a house built for the most part, we have been told, by the Indian princesses Wootonekanuske and Teweelema with their own hands. Some account of the family may be found in a book entitled "Families of Royal Descent," which relates to such people who have a residence in America.

One morning, Henry Laurens was surprised to see a modest, graceful lady, in full Indian costume, come from a path near the lake and enter the public highway. She carried a collection of small but very tasteful baskets.

"Who is that?" he asked of Charlie Leland.

"The Princess Teweelema," said Charlie. "She is a direct descendant of the family of Massasoit. Her mother lives near here."

"Let us go and visit her," said Henry.

The two boys entered the wood by the lake-side, Charlie leading. The woods were of oak, birch, and pine, and delightfully cool and shady. The placid lake could here and there be seen through the long arcades of trees.

They came at last to a strange-looking house, and were cordially received by an Indian lady nearly eighty years of age, but having the appearance of a woman of fifty. Here they purchased of her a book which she had published, entitled "Indian History and Genealogy." From this the boys learned that the good sachem Massasoit had a daughter named Amie. This princess was a sister to Alexander (Wamsutta) and King Philip (Mitaam). The son of Philip was sold into slavery after the Indian War, but Amie survived.

They further learned from this most interesting book that —

1. Amie had married Taspaquin, or the Black Sachem, chief of the Assawamsett Indians;

2. This Indian family were the descendants in the sixth or seventh generation from the heroic family of Massasoit and Taspaquin.

"The history of this royal family is a romance but little known outside of Middleborough, even in Massachusetts," said Mr. Leland, to whom the boys gave some account of their visit. He added:—

"This evening I will tell you a story of this royal family that is but little known, but that is as heroic and dramatic as anything to be found in American history."

Mr. Leland visited the Indian princesses that afternoon, and invited them to be present at the evening story-telling.

Early in the evening the Club filled the old red settle, and the guests of the hotel the piazza. Among the visitors was the beautiful Teweelema, in full Indian costume.

Mr. Leland introduced the stories of the evening with the following narrative.

A STRANGE CHAPTER OF INDIAN HISTORY.

Two years before the landing of the Pilgrims at Plymouth, Mass., a remarkable pestilence swept off the greater part of the Indians inhabiting that part of the country. The warriors of the three tribes of the Wampanoags, Massachusetts, and Pawtuckets were reduced to mere bands of men.

We do not know that any early historian has given a very circumstantial account of this remarkable event, the facts of which could have been obtained only from the Indians. Many of the early writers, however, allude to it; and these data, when collected, make an interesting if not a satisfactory history. Dr. Webster made a partial collection of such data, and published them in his work on " Pestilential Diseases." The Doctor says : " As this is one of the most remarkable facts in history, I have taken great pains to ascertain the species of the disease and the time of its appearance." He decides that the pestilence was the true American plague, called the Yellow Fever, and that the time of its appearance was the year 1618.

King James mentions the desolating effects of the pestilence as one of the reasons for granting the great patent of New England (Nov. 3, 1620) : " We have been further given certainly to know that within these late years there hath been, by God's visitation, a wonderful plague amongst the savages, those heretofore inhabiting, in a manner, to the utter destruction, devastation and depopulation of the whole territory, so as there is not left, for many leagues together, in a manner, any that do claim or challenge any kind of interest therein ; whereby we, in our judgment, are persuaded and satisfied that the appointed time is come in which Almighty God, in his goodness and bounty towards us and our people, hath thought fit that these large and goodly territories, deserted as it were by their natural inhabitants, should be possessed and enjoyed by such of our subjects and people as shall by his mercy and favor, and by his powerful arm, be conducted thither."

Belknap says in his " American Biography " (Life of Fernando Gorges) that Richard Vines and his companions, who had been sent by Gorges to explore

FIGHT BETWEEN A SETTLER AND AN INDIAN CHIEF.

the country, wintered among the Indians during the pestilence, and adds that the disease in no wise affected the English.

Purchas mentions that Captain Dermer, an English adventurer, who sailed along the northern coast in May, 1619, landed at several places where he had stopped a year before, and found many Indian towns wholly depopulated, and in others not a single person who was free from sickness.

Higginson, in his "New England's Plantation" (1613), thus refers to the disease: "Their subjects about twelve years since were swept away by a great and grievous plague that was amongst them, so that there are very few left to inhabit the country."

General Gookin in his "Historical Collections of the Indians," written in 1674, says of the "Pawkunnawkutts" (the Wampanoags): "This nation, a great number of them, were swept away by an epidemical and unwonted sickness, Anno 1612–13, about seven or eight years before the English first arrived in those parts to settle the colony of New Plymouth. Thereby Divine Providence made way for the quick settlement of the English in those nations." Of the Massachusetts: "In Anno 1612–13 these people were also sorely smitten by the hand of God with the same disease, which destroyed the most of them, and made room for the English people of Massachusetts Colony. There are not of this people left at the present day above three hundred men, besides women and children."

The date of this pestilence is given differently by different writers and antiquarians. Gookin, one of the best of the old authorities, gives it as 1612. General Fessenden, of Warren, R. I., the author of a very valuable paper on "Massasoit and his Family," fixes it at 1616. A letter from Captain Dermer, in Purchas, makes the time of the principal sickness the winter of 1618. Elder Cushman, in the dedicatory epistle to a sermon preached at Plymouth soon after the arrival of the Pilgrims and published in London soon after the establishment of the Colony, and which bears the date of 1621, says: "They [the Indians] were very much wasted of late by a great mortality that fell among them three years since, which with their own civil dissensions and bloody wars hath so wasted them that, as I think, the twentieth person is scarcely left alive." It seems to be certain that Dr. Webster is correct when he fixes the date of the greatest mortality at 1618. This, however, may be but the culminating point of a long pestilential period, as it is probable that Gookin (1674) had evidence of the appearance of the sickness in 1612.

But few facts remain concerning the nature of the disease. Hutchinson says that many of the early settlers supposed it to have been the small-pox. Captain Dermer (1618) speaks of it as the plague, and gives his reason that he had seen "the sores of some that had escaped, who described the *spots* of such as usually die." Prince's "Chronology" records that it produced hemorrhage from the nose. On this point, however, Gookin seems decisive. He says: "Doubtless it was some pestilential disease. I have discoursed with some old Indians that were then youths, who say that the bodies all over were exceeding yellow, describing it by a yellow garment that they showed me, both before they died and afterwards." This evidence sustains the views of Dr. Webster.

Morton, in his "New England Canaan," gives the following affecting account of the ravages of the disease, and of the scene presented by the depopulated wilderness: "Some few years before the English came to inhabit at New Plymouth, the hand of God fell heavily upon the natives with such a mortal stroke that they died in heaps. In a place where many inhabited, there hath been but one left alive to tell what became of the rest; and the bones and skulls upon the several places of the habitations made such a spectacle after my coming into these parts, that as I travelled in that forest, near the Massachusetts, it seemed to me a new-found Golgotha. This mortality was not ended when the Brownites of New Plymouth were settled at Patuxet; and by all likelihood the sickness that these Indians died of was the plague, as by conference with them since my arrival and habitation in these parts I have learned."

The tribe of the Wampanoags, a once powerful nation, inhabiting the eastern shores of the Atlantic from Cape Cod to the Narragansett Bay, which numbered thirty thousand people and three thousand warriors, and which was renowned for the beauty of its hunting-grounds and the valor of its braves, was reduced in a very brief period to less than five hundred souls. The powerful tribe of the Massachusetts, according to Hutchinson, lost more than twenty-nine thousand out of its thirty thousand people, and the Pawtuckets were almost wholly destroyed.

What a scene of desolation must the primitive forests of New England have presented in the temperate seasons of 1619! What strange emotions must have filled the bosoms of those who escaped the stroke of the great destroyer! The birds sung in the spring-time, but there were few to hear; the wild beasts multiplied and the fishes filled the warm currents of the bays and streams, but there were few to take the bow and the fishing-rod. The dreadful odor of decaying bodies filled the air, and unclean birds and beasts picked the bones of those who were once their natural enemies. The summer moons rounded, but looked down upon silent forests and oarless streams. The Indian maiden no longer disported in her birchen canoe, and the braves gathered no more before the villages with their hatchets and war plumes. The autumn sun shone on the uncultured maize-field, and the hunter's moon upon the old places of festivity, once alive with those who assembled to see the feats of the conjurer and dancer, but now frequented no more. The land was a still sepulchre, whitened with the bones of those who inhabited it.

The Indians who survived looked upon the terrible visitation with a resignation and fortitude worthy of a more enlightened faith. They spake of it as the work of the Great Spirit, who multiplied the nations, and whose wisdom the feeble creatures who people the earth could not divine or measure. The old Indian prophets had seen visions of great boats, with snowy wings, flying low on the luminous waters, and bringing strange people from unknown regions over the sea. The impression had long prevailed among the wise men of the tribes, that great changes were about to happen. Their faith in the wisdom and justice of the Great Spirit never faltered. The remnants of the tribes expected to meet the shades of departed friends in the regions that know no pestilence, amid shining streams, and in forests of eternal beauty.

The plague of 1618 may have been peculiar to the native races. Richard Vines and his companions who wintered among the Indians at the time of the greatest mortality, and who remained unharmed, seem to have held this view, — a view that is sustained by another very remarkable circumstance. "In 1762 the remnants of the Indian tribe dwelling on Nantucket and Martha's Vineyard were attacked by what seems to have been a milder form of the same sickness that had proved so fatal to their ancestors about a century and a half before. The Nantucket Indians numbered something less than four hundred. Two hundred and fifty-eight were seized with the disease, and of these only thirty-six survived. On Martha's Vineyard not a family escaped, and out of fifty-two patients thirty-nine died. "The disease," says Dr. Webster, "began with high fever, and ended with typhus in about five days. It appeared to be infectious among the Indians only; for no whites were attacked, although they associated freely with the diseased. Persons of a mixed blood were attacked, but recovered. Not one died except of full Indian blood. I am informed by a respectable authority that a similar fever attacked Indians on board of ships at a distance of hundreds of leagues, without any connection with Nantucket."

This indeed was the "pestilence that walketh in darkness" and the "destruction that wasteth at noonday." Fancy only can paint the scenes of these dark days. How strange a preparation for the Pilgrims was this destruction of the tribes; without it, the early Colonies must have been swept away in Philip's War.

Farmer Felix, to whom the whole history of the region was familiar, gave a picture of the romance of early New England in the following narrative. The story presented a very clear view of the early settlements during the Indian War.

QUEEN WETAMOO.

A NEGLECTED ROMANCE OF INDIAN HISTORY.

I spent my early years in Warren, R. I., — a town historically famous as Sowanes, the home of Massasoit.

My ancestors had lived at Mount Hope, in Bristol, R. I., and I had learned from the old members of the family many Indian romances, when I made the acquaintance of General Guy M. Fessenden, author of the history of "Massasoit and his Family," and was so much interested in the results of his historical researches as to seek to recover the story of Wetamoo, — an Indian Boadicea, whose name is familiar, but whose history is almost unknown.

As the traveller from Boston drops down Mount Hope Bay on one of the New York steamers from Fall River, he can hardly fail to be impressed with the picturesque landscapes on the east. This region, overlooking the calm inland seas and lifting its dreamy fields to a level with the brow of Mount Hope on the west, was once known as Pocasset. A part of Pocasset now bears the name of Tiverton.

The old sachem of Pocasset had two daughters, named Wetamoo and Wootonekanuske. One of the rustic palaces of Massasoit doubtless stood directly across the bay from the airy brow of Pocasset; and as Wamsutta and Pometacom (Philip) here spent a part of their youth, we may fancy that their light skiffs often shot across the bay to the dwelling of the beautiful princesses on the Pocasset shore. Alexander (Wamsutta) married Wetamoo, the more interesting of the two Indian maidens; and Philip (Pometacom) married Wootonekanuske, who was probably the younger. The wooing of the Pocasset princesses seems to have been the last romantic event in the history of the once powerful tribe of the Wampanoags.

Wetamoo became Queen of Pocasset. So far as we know, no historian has given a connected account of the life of this brave but unfortunate Indian queen. It is our purpose to write a brief sketch of her history, as far as the fragmentary data that remain concerning her will allow.

Massasoit regarded Alexander with deep affection, and associated him in the government of the Wampanoags. Several of the old deeds of sale given by Massasoit in his last years bear the signature of Alexander.

INDIAN ATTACK ON SETTLERS.

On the death of Massasoit, Alexander was invested with the sachemship. He was a noble Indian, prudent and considerate, but lofty in spirit and dignified in demeanor. He was a true patriot ; and he witnessed with alarm the expansion of the Colonies, and repented the sale of the beautiful hunting-grounds of his fathers, now passed from his control.

An altered spirit between the Indians and the Colonists began to manifest itself soon after his succession. The English, conscious of their power, ceased to be scrupulous and forbearing in their dealings with the Indians, as they had been with the great Massasoit in the infancy of the Colonies. Unprincipled men found their way to the frontier settlements, who defrauded the native inhabitants and treated them arrogantly. The Indian sages saw that the glory of the old tribes was departing, and their counsels advised that the rising tide of emigration be stayed.

Alexander treated the English respectfully, but coolly. He looked out on the dominion that had been his father's, and regarded it as despoiled ; he looked back on the long friendship of his father for the English, and saw in return that his people were despised. He felt the cloud of war darkening in the distance, and began to prepare for the storm. He numbered his warriors, determined to maintain those river-bright regions that God and Nature had intrusted to his keeping, and to defend, if need be, the liberties of his race. But we have no evidence that he ever intended to commence an aggressive war.

In 1661, not long after the death of Massasoit, rumors began to float through the air that the Pokanokets were preparing to make an attack upon the Colonies. Governor Prince at Plymouth received a letter from a friend, who had been called by business to Narragansett, which stated that Alexander was meditating hostilities, and was endeavoring to persuade the powerful sachem of the Narragansetts to unite with him against the English.

Governor Prince acted promptly. He ordered Captain Thomas Willet, one of his assistants, to go at once to Mount Hope, the royal residence of Alexander, and to inform the sachem of the reports that had reached Plymouth, and request him to be present at the next session of the Court at Plymouth, to vindicate himself from the charges that the Colonists were making against him.

Alexander received Captain Willet cordially and with dignity. He listened to the complaint respectfully, and replied that the accusation was false ; that the Narragansetts were his enemies, and that he had no wish to destroy the friendly relations that had so long existed between the Pokanoket chieftains and the rulers of Plymouth Colony. He agreed to the proposal made by Captain Willet, in behalf of the Governor, that he should attend in person the next Court at

Plymouth, and there publicly declare his pacific intentions, and satisfy the government that the charges made against him were untrue.

Alexander may have been sincere when he made this denial of the accusation, and this promise to answer in person to the charge before the Court at Plymouth. If so, reflection altered his purpose, and led him to regard the request of the Governor's messenger as a covered insult, and compliance with such a request as a departure from the dignity of the sachemship. Was he, the chieftain of the Wampanoags, — a tribe, time out of mind, glorious in peace and renowned in war, — to be held accountable for the acts of his government to parties of adventurers whom the generosity of his father had allowed to make their homes within the limits of his dominions? His lofty spirit, animated with all the fiery impulses of youth, recoiled from such an exhibition and fall. He looked upon himself, not as a cringing roytelet to be ordered hither and thither by those whom his family had pitied and spared, but as the rightful and proper head of all the river-cleft regions from the Narragansett to the sea.

The Court assembled, but Alexander did not appear. Instead of repairing to Plymouth, he went to his former enemy, the powerful sachem of the Narragansetts, doubtless to ask the assistance of his warriors for his own protection, and for the protection of the liberties of the Indian race.

Governor Prince, on hearing of Alexander's visit to the Narragansetts, called together his counsellors. Having received their advice and approval, he ordered Major Winslow to take a band of picked men, and to go to Mount Hope and surprise Alexander and bring him by force to Plymouth. Whether this act of hostility was wise and prudent, one cannot tell, for the motives and purposes of Alexander must remain forever a mystery ; but it proved the beginning of those dark scenes of New England history known as the Indian War, and in this case the English clearly were the aggressors.

Major Winslow immediately set out from Marshfield with a small body of men, for the royal residence of the Pokanoket chieftain. He intended to strengthen this force from towns near the bay. He needed but few men ; for the Indians, after nearly half a century of peace, had ceased to be suspicious, and the appearance of a company of English soldiers at any of their principal settlements would not have been regarded as a cause for alarm.

About midway between Plymouth and Bridgewater, Major Winslow and his men came to a smooth sheet of water, doubtless Moonponset Pond. Upon the bank was a rustic hunting-lodge, where a band of hunters were reposing and feasting after the toils of the chase. The Major soon ascertained that this was one of the transient residences of Alexander, and that the unsuspecting sachem was then there, with Wetamoo, banqueting with his friends.

ALEXANDER CARRIED A PRISONER TO PLYMOUTH

The Colonists lurked about the hunting-house awhile in silence. They discovered that the guns of the Indians had been left unguarded some distance from the entrance. Major Winslow ordered the seizure of these; then, with a few sturdy followers, marched directly into the cabin.

The Indians manifested no surprise on seeing the English, but greeted them cordially. Major Winslow requested Alexander to step out of the cabin with him for a brief conference. The sachem readily complied.

"I am ordered to arrest you for plotting against the English," said the major. "You must return with me, to answer to the charge at Plymouth."

The sachem seemed bewildered. He was slow to believe that such perfidy and insolence could be possible in the English. Major Winslow reaffirmed his order and his purpose.

Alexander's eyes flashed, and his heart palpitated. A moment's reflection kindled his wild passions; and he stood before his accuser, like a roused satyr of the forest, towering with rage.

"This is an insult!" he said on returning to his followers, "which my spirit cannot bear, and to which I never will submit!"

The Indians caught the hidden meaning of the declaration, and made ready to defend their chieftain. Major Winslow, understanding the movement, levelled his pistol at the captive's breast and said, —

"I am ordered to take you to Plymouth; and I shall do it, so help me, God. If you comply peacefully, you shall be treated kindly; if you resist, I will shoot you upon the spot."

The Indians outnumbered the English, almost ten to one; but they were disarmed. Seeing the helplessness of their situation, they urged Alexander to submit peacefully, and promised him, with true Indian fidelity, that they would accompany him to Plymouth.

Among the number was Wetamoo, young and beautiful, dressed in the fantastic habit of an Indian queen, in a manner to shed the utmost lustre upon her charms.

The Colonists began to return with their unhappy captive. Alexander, accompanied by his beautiful queen, led the retinue of Indians, sullen and silent. It was the warm season, and the day was sultry and oppressive. The English offered the sachem a horse that he might ride; but he declined the offer with dignity, saying that he preferred to walk with his family and friends.

Arrived at Duxbury, the illustrious captive was taken to Major Winslow's residence, where he was hospitably entertained, but guarded with scrupulous care. Here a sense of his wrongs, and the discovery of the true situation and the perils of his people, bore down his high spirit, and unsettled his mind. His mental anguish was so great as to destroy his health, and he fell a victim to a burning fever. His disease was rapid, and his sufferings were fearful to behold. The pride of the Indians who had followed him now gave way, and they begged piteously to be allowed to take their beloved chieftain home. Even the frigid spirit of the Colonist was not proof against such heart-rending appeals; and the Court at Plymouth, on receiving the report of the doctors concerning the actual state of the sufferer, consented to allow him to be taken back on the condition of the Indians sending them his son as a hostage for his reappearance at that place on his recovery.

The Indians mounted the quivering sachem on a litter upon their shoulders, and entered the cool trails of the forest. They travelled slowly, silent as stoics, the settled purpose of revenge smouldering in their hearts. There was pity in each eye, and the dark line of trouble on each brow, but they shed no tears. At length the forest solitude was broken by a calm river. They lowered their burden gently and tenderly, and placed it in one of the canoes lying upon the shore.

The light paddles lifted, and the boat dropped down the smooth river, now fanned by the airy boughs of marginal trees, now shining in the tempered light of the sun. Presently the paddles were suspended and fell tardily. A change had come over the chieftain: he was dying.

They took him to the shore, and laid him down under a spreading tree. The braves gathered around him in silence and in awe. Wetamoo bent over him, her bosom heaving in sympathy, and her hands performing the last wifely offices. His breath became feeble and faltered. Presently the last tremor of agony was over, and the son of Massasoit lay before the statue-like assemblage of his friends and followers — dead.

"They have poisoned him," said Wetamoo. "They shall bitterly repent the day."

The death of Alexander (1661) was followed by years of peace, but from that hour the Wampanoags became secretly the foes of the Colonies. And we may in justice remark that, with all the cunning imputed to the Indian character, the first wily stratagem of the New England Indian war was accomplished by the English, and that, with all the warlike propensities of which the Indians are accused by the early historians, the first act of open hostility is here directly traceable to the Colonists' own doors.

Philip succeeded Alexander in the sachemship, beginning his reign at Mount Hope, the ancient governmental seat of the dominion.

Wetamoo retired to her home in Pocasset, firmly bent on avenging the death of her husband. But the reign of Philip began peacefully, and the injured queen, having but limited power, contented herself for a time with living pacifically in her own romantic dominions. She married, in due time, Peter Nanuit, an Indian of fine natural endowments, and a friend to the English (1661–1675).

Fourteen years of peace elapsed between the tragic death of Alexander and the beginning of active hostilities; but the period was overshadowed by the rising cloud of war, and the peace was one that brought no feeling of security to the Colonists.

Philip prepared for the worst, quietly and methodically, during all these years; now laboring for the union of all of the Indian tribes against their natural enemy, now foiling the Colonists by a stroke of statesmanship that would have excited the admiration of a Metternich or a Talleyrand.

The killing of the executioners of Sassamon, a treacherous Indian, by the English, brought on the long-expected hostilities. The first signal for active war made Philip ambitious to unite under his leadership all of the neighboring tribes.

He went to the beautiful queen of Pocasset, whose airy cabins looked down on his council-fires from the evergreens over the bay, and appealed to her for the assistance of her warriors. Her husband, Nanuit, was on intimate terms with the English; she was at peace with the Colonists and with the sachems and sagamores near and far, and she seemed to hesitate to expose her dominion to the perils of war.

"Remember," said Philip, appealing to her pride, and opening an old wound by a well-timed allusion to an injury that she once had studied to avenge, — "remember that the English at Plymouth poisoned your husband and my brother."

The wild passions of Wetamoö were roused. She promised her warriors to Philip, and soon gave to the cause the romantic inspiration of a warrior queen. Her tribe numbered about three hundred braves. They were portly men, displaying upon their persons in war all the trappings of barbarian splendor, and they were proud of their queen.

Captain Church, the most conspicuous English officer in the first Indian war, visited Peter Nanuit at Pocasset just before the breaking out of hostilities. The Indian leader received him in a friendly manner, and he was the first to inform him of the certainty of war. He said that Philip had already begun to hold his dances, — those fearful revels that, according to the Indian custom, preceded the shedding of blood.

The lurid war-fires now in the still nights illumined the wooded rocks of

Mount Hope, and gleamed on the calm bosom of the bay. Dusky forms circled around the rose-colored flames, while light canoes danced on the palpitating waters. On the east lay Pocasset, her fair brow now crescented, now orbed, with the rising moon.

Captain Church held an interview with Wetamoo at Pocasset on the eve of the war. She lived on a hill a little north of what is known now as Howland's Ferry, — a place familiar to those who visit the attractive summer resorts, near Newport, on the outlets of the charming inland seas. She appeared very melancholy on the occasion. She said that her people had then gone across the water to attend one of Philip's dances, though without her approval. She seemed unwilling to converse, but affirmed that she saw on every hand the ominous signs of war.

Philip soon sent terror through the Colonies by the attack on Swansea, June 24, 1675, and on other exposed settlements. Wetamoo, true to her pledge, joined him at the head of her noble body of warriors. She followed him through the long trails of the forest, inspiring her men by her presence and example to do deeds of daring; she shared his privations and sufferings amid summer's heat and winter's snow.

Nanuit joined the English. Wetamoo disowned him when his alliance with the Colonists became known, and soon after her divorcement married Quinnapin, a Narragansett sagamore, engaged in the coalition against the English. Quinnapin is described as a "young lusty sachem," well skilled in the arts of war (1676).

Soon after the first attacks made by the Indians, Captain Church with a body of expert soldiers went to Pocasset to ravage the dominions of the warlike queen. She was at her own residence at this time, but, discovering the approach of the enemy, took refuge in an almost impenetrable cedar-swamp, near at hand, and so eluded her pursuer. Arriving at the place where Fall River now stands, Captain Church heard of the attack on Dartmouth. He hastened to the distressed town, but too late to avert the work of destruction. The Colonists, however, took one hundred and sixty prisoners, whom they induced to lay down their arms by promises of protection and kind treatment. These pledges were so well kept that the Plymouth authorities sold all of the captives into slavery, and received from the sale a comfortable sum to aid them in prosecuting the war.

Wetamoo joined Philip after the burning of Dartmouth, uniting her forces with his, probably in a thick forest on the river some miles below the old town of Taunton.[1] It was now midsummer in the dismal year 1675. The name of

---

[1] According to one authority, Wetamoo had about five hundred warriors.

DESTRUCTION OF PEQUOTS.

Philip had become a word to make the Colonists' hearts sink with terror in the long line of frontier towns. There was something so dark and fearful, so startling to the imagination, in the Indian mode of warfare, — in the war-whoop, in the taking of human life by the hatchet and the scalping-knife, in the indiscriminate slaughter of the young, the helpless, and the old, in the levelling of homes, in the burning of towns, — that the solitary settler seemed to see wild visions by day and by night, and to start back from the reflection of his own fancies as from lurking foes. Cotton Mather tells us, with all the gravity of a historian, that the report of a cannon and of small guns, the hissing bullets, and the rolling of drums had been heard in the air "in a clear, still, sunshiny morning;" and other early writers speak of an Indian bow that appeared on the face of the sky, and of an eclipse in which the outline of an Indian scalp was seen imprinted on the disk of the moon.

When the inhabitants of Taunton learned that Philip and Wetamoo with their united forces were concealed in one of the great Pocasset swamps on the river, below the town, they abandoned their homes, and gathered together for defence in eight garrison houses. On the 18th of July a body of soldiers from Plymouth and Taunton appeared before the Indian encampment. They found about one hundred wigwams fantastically constructed of green bark, but discovered but few warriors. They cautiously penetrated a miry and tangled thicket, whose dense foliage bending from tree and shrub and interlacing vines obstructed the view. Philip and his warriors retreated silently and unseen, a little way before them, as they advanced; an expert now and then exhibiting himself to lure the Colonists on. The latter, becoming excited by this singular warfare, as the hunter becomes animated when breaking through the thicket in the chase, quite lost their wonted prudence and self-possession. Their progress was suddenly arrested by a volley of bullets poured upon them through the covert of a dark, matted growth of underbrush, from an invisible foe. Fifteen of the English fell dead on the spot. The rest, seeing the peril of their situation, fled precipitately, "finding it ill," says an old historian (Hubbard), "fighting a wild beast in his own den."

The English now surrounded the swamp, a gloomy tract of country seven miles in circuit, in the hope of starving the Indians and capturing Philip and the terrible Pocasset queen. Here they held a blockade thirteen days, when they found that Philip had floated his warriors on rafts, one moonless night, past the drowsy sentinels, and himself with Wetamoo had gone far away into the wilderness in the heart of Massachusetts.

Philip ravaged the western frontier of Massachusetts during the autumn, but the old chronicles afford but casual glimpses of the interesting Wetamoo.

During the ensuing winter the colonial army made the famous attack on the winter quarters of the Indians at South Kingston, R. I., capturing the fort, and imitating the example of the "barbarians" and "pagans," by killing women and children without mercy, and applying the torch to the dwellings. "They were in much doubt," says the manuscript of the Rev. W. Ruggles, "and they afterwards made it a subject of inquiry, whether burning their enemies alive could be consistent with humanity and the benevolent principles of the Gospel." But they were fighting for their lives, and for the lives of their families, with a terrible foe, and they did not stop to decide this nice moral question until well after the close of the war.

We here lose sight of Wetamoo for a time. We only know that she shared the fortunes of Philip, and that the work of destruction went on. Feb. 10, 1676, a party of Indians attacked and burned the town of Lancaster, Mass. They took a number of prisoners; among these, Mary Rowlandson, the wife of the Rev. Joseph Rowlandson, clergyman at that place. The English had made slaves of the captive Indians; and to remove them from scenes which ever would have appealed to their patriotism and pride, they had sold many, including both women and children, into a servitude more cruel than death, — that of the West Indian plantation. As the English had imitated the "barbarians" in killing women and children, so the Indians sought to follow the example of their enlightened combatants in the treatment of captives, and accordingly copied the beauties of civilization by selling them into bondage. Mrs. Rowlandson was sold to the lusty young sagamore Quinnapin, who bought her for a dressing-maid to Queen Wetamoo (February, 1676).

Mrs. Rowlandson published a narrative of her captivity, which, like many old accounts of the kind, is made up largely of perverted passages of Scripture to show the barbarities of the "pagans," without, however, very frequent allusions to the Sermon on the Mount, which seems to have fallen into disuse during the war. She complains bitterly, deeming it an act of extreme barbarity that her little daughter Mary was sold by a *praying* Indian *for a gun*, but makes no allusion to the source of such mischief; nor does she seem to have comprehended at all how nearly equally balanced in this war was "man's inhumanity to man."

Mrs. Rowlandson gives us the following description of her new mistress, the Pocasset queen : " A severe and proud dame she was ; bestowing every day, in dressing herself, near as much time as any of the gentry of the land ; powdering her hair and painting her face, going with her necklaces, with jewels in her ears, and bracelets upon her hands. When she had dressed herself, her work was to make girdles of wampum and beads."

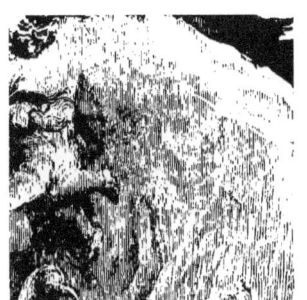

The following anecdote, which we copy for the sake of completeness, leaves no pleasant impression of the disposition either of the Indian queen or of her maid:—

"As I was sitting once in the wigwam, Philip's maid came with the child in her arms [the son of Philip, made a prisoner July 31, 1676, sold into Spanish slavery, when a child, by the Colonists], and asked me to give her a piece of my apron to make him a garment. I told her I would not. Then my mistress told me to give it, but I said no. The maid told me if I would not give her a piece she would tear a piece off it. I told her I would tear her coat then. With that my mistress rises up, and takes up a stick big enough to have killed me, and struck at me with it; but I stepped out, and she struck the stick into the mat of the wigwam. But while she was pulling it out, I went to the maid and gave her my apron, and so the storm passed over."

Once, when Mrs. Rowlandson had received for some work which she had done for some Indians a quart of peas and a sirloin of bear's meat (both Philip and the Indians *paid* Mrs. Rowlandson for whatever work she found time to do, aside from her special duties), she prepared a nice dinner, and asked her master and mistress, Quinnapin and Wetamoo, to dine with her, as Philip had once asked her (the queen's maid) to sit at a nice table with him. The queen and sagamore came, seemingly much pleased. Mrs. Rowlandson set before them the repast in a single bowl. Now Wetamoo was a queen and Quinnapin was a sort of prince, inferior in rank, and merely the queen's husband. The former was not used to this style of service, in which she and her husband were treated as equals; and she left the table with injured pride, and refused to eat a morsel.

Quinnapin was the sagamore who brought the message to Mrs. Rowlandson that she might go to the foot of Wachusett Mountain, where arrangements were making for her ransom.

Mrs. Rowlandson gives an interesting account of an Indian dance that took place soon after their successes at Sudbury and other exposed places. The cotillon was performed by eight persons in the presence of the braves and a great concourse of people. Quinnapin and Wetamoo were among the gayest and the most elegantly dressed of the dancers. Quinnapin was decked in a white linen robe, bordered with lace and ornamented with silver. He wore on his head a turban composed of girdles of wampum, and on his feet white stockings with pieces of silver tinkling from the ties. A magnificent girdle of wampum passed over his shoulders, and clasped his waist.

Wetamoo was arrayed as fantastically, in an ornamented blanket, with bracelets on her arms, jewels in her ears, and many necklaces falling from her shoulders. Her face was painted red, and her hair powdered white. She wore red stockings and white shoes. The merry party danced to the music of a brass kettle.

All of this seems shocking in barbarians; but we have read of other dances at very serious times, — one at Brussels when Europe had reached the height of military splendor, and others neither in lands nor in periods remote.

Philip did not join in the dance, but stood aside, looking on, careworn and thoughtful. When the revel was done, he sent for Mrs. Rowlandson, and said to her kindly, " Would you like to hear good news ? I have something good to tell you. You are to be released and to go home to-morrow."

We again lose sight of Wetamoo. Philip carried destruction into the very heart of the Colonies, and was for a time successful. Then the fortunes of war varied, then turned. His powerful ally, Nanuntenoo the Narragansett (the friend of Roger Williams), was captured by the English and executed, dying, as he said he wished to die, " before he had done anything unworthy of his character." Philip attempted, but failed, to raise the Mohawks against the English. Awashonks, another interesting Indian queen, detached the Seconets from his cause, and united her warriors with his enemies. It is said that after the defection of the Seconets he was never seen to smile. His own warriors deserted him, and the colonial army everywhere pursued him and occupied his dominions. Wetamoo remained true to him in all the vicissitudes of war.

In July, 1676, Philip and Wetamoo, with the remnant of their warriors, attempted to return to their old homes at Mount Hope and Pocasset. They were attacked on the 1st of August by Captain Church near Bridgewater, and totally defeated, losing one hundred and thirty of their men. Among the prisoners taken by the English in this decisive battle were Philip's wife, Wootonekanuske (Wetamoo's sister) and his son. Wootonekanuske seems to have been a quiet woman, and to have held to the last the affection of her chief. When Philip knew of her capture, he said, " My heart breaks ; now I am ready to die."

Philip and Wetamoo were now fugitives. In the listless August days they pursued their way through the shadowy swamps, towards those river-cleft regions where reposed the bones of their fathers, now no longer their own. Wetamoo longed to see the shores of Pocasset once more before she died ; and she travelled through tangled forests and forded hidden streams in the hope of resting her eyes once more on the scenes of her happy maidenhood. She reached Swansea on the 5th of August, or about that date, and hastened to a wooded peninsula overlooking the bay, now known as Gardiner's Neck. Here she beheld Pokanoket and the green declivities of Pocasset, glimmering in the

PHILIP'S HEAD BROUGHT TO PLYMOUTH.

sunset, for the last time. She had left Pocasset with three hundred warriors; she returned in sight of its shores with but twenty-six followers.

On August 6 an Indian who had deserted Philip sought the protection of the Colonists at Taunton, and to secure terms for himself, offered to conduct the English to the place where Wetamoo was resting after her wearisome marches, with a few faithful warriors. The English, following this guide, came upon the encampment, and made prisoners of the warriors. The heroic queen, seeing her helpless situation, determined not to be taken, but to die free. She seized a piece of wood, or raft, and threw herself into the river. The poor creature struggled awhile to reach the opposite shore; but her strength was already spent by reason of fatigue and scanty food, her arm failed her, and she sunk to rise no more.

The captive warriors were taken to Taunton.

A short time after this event a party of English discovered on the Mattapoisett shore the dead body of an Indian woman, remarkable for its symmetry and beauty. They cut off the head, and took it to Taunton to exhibit it on a pole in their streets, but without knowing, according to Cotton Mather, whose head it was. When the captives saw it, "they made," to use the choice and sympathetic expressions of the enlightened old chronicler, "a most horrid and diabolical lamentation, and fell into such hideous howlings as can scarce be imitated, crying out that it was their queen's head" (1676).

The destruction of Philip soon followed.

It was the night of August 11, 1676. Philip stood on the summit of Mount Hope in the evening overlooking the dusky landscape, in order to catch the first indication in the far, far distance of the approach of his pursuers. The great outlets to the sea stretched southward like bars of living light, while below rolled the bay like a sheet of silver, mirroring the moon.

What reflections must have crowded upon him in this last solitary vigil! Just below him were the graves of his fathers, and the bones of the sachems and warriors of old. Over the bay lay Pocasset, the scene of his early wooing. On the west glimmered Sowanes, the royal residence of his father. The Kickmuit went shimmering to the north; but the lovely old Indian town on its banks was gone, forever gone. The low winds breathed through the cedars below, and the brightening moon scattered over them her night-beams.

The sachems were gone, all gone. His warriors had perished, one by one; fallen like the leaves of autumn, till the tree was bare. His wife and child were no longer his own. The faithful Wetamoo had died, hunted like a beast, in sight of her own sun-bright rivers, dreamy hills, and shady forest-retreats. He saw the moon sinking low on the tide; he never saw the sight again.

The story of the tragic death of Philip is too well known to need repeating here. He perished the next morning, when the autumn sun was just trembling on the verge of the sky, and the night dews lay thick on the woodlands and the meadows.

We will say, however, in order to aid the tourist who may visit Mount Hope, that the great sachem was surprised and killed at a little knoll, at the foot of the eminence, on the southwest side. The last scene that Philip beheld was doubtless the broad bosom of the Narragansett, lighting up in the morning sun.

We cannot to-day understand the low brutal spirit that led enlightened men to take pleasure in mutilating the dead bodies of their foes. When Nanuntenoo was killed — for an Indian, a man of lofty character, aspirations, and aims, who protected the home of Roger Williams when the town of Providence was burning, and who refused to ransom his own life by surrendering the adherents of Philip in his own dominions to the English — his head was cut off, and his body was quartered and burned. "The mighty sachem of the Narragansetts," says Cotton Mather, "the English wisely delivered unto their tawny auxiliaries for them to cut off his head, that so the alienation between them and the wretches in hostility against us might become incurable." Hubbard, an old historian, speaks of Nanuntenoo's fate as "the confusion of that damned wretch," etc. The beheading of the remains of Wetamoo, and the exhibition of her dead face in the streets of Taunton, have already been told. The dead body of Philip was treated with greater indignity than either. Said Captain Church, as his victim lay stretched upon the ground before him, "Forasmuch as he has caused many an Englishman's body to lie unburied and to rot above ground, not one of his bones shall be buried." An old Indian cut-throat was ordered to bisect the remains and to quarter the trunk. He performed the work with a relish that shows how nearly a man may approach to the character of a demon, delivering a speech which startles the reader of old histories with its obscenity, making one wonder at the strange morality of the age, — a choice morsel, no doubt, to those old readers whose hatred of the native tribes overstepped the decent limits of death. Philip's hand was given to the Indian who shot him, and was preserved in rum, and carried about the Colonies for a show. His head was sent to Plymouth, and exposed upon a gibbet. Cotton Mather thus feelingly moralizes on the disposition made of the fallen chieftain's members: "And in that very place where he first contrived and commenced his mischief, this Agag was now cut in quarters, which were then hanged up, while his head was carried in triumph to Plymouth, where it arrived on the very day that the church was keeping a solemn thanksgiving to God. God sent them in the head of a Leviathan for a thanksgiving feast." The four quarters of Philip's body were hung upon four trees, where they blew about in the river-winds, until they wasted away and dropped to the ground.

So perished the last queen of Pocasset and the last sachem of the Wampanoags.

The story of Queen Wetamoo greatly interested the Laurenses in the places in Massachusetts and Rhode Island where the tragic and heroic events took place.

Charlie and Henry began to make daily excursions to the old towns on this historic ground. The whole district is a network of railroads, with swift trains and easy connections; and the two boys found the long summer days adapted to such picnicking. They went together to Mount Hope at Bristol, R. I., where Massasoit lived; to Massasoit's spring in Warren, R. I.; to "Wyllett's" tomb in Barrington, R. I.; to the supposed Northmen's Rock in Dighton; to Bowers's Shore, where once the liberator of Hayti breathed the air of liberty; to the landing-place of Roger Williams; and finally, to Newport, the scene of the "Old Mill" and the residence of the prophetic Berkeley.

On July 4 they made an excursion to Taunton, visited Annawan's Rock, and the place where the first flag of Independence was thrown to the breeze by the American Colonists.

Evenings of story-telling on the old red settle followed these excursions.

"I wish you to make me a present," said Mrs. Laurens to Mrs. Endicott, one evening near the close of her visit to Lakeville.

"That is what I would like to do. What would you have?"

"The old red settle."

"Is that all? You are very welcome to it. I only brought it out as a curiosity. What would you do with it?"

"Send it to my home at St. Augustine, and use it for story-telling, as you have here. You have given me so good a view of the early times of the Plymouth and Massachusetts Bay Colonies, by the of the old settle, that I would be glad to give you a view of early times of St. Augustine and the South in the same way."

THE FIRST FLAG OF LIBERTY.

OCTOBER, 1774.

The grand years have numbered one hundred and ten
  Since the first flag of freedom ascended the sky,
And the fair Green of Taunton made heroes of men,
  As men saw the ensign unfolding on high.
The motto of " Union and Liberty " rolled
Out into the sun-tides vermilion and gold,
And loud cried those heroes of liberty bold :
  " We 'll defend it with valor and virtue and votes,
      The red flag of Taunton,
      That waves o'er the Green ! "

'T was autumn, bright autumn ; and glimmered the weir ;
  The Taunton flowed full on that beautiful day,
And kirtled wives gathered the flag-pole a-near,
  'Mid the old men at prayer, and the children at play.
They saw the red flag in blue liberty's dome
Wave o'er the valley, Equality's home,
And they heard the men say, while their own lips were dumb :
  " We 'll defend with our valor and virtue and votes
      The red flag of Taunton
      That waves o'er the Green ! "

The Taunton flowed swift through the shimmering weir,
  Past the rock where the Northmen came in from the Bay ;
In the forest the red leaves were falling, and sere,
  Where Annawan perished. The stone church to-day,
The loveliest church e'er the traveller saw,
  With its sentinel pines and its ivy-wreathed tower,
Stands hard by the place where the women in awe
  Heard their husbands cry out in that glorious hour :
" We 'll defend with our valor, our virtue, and votes
      The red flag of Taunton
      That waves o'er the Green ! "

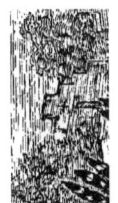

The old parson stood by the church near the Green,
   And looked to the sky on that sun-flooded day;
The forest primeval encircled the scene,
   And shaded streams rolled o'er the rocks to the Bay.
He lifted his hand like a white cross in prayer,
   And said as the flag like an angel's wings spread:
"It is God who has written those words on the air;
   By the Hand that has led you, ye still shall be led.
Long may valor and virtue defend with their votes
        The red flag that Taunton
        Has raised o'er the Green!"

O'er the red oaks it hung while the autumn sun burned,
   And turned the green sea of leaves russet and sere;
And toward it the yeomen's eyes wondering turned
   From far lattices open on valley and weir.
There the old parson stood, his white hand in the air,
   And men gathered near in silence of prayer,
And said, as their brows 'neath the flag they made bare:
   "We'll defend with our valor and virtue and votes
        The red flag of Taunton
        That waves o'er the Green."

"Behold," said the parson, "its folds in the sky,
   In the eye of the sun,—do you know what you do?
The hand that sets Liberty's watchword on high
   Must to valor be pledged, and to honor be true.
Ye have set yonder flag for a sceptreless hand.
While God ye shall honor, your nation shall stand;
For truth is puissant, though led by a band.
   Defend with your valor and virtue and votes
        The flag ye have lifted
        To-day o'er the Green!"

"Peace,"—how calmly the light of the past noontide shone
   On the orchards of Taunton that glorious day,
As the mellow word rung like an altar-bell's tone;
   "Peace, peace, men of Taunton; 't is time we should pray.
O Thou whom all sceptres dost strengthen or break,
Yon flag to the hand of thy providence take,
In battle victorious, in peace glorious make,
   Defended by valor and virtue and votes,—
        The flag we have lifted
        To-day o'er the Green."

A young farmer came from his cot in the wood,
    The forest retreat that Pometacom loved,
And under the flag as a sentinel stood,
    And watched the slow feet as they tarried and moved.
" O sentinel, sentinel, stand at your post,"
The old parson said, and moved by like a ghost;
" The cause of the people can never be lost,
    If they give to it valor and virtue and votes.
        Stand, sentinel, stand
        By the flag o'er the Green!"

Oh, whence came the Spirit that then thrilled the land?
    The flag was the blossom, but whence came the seed?
From Cambrian mountains a shelterless band
    Here planted their cause, and here prayed in their need,
'Mid Swansea's green oaks, and tent-groves of pine
    By the still Narragansett, the chrysolite sea;
And Williams in exile his message divine
    Here uttered, and rose the red flag of the free,
Defended by valor and virtue and votes, —
        The red flag of Taunton
        That waved o'er the Green.

Here Vane, freedom's commoner, captain, and seer,
    For the birthrights of man scrolled his letters of fire,
To dream on the Scilly Isles, sunless and drear,
    Of the land where his spirit would never expire.
Here, shores of Rhode Island, here freedom was born,
    Here her twilight of gods first humanity cheered;
Here her prophets beheld the first star of the dawn,
    Till Equality's knights their first watchwords upreared,
Defended by valor and virtue and votes,
        On the red flag of Taunton
        That waved o'er the Green.

Those days have departed; the shaded waves creep
    By Taunton, fair Taunton, as on that old day.
Those men have departed; unmindful they sleep
    When the peace-trumpets blow and the war-bugles play.
The house where they worshipped is gone, and one sees
A poem of stone in its stead 'mid the trees;
And stars fill the banner that drifts on the breeze,
    Defended with valor and virtue and votes,
        Like the old flag of Taunton
        That waved o'er the Green.

The red flag of Taunton at old Brandywine
  Gave place to the flag of the Stripes and the Stars,
And the bold words of " Union and Liberty " shine
  No more as of old 'mid the smoke-cloud of wars.
Here Liberty reigns and her triumphs increase,
And our Union of States is the empire of peace.
And the sentinel's watch 'neath the flag does not cease;
  But virtue defends it with valor and votes,
            Like the heroes of Taunton
            That stood on the Green.

O sentinel, sentinel, stand, as of old,
  By the green earth beneath you, Equality's home ;
By all that ye owe to the future untold ;
  By the blue sky above you, our liberty's dome !
From the doctrinaire's art, from the sectionist's hate,
From passions that follow the demagogue's prate,
From men who grow rich on the spoils of the State,
  Defend it with valor and virtue and votes,
            Like the sons of the heroes
          . Of fair Taunton Green.

The grand years have numbered one hundred and ten
  Since the old flag of freedom ascended the sky,
And the fair Green of Taunton made heroes of men,
  As men saw the ensign unrolling on high.
One hundred and ten, and the new summer fills
Her gold horns of plenty and banners the hills,
And the spirit of old still the patriot thrills ;
  Still calling for valor and virtue and votes,
            While a million flags fly
            For that one on the Green.

CHAPTER V.

THE OLD RED SETTLE GOES SOUTH.

THE old red settle went South, to the broad cool veranda of an ancient mansion overlooking the Gulf, in the oldest town in America.

"We shall meet on the old red settle next winter," said Mrs. Laurens to Mr. Leland and Charlie, on leaving the East; "and there we will tell you the stories of old Florida, a district as rich in tales as yours. Florida, you know, once extended to the Carolinas, and was the scene of the romances of the Yemassee."

The Lelands went South during the month of February, beginning their historic visits at Washington.

More than a century ago a young surveyor looked down from the hill where the Washington Observatory now stands, and in the landscape beheld with prophetic vision the site of a city. In his young mind, then and there the American Capital was conceived. He became the liberator of his country; he planned the city and rejoiced at its birth, but he never entered it as the capital of the United States.

Humboldt declared that the site of the city of Washington is the finest in the world; and there is no more beautiful building on earth than that mountain of pure white marble that we call the Capitol.

CAPITOL AT WASHINGTON.

Enter Washington on a moonlight night, when the white garments of the Capitol glow, and the building itself seems fit for a palace for Selene! How the majestic structure seems to stand over the city! Then the city seems under its dominion like an ancient army under the glittering shield of its queen. Go where you will, the white Capitol seems to stand in the air. Under the full moon it is one of the most beautiful structures on earth.

French arms brought independence to the United States; and the Capital was planned by a Frenchman, Peter Charles l'Enfant, a gentleman of the best art-culture, who was born in France in 1755. He met with much opposition at first; but the Washington of to-day, with its wheel of avenues, is the fulfilment of his poetic dream.

Mr. Leland and Charlie had been in Washington before. They did not go there to see its modern wonders, but to begin an historic journey. A Zigzag journey it proved to be, indeed, — from the fine city that stands for America's heart and brain to the queen city of the Antilles, where the bones of the discoverer of America rest.

One of the first détours was to Winchester, Va., to visit Greenway Court, where old Lord Fairfax lived, and the church where that fine old gentleman was buried. In connection with this excursion Mr. Leland related —

THE ROMANCE OF LORD FAIRFAX.

There are many interesting reminiscences connected with the life of this nobleman, whose name to this day is highly respected among the aristocratic families of the "Old Dominion," yet few are aware of the untoward circumstances which threw him upon our shores.

Lord Fairfax was a descendant of the old Fairfax family so renowned in English history during the reigns of the Charleses and the Georges, — a family loyal to kings and heroic in knightly deeds.

In his youth Lord Fairfax was a gentleman of fashion in the highest circles of London society, with no greater ambition than to sip the sweets of life and be considered a wit. As he grew older he had literary aspirations which tended to increase greatly his reputation. Yet we know nothing of his productions, although it is a matter of history that he was engaged in literary labors with Addison and was a firm friend of Steele.

When he was about thirty years old, the lady to whom he was affianced, and upon whom he had expended a small fortune in expensive wedding-presents, rejected him on the eve of marriage and accepted a wealthier suitor. This terrible blow produced a great change in his disposition and habits, transforming the gay, social man into a disappointed recluse.

About the same time he was extremely mortified at the loss of some of the Fairfax property in England, which had been entailed; and thus weighed down by disappointment and wounded pride, he resolved to retire from the scenes and associations which had now become distasteful to him. After a final settlement of his affairs in England, he embarked, in the year 1750, for his far-away possessions in America. These unvisited estates he held in right of his mother, the daughter of Lord Culpepper, who received this land grant in Virginia from Charles II. as early as the year 1664.

The house "Belvoir," to which Lord Fairfax came, and which was occupied by his cousin Sir William Fairfax, who had the management of his property, stood upon the Potomac River, a few miles below Mount Vernon; and it was here the intimacy between this nobleman and George Washington, then a boy of sixteen, commenced. Lawrence Washington, the elder brother of George, had married a daughter of Sir William Fairfax, which tended to throw the sorrowful man and bright, intelligent boy intimately together as relatives, and afforded Lord Fairfax abundant opportunity to read the great possibilities in the character of his young favorite. He influenced the lad by his discreet example and judicious advice to such a degree that to him, probably more than to any other person, do we owe the development of those great characteristics which ultimately made him a ruler among men, the father of this great country.

The possessions of Lord Fairfax covered an immense area of land, spreading far beyond the Blue Ridge, comprising the beautiful valley of the Shenandoah, which had never been surveyed, and which had become the prey of "squatters," who even then considered that property-holders had no rights they were bound to respect, and who had planted themselves upon some of the most beautiful, fertile sites in the valley. Their audacity aroused Lord Fairfax to the necessity of making his title good. Herein opened the career of George Washington, which hardened his muscles and "toughened his manhood" for the leadership of the

GEORGE WASHINGTON.

Revolution. Lord Fairfax could have advanced his favorite's interests in almost any channel; but with prudent foresight he engaged the boy who, although only eighteen, thoroughly understood surveying, to undertake the difficult and in those days perilous commission of mapping out his possessions. Young Washington remained three years in this occupation, for which he received as high as a doubloon and sometimes six pistoles (about twenty dollars) a day.

After completing his commission, Washington returned to Lord Fairfax, whom he so delighted by his glowing accounts of the Shenandoah Valley that he at once removed beyond the Blue Ridge, and built a house known as "Greenway Court," similar to the usual home of the pioneer settler, — a log-cabin. A fine mansion was subsequently built near the present village of Millwood ; but in the humble cabin, surrounded by his dogs, Lord Fairfax spent the remainder of his life.

The Indians dearly loved this beautiful hunting-ground, and gave it the sweetest, most musical name in their language, — Shenandoah, "the Daughter of the Stars." Its wild, picturesque beauty was then at its height, undisturbed by the tread of civilization.

After spending thirty years in this lovely region, assiduously devoting himself to his duties as a landed proprietor, Lord Fairfax passed away in 1781, after the surrender of Cornwallis at Yorktown.

His death was remarkable. He was nearly one hundred years old, or more than ninety. He had remained a Royalist, and was grieved to see the boy that he had loved and befriended the commander of the American army.

They brought him the news of the surrender of Lord Cornwallis.

"Joe," he said to his faithful colored servant, "it is time for me to die."

He was taken to his bed, from which he never arose.

The body of Thomas, Lord Fairfax, Baron of Cameron, the sixth of the name, lies in the little Episcopal church at Winchester, Va., the ground of which he gave to the church.

The Lelands made another visit to a spot as interesting, — more sacred, if not so romantic. It was to Fredericksburg, to see the places associated with Washington's mother, and especially the place where she was buried. And here it is proper to give some account of —

THE TOMB OF THE MOTHER OF WASHINGTON.

The mother of Washington passed her last years in Fredericksburg. She was a prayerful woman, trustful and devout. Near her residence were some picturesque rocks overshadowed by trees. A lover of woods, birds, and flowers, she used to retire in pleasant weather to this lovely spot for meditation and prayer. She there tasted the sweetness of which Cowper sings, —

> " The calm retreat, the silent shade,
> With prayer and praise agree,
> And seem by Thy sweet bounty made
> For those who follow Thee."

Here the still twilights of the summer days during the stormy period of the American Revolution found the mother of Washington praying.

The burden of her prayers is known only to God. No step followed her to that leafy sanctuary. One cannot doubt that she prayed for her country and for her son, and that her prayers were heard in heaven. This place of devotion became to her one of the dearest spots on earth, and she selected it for her grave.

The spring of 1789 found her at the age of fourscore and five years suffering from an incurable disease. Just before entering upon the duties of the presidential office, Washington hastened to Fredericksburg to make her a visit. It was their last interview.

"The people," said Washington, after the first emotions incident to such a meeting had subsided, " have been pleased to elect me to the magistracy of the United States. I have come to bid you farewell. As soon as the business of arranging the new government is over, I shall hasten to Virginia and — "

" You will never see me more," said the venerable woman. " My great age and the disease from which I am suffering warn me that I shall not be long in the world. I trust God I am somewhat prepared for a better. But go, George, fulfil the destiny Heaven assigns you; and may Heaven's and your mother's blessing be with you always ! "

Washington wept like a child, kissed her furrowed cheek, then went forth to the great work before him. Her grave was long neglected. As Mrs. Sigourney sweetly and touchingly told the tale, —

> " Nature stole
> In her soft minstrelsy around thy bed,
> Spreading her vernal tissue, violet gemmed,
> And pearled with dews.

THE OLD RED SETTLE GOES SOUTH.

" She bade bright flowers spring,
Gifts of frankincense with sweet song of bird;
And Autumn cast his reaper's coronet
Down at thy feet, and stormy Winter speak
Sternly of man's neglect."

In 1833 a monument was commenced over her grave, the corner-stone of which was laid by President Jackson. On it is the inscription:—

MARY, THE MOTHER OF WASHINGTON.

The monument stands near the rocks associated with her devotions. It is picturesque, but unfinished.

The Lelands' visits to the public buildings need not be described, as such visits have little to do with the purpose of our narrative. The city of Washington recalls the events of the lives of all the Presidents. Pennsylvania Avenue has been walked by them all, even by Washington before it received its name.

THE WASHINGTON MONUMENT.

More than a century ago, in the year 1783, the Congress of the United States passed resolutions providing for a memorial to General Washington. This memorial was to be erected at the permanent seat of government of the United States, — then a newly created nationality. The War of Independence was ended, and the country was universally grateful to the noble leader to whose efforts they justly ascribed a great measure of its success.

Ten years later, the Commissioners who laid out the District of Columbia set apart a tract of land between the site of the President's mansion and the Potomac River as the spot where this national tribute to Washington was to be erected; and their report in which this reservation was established President Washington himself transmitted to Congress.

He died in 1799, in the belief that on that pleasant slope, overlooking the broad Potomac, his services to the country would be commemorated. The whole project slumbered until 1833, — fifty years after Congress had voted to make a memorial to him, — and then it was revived again by private enterprise.

A meeting of citizens of Washington was held in September, 1833, and an association was formed for the purpose of erecting a national monument to Washington. The original plan was to procure the money by subscriptions of one dollar each. The amount raised was not large. A new subscription was begun in 1846, and by the year 1854 a sum of a little more than a quarter of a million dollars had been obtained.

Work had been begun, however, some years before; and the corner-stone of the monument was laid on the 4th of July, 1848, on which occasion a fine oration was delivered by the Hon. Robert C. Winthrop, then Speaker of the House of Representatives. The contributions, however, began to fall off; and finally, when the monument had reached the height of one hundred and eighty feet, construction ceased.

A period of neglect and indifference followed, ending in the Civil War and the exciting questions which were at issue after the war closed, causing the shame of this unfinished monument to be forgotten. But in 1876, — the centennial year, — Congress made an appropriation towards the completion of the monument.

The foundations were examined and found to be defective. The work of enlarging and strengthening them was not completed until 1880, when construction upon the monument itself was resumed.

The monument is the most lofty structure ever erected by man. Its height was originally intended to be six hundred feet; but owing to its enormous weight, it was not deemed wise to carry the monument so high. Its height is five hundred and fifty-five feet. Its exterior is of Maryland marble, and the interior is Maine granite.

The foundation is one hundred and twenty-six feet six inches square at the base. The obelisk itself is fifty-five feet square at the base, and tapers to the top. The walls are fifteen feet thick at the bottom, but gradually become thinner until at the top they are only one foot six inches thick, and the monument is there thirty-four feet square.

Each State in the Union sent a block of stone to be set in the interior, and many cities as well as several foreign countries have done likewise.

These contributions, many of them highly polished and elegantly inscribed, make the monument a museum of mineralogical treasures.

Of the beauty of the monument there is not much to be said. It is not graceful or elegant. Those who wish to find beauty in it, however, will say that it befits republican simplicity and the rugged honesty and virtue of Washington. But if it does not gratify æsthetic taste, it will none the less serve as a memorial to recall to all future generations the heroic life and noble character of the first and greatest of Americans.

FORD'S THEATRE.

The place that interested the Lelands the most in the city of Washington, having seen the great buildings on a previous visit, was Ford's Theatre, the scene of the awful tragedy of April 14, 1865.

The building is no longer used for a theatre, but as a place for medical stores and a medical museum. The house where Lincoln died was found to be more interesting than the grim-looking storehouse, and awakened more tender associations.

An incident said to have been related by Mr. Lincoln to a friend was recalled by Mr. Leland.

"I am weary of the cares of State," said Mr. Lincoln to his wife after his second inauguration and before the tragedy. "When my term is over, I mean to go to Palestine, and visit the places where Christ lived." The dream seemed to glow in his mind like a rainbow, and to haunt him.

GOLDEN HORSESHOES.

The story of Governor Spotswood and his heroic march over the Blue Ridge, and his knightly order of golden horseshoes was suggested by these détours about Washington and in Virginia.

Spotswood carved the name of King George on one of the highest points of the Blue Ridge.

"Let him hereafter who would drink to the health of the King, drink here," he said to his explorers. "He shall have a golden horseshoe who drinks the King's health here, and penetrates into the regions beyond," he afterward proclaimed. The cavaliers won their colors, but the pioneers of a later date are more worthy of golden horseshoes.

Washington! The dome of the Capitol crowns it, — a white crowned god! But how has a place in its national halls proved the coronation of men of noble aspirations and struggles!

Mr. Leland related to Charlie stories of the grand old days of the early Presidents and Congressmen who had represented the American struggle for development, — men from the farm and shop, — boys who were laughed at, and who rose on the rounds of the ladder of their own efforts.

THE BOYHOOD OF EMINENT CONGRESSMEN.

"It ought to encourage some poor boy who desires to prepare himself for the best callings of life," he said, "to know that some of the men who have been prominent in our National Congress were not the sons of wealthy parents, but were obliged to work for their own

GOVERNOR SPOTSWOOD ON THE BLUE RIDGE.

support, and under this disadvantage to find time for the improvement of their minds.

"It is a remarkable fact that a large number of American statesmen have been farmer boys and apprentices. It is also an interesting fact that these boys acquired the rudiments of their education by resolute self-denial, working at their books while others were playing, idling, or sleeping.

"The course pursued by many of them was to obtain an education sufficient to teach a district school, and to earn money enough by teaching to pay for instruction in academic and professional studies. Self-instruction, teaching, and a course of professional training have been the three steps upon which numerous Americans have reached the most honorable positions of statesmanship.

"George S. Boutwell, James Brooks, Horace Greeley, Hannibal Hamlin, John B. Henderson, James K. Moorhead, James H. Woodworth, Henry G. Raymond, Samuel A. Smith, Silas Wright, Sam Houston, Lewis Cass, James A. Garfield, Abraham Lincoln, and many others whose names have filled less conspicuous places in American political history, were hard-working farmer boys. They earned their bread by farm labor, and used their spare hours for study.

"Benjamin F. Wade, only twelve years before he was elected to Congress, was employed with a spade and wheelbarrow on the Erie Canal. But his mind was at work as well as his hands; and with the feeling that God had given him mental qualities that should be used to influence others, he struggled until his aspirations were realized.

"Daniel Webster knew what it was to use the axe and the hoe, and his hands bore the marks of honorable toil; but it must be admitted that he was not much of a farmer. His brother used to say that his father sent Daniel to college to make him equal to the rest of the family.

"George S. Boutwell, Allen A. Bradford, Henry L. Dawes, Daniel S. Dickinson, Cyrus L. Dunham, Sidney Edgerton, John B. Henderson, Edward H. Rollins, Owen Lovejoy, Thomas Ewing, Henry G. Raymond, Benjamin F. Wade, and very many other Congressmen paid wholly or in part for their literary education by teaching. Each of these knew the vicissitudes and struggles of poverty, or the pressure of limited circumstances in early life.

"John B. Alley was apprenticed to a shoemaker when a lad, but he put his mind at work with his last. James M. Ashley was self-educated, having been thrown upon the world to make his own fortune at the age of fifteen. He found employment for a considerable period on one of the Ohio and Mississippi steamboats. He repaired in part the defects of his early education by obtaining employment in a printing-office.

"Joseph Bailey, one of the twelve Democrats who voted for the Constitutional Amendment abolishing slavery, acquired by his own exertions all the education that he ever received.

"George N. Briggs learned the trade of a hatter, and his early life was full of generous inspirations and manly struggles. Nathaniel P. Banks was a bobbin boy. He aspired to be a public speaker even when he was at work amid the din of machinery and the flying of spindles, and sought to cultivate his forensic tastes by attending the meetings of a debating-club.

"Andrew Johnson, who was really a noble boy, was hungry for books and learning during all his early days of toil, but he was never able to attend school. He was apprenticed to a tailor. Few men ever worked more resolutely for self-improvement than he.

"John B. Alley, Isaac Hill, James K. Moorhead, Millard Fillmore, Roger Sherman, and many others were apprentices. Erastus Corning was a clerk. Thomas Corwin was a penniless boy. John S. Carlyle and Thomas Ewing were thrown upon their own exertions in boyhood. The former was educated by his mother; the latter by his sister.

"A number of distinguished Congressmen were left orphans at an early age, and were obliged in youth to bear the burdens that belong to mature years. Among these we may mention Augustus C. Baldwin, Simon Cameron, Alexander H. Stevens, the lamented Senator Baker, who fell at Leesburg, and Stephen A. Douglas.

"Vice-President Colfax was left an orphan in childhood, and when about eleven years of age he began to contribute towards his own support and the support of his mother by working in a store.

"These eminent men worked with young hands as well as with young brains. There was no sunny, dreamy period in their lives, free from care, which answers our poetic conceptions of youth. The cares and responsibilities of life came upon them at once. They were schooled in realities, and not in pleasure-seeking.

"The lesson of these examples is that success is within the reach of earnest minds, however great may be the obstacles in the way of its attainment. Poetry never sang more truly than in the following lines of Coates Kenney: —

> "Destiny is not
> Without thee, but within.
> Thyself must make thyself ;
> The agonizing throes of thought, —
> These bring forth glory,
> Bring forth destiny."

TO JAMESTOWN AND RICHMOND.

Mr. Leland and Charlie went to Richmond by the way of Norfolk and the James, passing Mount Vernon.

They approached Jamestown with deep interest.

"It is yonder," said a friend on the boat. A solitary tower appeared, — a ruin.

"Is that all that is left?" asked Charlie.

"Yes, all."

Yet there America began. There assembled the first House of Burgesses, and there the first white child in America was born. There rose the fabric of the young nation out of the dreams of Sir Walter Raleigh, and there Virginia received its name in honor of the virgin queen. There Powhattan was made king by an English coronation, and there were the scenes of a most romantic Indian history. Vanished all, — the only monument a ruined tower!

Mr. Leland recalled, while passing the ruin, the story of the sending of wives by the old Virginia Company to the bachelor colony.

"They were women of good credit," he said, "selected from the working families of London and other places. They were as eager for husbands as the planters were for wives. The company sent them over at its own expense, and it was stipulated that no man who was not able to support a wife should court one of them. Their coming was eagerly awaited, and they had hardly landed when the wooing began. Such sudden courtships and marriages were rarely if ever known before in any colony. The marriages, however, seem generally to have proved happy."

Richmond is full of life and enterprise. But it was the Richmond of the long past that our friends came to see. One of the most interesting places to them was the St. John's Church.

"We must fight! I repeat it, sir, we must fight! An appeal to arms and to the God of Hosts is all that is left us!"— These words are part of a speech by Patrick Henry, delivered in 1775, which is to be found in almost every school Speaker. We have heard it spoken by boys many times; all utter these words in the wrong way. There are still old men in Virginia whose grandfathers heard this speech in 1775; and those words, they say, were not spoken in a loud, vehement manner, as boys usually speak them, but in a low tone and with the deepest solemnity.

St. John's Church, in which the speech was spoken, is still standing at Richmond. It is a small church, built at a time when Richmond was only a village, and it was intended to seat about two hundred persons in its oaken pews.

WIVES FOR THE SETTLERS.

If Patrick Henry had shrieked those sentences, as I have heard some boys shriek them, the effect would have been more laughable than impressive in so small a room.

It was a time when every patriot in Virginia was most anxious for his country. The first Congress had sat and adjourned, and it seemed to many that the Colonies had then done all that they could to bring the King of England to his senses. The feeling was general that it was impossible for the Colonies to contend with Great Britain in arms. Patrick Henry thought otherwise, and he supported his opinion with a number of powerful arguments.

But this great orator had a way of putting his whole speech, after he had argued the matter, into one electric sentence, which pierced every ear, and remained in the memory ever after. He did so on this occasion, when he said in the lowest tones of his wonderful voice, —

"We must fight! I repeat it, sir, we must fight!"

He spoke for America. His was the voice of destiny. The voice makes the church a monument; and the church, like the Old South in Boston, should be eternally sacred to the heart of the great Republic.

THE STORY OF WASHINGTON'S LIFE AT HOME.

It is one hundred and fifty-four years since George Washington was born, on the 22d of February, 1732, and a little more than eighty-six years since he died, a retired Virginia farmer, at Mount Vernon, on the 14th of December, 1799. Whenever we approach the anniversary of his birth, it is pleasant to look at him not as a public man, but as he appeared in ordinary occupations of his life at home and as a Virginia planter. It is said that when at Mount Vernon, it was his habit to rise before the dawn of day in the dark mornings of winter. He struck a light in his tinder-box and kindled his own fire when the morning was cold, and lighted also the tallow candles, made under Mrs. Washington's superintendence.

Contrary to the custom of the wealthy planters of Virginia, he dressed and shaved himself, except that a servant combed his hair and tied his queue.

His shaving apparatus has been preserved to this day by the descendants of his step-son, Mr. Custis.

As soon as he was dressed, he usually wrote some of his business correspondence, made entries in his diary, and wrote out directions for his overseers. Desk-work he disliked, but he performed it with care and exactness.

This irksome labor done, he went to the stable near the mansion house, and enjoyed a long inspection of his horses, of which he was extremely fond. He

WASHINGTON'S HOUSE AT MOUNT VERNON.

usually had about twenty carriage and saddle horses in the home stable, beside fifty or sixty draught-horses on the farms which composed his estate. A love of the horse was hereditary in the Washington family. His own mother, it is said, was as good a judge of a horse as any man in Virginia.

Upon returning from the stable, Washington sat down to an old-fashioned Virginia breakfast, which consisted chiefly of the four h's, — hominy, ham, hoe-cake, and honey, — with a cup or two of tea or coffee. He was a good eater, but preferred honest, plain food; and almost everything he ate was produced on his own estate.

Breakfast over, he entered upon the business of the day. Generally, in fine weather, his horse was ready saddled for him as soon as he had left the table,

WASHINGTON'S GRAVE AT MOUNT VERNON.

and on most days he had business which required attention at some distant farm. His estate consisted of three thousand two hundred and sixty acres, divided into five farms, each having its own overseer, its own barns, stables, and negro quarter. His slaves usually numbered between four hundred and fifty and five hundred, who were like so many children in having to be clothed, fed, doctored, housed, and directed by their master.

Under Mrs. Washington's own eye all their clothes were cut and made; and if sickness broke out in one of the quarters, it was the General himself who commonly visited and prescribed for them, often giving them their medicine with his own hands. Sometimes, in periods of epidemic, he would spend many hours of the night in their huts.

All good planters did so; and indeed we may justly boast that no slaves were ever so well cared for as those of the Southern States. That is not saying much, but so much we can say.

We may imagine, therefore, that General Washington had a great deal of hard riding to do when he was at home. Mr. Custis, his step-son, records that he rode about his farms unattended by a servant, although he often had to dismount to let down the bars.

His morning ride on farm business averaged from twelve to fifteen miles; but he frequently stopped on the way, and did not usually return much before dinner-time, which was two o'clock. A gentleman once rode out in search of him, and asked Mr. Custis how he should know the General when he met him. The young man replied, —

"You will meet, sir, an old gentleman riding alone, in plain drab clothes and a broad-brimmed white hat, with a hickory switch in his hand, and carrying an umbrella with a long staff, which is attached to his saddle-bow. That person, sir, is General Washington."

Mr. Custis explains that the General's skin was tender, and he carried the umbrella as a protection against the sun. Upon the whole, he was an excellent farmer. To be sure, he complained on one occasion that although he had a hundred and one cows, he was obliged to buy butter for his own table. On the other hand, he produced such excellent wheat and put up his flour so carefully that a barrel of flour bearing the brand of GEORGE WASHINGTON, MOUNT VERNON, was admitted into West India ports without inspection.

Like Jefferson and Madison, and the other noble farmers of that period, he was very zealous in raising superior breeds of farm animals, — a matter of great importance then, when the common breeds had become exceedingly degenerate. He tried the English sheep, the Berkshire pig, and horses bred from Arab stock.

Perhaps he succeeded best with the mule. The King of Spain, knowing his tastes, gave him a small drove of very superior asses, and sent with them a man acquainted with the whole business of raising mules. A little later, the Marquis de Lafayette sent him a number of the same animals from Malta. In a few years the mules of Mount Vernon became famous all over Virginia ; and some of them were sold for two hundred dollars each, which was at that time more than double the price of a good working-horse.

Dinner at Mount Vernon was generally at two ; on ceremonious occasions, at three; and the General waited for no man beyond five minutes, which he allowed for the difference of watches.

"My cook," said he, "does not ask whether the guests have arrived, but whether the hour has."

He did not always dress for dinner. This we know because he owed his death to sitting down to the table in his wet clothes after a long morning ride. Usually, however, he did so, as every one should who fairly can.

He liked all the good old Virginian dishes, particularly Virginia hams, famous then as now. Mr. Custis records that on one occasion the ham did not appear at the dinner-table ; and Mrs. Washington, with some irritation, inquired the reason. The truth had to be told, which was that the General's favorite hound Vulcan had come into the kitchen while the ham was smoking in its dish, and carried it off into the woods in defiance of the whole kitchen. The lady of the mansion did not relish the incident, but the master and all his guests laughed heartily.

The General liked to sit long at table, eating hickory nuts and talking over his farming, his fox-hunting, and his early campaigns.

His guests seldom succeeded in making him talk of the Revolutionary War ; but nothing pleased him better than to relate incidents of the Braddock campaign, and of his early adventures as a surveyor and volunteer soldier.

In the evenings, when there was no ball at Alexandria, he loved a quiet game of cards, but went to bed soon after the primitive hour of nine.

We have two night anecdotes of his Mount Vernon life. One guest, who slept in the room next to that of the General and his wife, separated from theirs only by a thin partition, reports that he overheard the lady giving her husband a curtain lecture, which he received in becoming silence, and when it was over, gently remarked, —

"And now good sleep to you, my dear."

The Lelands went to Fayetteville, N. C., and there visited the old place where Flora Macdonald had lived. They then went to Charleston.

CHAPTER VI.

CHARLESTON, AND THE STORIES OF WILLIAM GILMORE SIMMS.

PORT ROYAL, S. C., was the sister of Plymouth, Mass., in the pioneer sisterhoods of American settlements. To the former came the Huguenots, to the latter the Puritan; the gentle blood and tender conscience of France to one, and the strong will and heroic aim of England's best yeomen to the other. Each community sought to be governed by God.

Grand names are those that appear on the early records of the history of South Carolina,—the men who came to Port Royal to build New France, and fulfil Coligny's glorious dream. A Palatinate was established, and the eldest of the Lords Proprietors was constituted Palatine by the number of his years,—an election of fate that was supposed to bring with it the wisdom of experience. Then came the English; and John Locke, the greatest of England's philosophers, framed the constitution for the province after the pattern of Plato's model Republic.

The new colony of French and English never stained their record by religious persecutions. South Carolina struck boldly with Massachusetts and Virginia for independence in Revolutionary days, and Rhode Island sent to her that wonderful hero, General Greene.

Marion, famous in song and story, became her hero,—a solitary man, all soul and purpose, who was ready to starve for a cause. He and his men gave up everything for liberty. There is no romance of the Revolution like his.

Mr. Leland and Charlie were introduced at Charleston to the greatest poet that the South has produced, — a slender-looking but

CHARLESTON.

most courtly and gracious man, Paul Hamilton Hayne. Poets are the voices of their places and times, and in Mr. Hayne the South has found a voice that will always be heard in history.

Mr. Hayne is of gentle blood and historic family. His ancestors were noble in England, and the family have been conspicuous in political events through all the years of South Carolina's history. He was born in Charleston, Jan. 1, 1830. He lost his property by the war, became an invalid, and was compelled to go away from the coast to the Pine Barrens. He lives in a rural cottage at Copse Hill, Augusta, Ga. His wife is a daughter of an eminent French physician who received a gold medal from Napoleon III., and his only son is one of the most promising of America's young poets.

Mr. Leland and Charlie asked Colonel Hayne for some incidents of the life of William Gilmore Simms, the novelist. Mr. Simms was a friend of Colonel Hayne in the latter's early days, and the invalid poet's recollections of him were most sympathetic.

WILLIAM GILMORE SIMMS.

When I was a schoolboy in the venerable city of Charleston, — my native place, — I observed one morning at recess, while engaged with a score of my companions in the animated game of "shinny,"[1] that a certain classmate of ours, noted generally for his love of sport, had withdrawn himself from us, and was busily reading some mysterious volume in a corner of the playground.

I knew very well it could not be a school-book, a Cæsar or Xenophon, because Martin Mayham, although a clever lad, rather disliked Latin, and for Greek he entertained a mortal aversion.

In a pause of the game I approached him, where he sat comfortably tilted back in his chair against the trunk of a great, blossoming Pride-of-India tree.

"What book is that, Mayham?" I inquired.

"Don't bother!" was the uncourtly rejoinder. "Wait till I see which one of these two fellows is going to get the better of the other."

But a puff of wind at that moment blew the leaves of the work over towards the titlepage, upon which I saw in big capitals, "THE PARTISAN, A Romance of the Revolution. By William Gilmore Simms." Surely an inviting

---

[1] The game with this uncouth name was very popular among Southern schoolboys thirty or forty years ago. A score or two of lads armed with long sticks curved at one end would divide into companies of equal number, and fronting each other would strive to see which side could drive to a previously appointed goal a ball dropped between them. Of course there never were two goals in opposite directions. The cant term "shindy," as used to signify a promiscuous fight or struggle, may have suggested the title of this game.

title, with fascinating suggestions of battles, of vivid movement and dramatic adventure!

It captured my fancy; and therefore, when the youthful reader then devouring its chapters came to " Finis " the next day, I borrowed the tale of him, and grew equally interested in it myself.

Indeed, the story proved so absorbing that I neglected my studies, and under cover of the uplifted lid of a large desk perused its pages assiduously during school hours.

Our teacher, Mr. Christopher Coats (he always used to sign his name, as it seemed to me with great irreverence, " *Christ*. Coats ") had, like Old Squeers in " Nicholas Nickleby," but one eye. Yet this solitary optic was wonderfully piercing and far-sighted.

It detected my wrong-doing, of course; and very rudely was I awakened from the charms of fiction by an ominous whizz in the rear, and such a shower of blows across back and shoulders that the bare memory of them is enough to make the flesh shrink!

Pedagogues in those benighted times dealt not in " moral suasion," but in stout Malacca canes.

Thus my introduction to the genius of Simms was signalized by quite a striking circumstance, as impressive physically as mentally.

SUMTER.

And now I will tell you something of the life and literary career of this remarkable man, the " Fenimore Cooper of the South."

He was born in Charleston, S. C., in the April of 1806. His father was of Scotch-Irish extraction, and bequeathed to him a lively, enthusiastic temperament and a powerful physique; from his mother — one of the Carolina Singletons — he probably derived the finer traits of imagination, sensibility, and artistic force.

The mother died during his early childhood; and the elder Simms emigrating soon after to the West, his son was left to the sole care of the paternal grandmother. She appears to have been a shrewd and sensible old lady.

Repeatedly I have heard Simms — with whom I became personally intimate in later years — allude to her, not merely with affection but with admiration.

"I don't believe," he used to say, "that Haroun-al-Raschid was ever so charmed by the tales of Scheherezade, as I, when a boy, by the narrations of my grandmother about Whigs, Tories, and Indians, and all the stirring scenes of the Revolutionary conflict! She herself was a red-hot Whig, or patriot; and grew particularly indignant in describing how my father, a mere lad, was hurried, together with forty other citizens of Charleston, on board a British prison-ship, where hundreds died from ill-treatment and close quarters."

When but eight years old, Simms composed verses, — ballads of war and chivalry. He published nothing, however, until he was seventeen or eighteen, when a "Monody" appeared "upon the Death of General Charles Cotesworth Pinckney," — a Revolutionary celebrity. This was speedily followed by two volumes of "Early Lays," exceedingly clever and full of poetical promise. The author, in fact, possessed the instinct and endowments of the true poet, but unfortunately lacked both leisure and patience for that *labor limæ*, or polishing "work of the file," which is essential to permanent artistic success. Many a diamond of thought and expression may be found in his poems; only they lie imbedded in a mass of crude, diffuse, half-chaotic matter, and few are willing to take the trouble of *unearthing* them!

His fame must therefore rest upon his prose works chiefly.

It was in 1835 that the Harpers published the book already mentioned, "The Partisan." This production opened a new vein of romance, — the Revolutionary and social life of the South, — and proved wonderfully popular. It constituted the first of a Trilogy, of which the concluding tales were "Mellichampe" and "Katherine Walton;" all of them characterized by a vivid and picturesque style, intensity of action, and fine dramatic contrast.

One feels, in reading them, as if "the times which tried men's souls" had returned, and we ourselves were actual spectators of the strife, the agony, or the triumph. As historical pictures they are invaluable. Moultrie, Marion, Sumter, Pickens, and other distinguished Americans are brilliantly portrayed; while upon the British side, no less clear and full of *vraisemblance* are the portraits of Cornwallis, Tarleton, Proctor, and Balfour.

"Katherine Walton" is particularly noteworthy, as the only work we know which gives a perfect idea of the society in Charleston, military and civil, during the occupation of that city by the British troops. Despite the war, there was a great deal of gayety. The English officers gave balls and parties to which the ladies were specially invited, — even the Whig ladies, whom they wished to conciliate. We hear much of the rival beauties of that day.

The prettiest of the fashionable Tory belles, a charming brunette, was named Paulina Phelps.

CHARLESTON. 175

"Mad Archie Campbell," an English captain distinguished for his eccentricities, fell in love with her, and though he received but little encouragement, had the impudence to make a bet with the major of his regiment, to the effect that on a certain day he would marry Paulina, whether she liked it or not! And how do you think that he managed to accomplish his purpose?

He called one fine afternoon upon the young lady, in a stylish gig, just large enough for two, and drawn by a blooded horse as swift as he was graceful and well-trained.

"Miss Paulina," said Campbell, "may I have the honor of taking you for a drive some few miles out into the country?"

She consented, and no doubt enjoyed herself at first, since the spring weather was exhilarating and the landscape attractive. But soon she began to notice a peculiar wildness in her companion's manner.

He drove very much at random, grazing a tree here and a ditch there; and finally, having reached a neglected graveyard, with its walls down on the side of the road, actually urged his horse among and even over the crumbling tombstones, at the risk of breaking not only the vehicle, but his fair partner's neck! He behaved so badly, indeed, as fully to justify his nickname; and you may be sure that Paulina was relieved when at length he drew rein at the gate of the country parsonage.

MARION.

"Alight and rest yourself," said Campbell, offering her his hand with the utmost nonchalance. She would not observe it, however, and being a tall, dignified young woman, walked past him in haughty silence, though still internally quivering with fear, to the parsonage porch. There her cavalier joined her, and they entered the house together. The clergyman met them in the hall, loosely slippered, and altogether *en déshabillé*, not having expected visitors.

"We are here to be married," said Campbell, abruptly. "Come, your Reverence, perform the ceremony! Time presses."

Paulina laughed a little, trembling, contemptuous laugh; and assured the clergyman that she was not engaged to Captain Campbell, that he had been unpardonably rude and reckless, and that she placed herself under his (the clergyman's) protection.

"We are to be married," rejoined the soldier, whose "madness had a method" in it, "and that immediately! Don't let us burn daylight on waste words."

Expostulation followed on the parson's side, and tears on the lady's; but the soldier of fortune was obdurate.

Very coolly he produced a horse-pistol, and told the elderly churchman "to marry him on the spot, or submit to a leaden pill!"

The ceremony was performed under protest; and Campbell returned to the city, the possessor of a lovely though reluctant bride, and the winner of a bet which covered, it is said, a considerable amount. The oddest part of the affair is that he does not seem to have been called to account for his brutal conduct by any one of Miss Phelps's relatives. But in less than six months after, "Mad Archie," having been taken prisoner by the Americans, and refusing to submit to any control, was shot and killed by one of his captors. Therefore, as the Scotch say, he was made "to dree his weird" at last!

Simms's novels abound in curious and entertaining stories and traditions clearly illustrative of the manners and incidents of the "olden time."

"The Scout," "Woodcraft," "The Forayers," and "Eutaw" were subsequently added to the Revolutionary series; while of his border tales, "Beauchamp," founded upon a Kentucky tragedy, is the most vigorous and artistic. His principal colonial romances are "The Yemassee" and "The Cassique of Kiawah." The former shows his appreciation of Indian character, and a force and skill in portraying it not unequal to Cooper's. "The Cassique" is so rapid in movement, so adroit in disposition of events, so picturesque, dramatic, and true in minutest detail to the period and people introduced, that, for my part, I have perused it a dozen times over with undiminished interest.

Biography is indebted to this indefatigable worker for admirable lives of General Francis Marion, the famous Carolina "swamp fox;" of General Nathaniel Greene; of John Smith and Pocahontas; and finally, of the illustrious Chevalier Bayard.

As for his miscellanies — political, historical, social, and philosophical — their name is legion.

Altogether, he was a more voluminous author than Walter Scott, rivalled in this respect Alexandre Dumas Père, and may almost be compared in exhaustless fertility of fancy to Lope de Vega himself!

Simms was one of the finest-looking men I ever saw; tall, erect as a poplar, with a superb forehead, and a bluish-gray eye, which in moments of excitement flashed like a scimitar.

He delighted in the society of intelligent young men. An informal club, literary and social, was organized in Charleston, of which he was made President. We met during the summer months at each other's houses to discuss a hundred different topics of art and letters. We also discussed certain appetizing little dishes, well known to the Southern cuisine. Simms reminded one then of a great boy out of school! How he jested and laughed over his own racy anecdotes! Care and trouble for the time were scared away. It might have cheered a misanthrope to hear his sonorous "Ha! ha!" loud and joyful as the consign of Denis of Burgundy in Mr. Charles Reade's famous mediæval novel, "The Cloister and the Hearth,"—"Courage, mon ami, le diable est mort!"

During the winter Simms resided in the country at his place called "Woodlands," about eighty miles from the seaboard. Such a host as he was, — so considerate of one's comfort, so free-handed and cordial, and altogether kind-hearted, despite a frequent dogmatism of manner when arguments ran high! "Woodlands," indeed, could justly have been styled "Hospitality Hall." In the zenith of Simms's fame the house was often thronged with guests for weeks together. Distinguished persons from the North and abroad visited him: among these were William Cullen Bryant, with whom he was intimate; James, the English novelist; and scores of other notabilities.

On the ground-floor of his substantial English-looking mansion was a spacious study, the author's *sanctum sanctorum*. I have seen him there standing by his desk and busily composing from nine o'clock A. M. until the bell sounded for dinner.

Then would he give his thoughts a brief holiday!

A sad domestic affliction — the death of his wife — in 1863 permanently affected his spirits, though not his mental energy. He labored to the very last with unconquerable resolution.

In a letter now before me of March, 1867, he observes: "I have six children left out of fifteen, and three grandchildren. Now I wish to live long enough to see them fairly embarked in the voyage of existence, with a proper knowledge of the helm. After that, what matters? Beyond these, life has few objects for me; yet these suffice to make me desire that I may be permitted to die in harness, spurs at heel, lance in rest, and in the heat of a desperate charge! Sinking 'into the lean and slippered pantaloon,' dealing in old saws and drowsy proverbs, does not suit my taste. I am for *action* to the last; for life is so much warfare against sin, temptation, and the devil!"

In the autumn of 1868 Simms visited New York, and there took a contract for three romances, all to be worked at the same time!

"I went rigidly to work," he says, "concentrating myself at the desk from the 20th of October, 1868, to the 1st of July, 1869, nearly nine months! . . . I finished two of these books, but broke down upon the third, having penned during that period three thousand pages of manuscript."

So tremendous an effort was fatal to his already undermined constitution.

Passing through Charleston a few months previous to his decease, I called to see him at his daughter's home, and was shocked by the great change in his appearance. His once ruddy cheeks were emaciated and pale, his limbs gaunt and wasted, his hair white as snow; but he still stood erect, like some storm-smitten pine which the elements might break, but could not bend! There was muscular force still in the hearty grasp, although it quivered slightly; and from the sunken eyes would dart now and again a flash of the old enthusiasm.

PICKENS.

I look back upon the last evening spent in his society with a strange, dream-like, melancholy feeling. I knew then that on earth we would meet no more; and a choking sensation mastered me, as his hand fell from mine, unloosened in a final grasp of friendship.

The old man had insisted upon accompanying me to the door; and my last glimpse of him rested upon his gray but stately head, somewhat elevated, his mournful eyes gazing forth into the misty night, and the long patriarchal beard glittering in the lamplight!

On a quiet summer's afternoon in the month of June, 1870, in the beautiful old city he had loved so passionately, with his family and friends around him, and his dying eyes fixed on the Redeemer's cross, he passed tranquilly away.[1]

He lies at peace in one of the loveliest of Southern cemeteries, "Magnolia," near Charleston, — breezes from the ocean and the river rustling among the ancient oaks which bow majestically above his grave. His career was one of

[1] There is a strange and most pathetic circumstance associated with Simms's death. A lady friend who had been most attentive during his last illness wrote me as follows: "I made garlands of laurel and bay, and wove too a cross of white immortelles, which I placed in his poor emaciated hands, as he rested in the last slumber. The fingers refused to take any other position than their natural one, — drawn up as if to write!"

difficulty and trial, but "after life's fitful fever he sleeps well!" Unconventional and even rough occasionally in manner, his nature was sterling and sound to the core.

As for his works, the best of them have taken their place in the permanent literature of America; nor are they unknown in Europe. Several of his Romances have been translated into German; and in 1883 the "London Quarterly" referred to him as a writer of "powerful sketches of genuine American incident, — productions of permanent value because of their fidelity and force of characterization." This reviewer concludes, and justly, that "the United States have thus far produced few imaginative authors of greater desert than Simms," and he maintains that "so meritorious a writer is not likely to be forgotten by his countrymen."

The frequent lack of art in his style — his too hasty and careless mode of composition — has subjected him to the ridicule of a certain class of finical and fastidious critics, to whom a perfect style is more important than original creative power and virility of imagination. We think he will survive their contempt.

"NON OMNEM MORITURAM!"[1]

---

[1] This account of Simms was generously furnished by one of the novelist's intimate friends, Colonel Paul H. Hayne, of Augusta, Ga. A part of the narrative was originally published in the "Youth's Companion."

CHAPTER VII.

BEAUTIFUL SAVANNAH, AND SOUTHWARD.

SAVANNAH is one of the most beautiful cities in America. Its early history is a poem.

Non sibi sed aliis, was the motto of the noble English company that founded Georgia, — " Not for us, but for others."

Governor Oglethorpe, one of the world's benefactors, great in mind, in heart, and in inspiration, came to America in the spirit of the motto of the English company. He ascended the Savannah River some eighteen miles, saw a fine bluff, and on it he resolved to found a city, and make that city a home for the oppressed people of the earth.

The Yamacraws lived in their beautiful region of bearded oaks, magnolias, and palmettoes.

Their chief, dressed in fantastic attire, came to meet Oglethorpe on his arrival.

" Here is a little present," said the chief, offering a buffalo skin, painted on the inside with the head and feathers of an eagle. " The feathers are soft, — they mean love; the skin is warm, — it means protection. Therefore love and protect the Indian race."

The speech was a poem, — a true poem, amid a region that was all poetry. To the bluff, Oglethorpe brought his colony; and the forest city was begun on the first day of February, the time of the real Southern spring.

OGLETHORPE WITH THE INDIANS.

Thither came the Moravians, singing their hymns as they journeyed along the Rhine, and set forth on the sea,—a noble people, of whom their own country and time were not worthy.

People fleeing from religious persecution continued to come, and the city grew.

SAVANNAH HARBOR.

Savannah was a truly American town from the first. She sent to Boston the powder that was used at the battle of Bunker Hill.

Rhode Island sent to Georgia her young and heroic general, the friend of Washington, Nathaniel Greene. Georgia presented Greene with a grand estate near Savannah after the war. Here the hero of Eutaw died at an early age.

Count Pulaski was buried in the Savannah River, and his monument in Savannah is one of the finest memorial shafts in the country. Savannah has always remembered and honored her heroes.

Savannah is a city of squares and groves, — of airy homes surrounded with gardens of flowers that bloom all the year.

One of the most beautiful resorts is Bonaventure Cemetery, about four miles from the city. This spot has been well named Arcadia.

FOUNTAIN IN FORSYTH PARK, SAVANNAH.

No cemetery in the world is so endowed by Nature with poetic beauty. The broad avenues of live-oak draped in waving moss seem formed to lament the dead and console the living. The place reminds one of Bryant's lines in his " Ode to Freedom," —

> " Here are old trees, tall oaks, and gnarlèd pines
> That stream with gray green mosses."

People from New England find a favorite route to Savannah by the Boston and Savannah Steamship Company's elegant boats; and to Florida by taking these boats to Savannah, and rail to Jacksonville. The fare from Boston to Jacksonville is from $25 to $30, or $20 to Savannah by boat, and some $10 to Florida, the round tickets being subject to reduced rates. The usual fare, by many routes, from Boston and New York to Florida (Jacksonville) and return, is $50. A tourist, by taking the Ward line of steamers, may go to the Bahamas (Nassau, N. P.), and thence to Jacksonville. The fare to the Bahamas is about $50; from Nassau to Jacksonville, about $25. He may return by way of Savannah, Augusta, Columbia, Wilmington, Richmond, and Washington to New York or Boston, at a fare of about $25, thus making, for $100, a Southern tour as historic and romantic as it is warm and flowery. The time for such a tour is in February and March, thus following the spring birds and flowers northward.

SOUTHWARD.

From Savannah, carrying with them delightful memories of Forsyth Park, our tourists went on their way to Fernandina, an old Spanish American city whose harbor is the finest of the South Atlantic coast. Many travellers go from Savannah to Fernandina by water, through the lagoons of the Sea Islands, passing Dungeness on Cumberland Island, once the home of General Nathaniel Greene and a place of romantic traditions. People desiring a long sea-voyage find the steamers from New York to Fernandina a healthful route to Florida.

Jacksonville is really a city of the North, a great Northern hotel, on the old river May, as the St. John's was originally called. What the White Mountains are to New England in summer, Jacksonville and the St. John's are to the East in winter. The city is a flower-garden, or the porter's lodge to a park that is four hundred miles long, — the most beautiful park in North America.

Mr. Laurens and his son met the Lelands at Jacksonville; and the leading members of the Assawamsett Club were thus united, and after the most hearty greetings went on their way — a way all sunshine and greenery and flowers in February — to the ancient city of St. Augustine.

The home of the Laurenses was a few miles from the city, and overlooked the ocean.

VIEW OF JACKSONVILLE HARBOR.

Thirty-six hours from the frozen North may find the traveller in Florida, by the fast service, — from the lands of snow to the lands of sands hot with the sunshine!

The Lelands found the air like June. The sky was cloudless; and the ocean winds, as light as the fanning of birds' wings, were full of odors.

NATURAL FOREST.

The home of the Laurenses was old and elegant. Over a tract that seemed like ploughed sand, and through an orange grove, the Lelands came upon it, and caught a view of its broad verandas.

A red object caught Charlie's eye, — the only thing he had seen in the journey to remind him of the North.

"The old red settle!" he exclaimed.

Mrs. Laurens appeared on the veranda, and there welcomed her Northern friends, and invitèd them to a seat on the settle.

"And here," she said, "it will give us pleasure to tell you some tales of old Florida and of Southern life; and if we are able to entertain you as delightfully as you did us at Lakeville, our acquaintance will be agreeable and profitable indeed."

The yard around the house was threaded with lovely walks. On one of them were some baskets heaped with oranges. Beyond were live-oaks streaming with Spanish moss. In an open flower-garden were century-plants and gigantic cacti. About the out-buildings were jessamines of starry gold, and crimson honeysuckles.

Beyond one garden rose another, flaming with bloom. The land seemed pouring out blossoms from unseen cornucopias. Everywhere was sunshine, everywhere birds, greenery, gray moss, and flowers.

"This is not like the old Assawamsett Hotel," said Charlie to Henry. "How could you have been so pleased with the tame scenery there, when your own home was in such surroundings? Life here does not seem real, — it is hard to believe that all I see is not a dream."

Pointing to an old orange-tree, he asked, —

"How many bushels does that bear?"

"I do not know how many bushels it bears," said Henry; "it usually yields about a thousand oranges a year!"

"A thousand oranges!"

The story-telling in this New Sicily began on the first evening after the arrival of the Lelands, Mr. and Mrs. Laurens being the story-tellers. During the narratives the moon rose over the ocean, and changed the vegetation into towers and palaces of silver. The air was full of odors, borne on the light winds from the sea.

The first story was told by Mr. Laurens, and related to the personal history of the discoverer of Florida.

THE STORY OF A PALM SUNDAY.

Florida boasts many beautiful and even magnificent flowers; but it was not for that reason that its Spanish discoverer gave it the name it now bears, which both in Latin and Spanish means "flowery." The aspect of its Atlantic coast as seen from the ocean is not suggestive of the word. Nor is it probably true, as so many of our books assert, that the land was first descried by white men on the flowery day of the Christian year, Easter Sunday. Ponce de Leon sighted it on Palm Sunday, the Sunday before Easter, according to excellent authorities.

Palm Sunday, long celebrated in Europe with peculiar and impressive ceremonies, is called by the Spaniards the Flowery Passover (Pascua Florida). The French commonly style it Branch Sunday, but they too often speak of it as Pâques Fleuries, or Flowery Easter.

It was upon Palm Sunday, then, the 27th of March in the year 1512, that three small ships under the command of the tough old Spanish explorer, Juan Ponce de Leon, arrived off the coast of this unknown land. These ships had sailed three weeks before from Porto Rico, and they were bound for the imaginary island of Bimini.

The voyage had been pleasant, with tranquil weather and favorable winds; but no sooner had they come in sight of the strange coast than a storm arose which kept them for several days beating up and down, unable to cast anchor. It was not until the 2d of April that Ponce de Leon and his men went ashore and took possession of the land in the name of the King and Queen of Spain.

They found it a beautiful country, filled with flowers and blossoming vines; but it was not the Bimini of which they were in search, — where, as they had been told, gold abounded in the rocks and streams.

In Bimini, too, sprang the fabled Fountain of Youth! But of all the springs in the new land, which the grizzled old Ponce de Leon went about anxiously tasting, none, alas! made him younger by a single year. He learned from the

WATER-CARRIER.

BEAUTIFUL SAVANNAH, AND SOUTHWARD.

Indians that the country was called Cautio. He renamed it Florida because he had first seen it on Pascua Florida. In June he sailed away again, a sadly disappointed man.

The history of the romantic old captain who thus named Florida is strange and eventful. In boyhood he was page to a Spanish nobleman, and while still a mere youth saw hard service in several campaigns against the Moors of Granada. He accompanied Columbus in his second voyage to the New World in 1493, and distinguished himself in the many needless and cruel conflicts which occurred between the Spanish explorers and the natives of Hispaniola. After serving for some time in a subordinate capacity, he was appointed governor of the province of Higuey, situated at the eastern end of the island, opposite to Porto Rico, then known only by its Indian name of Boriquen. This island had not yet been explored. Its green and lofty mountains, about twelve leagues distant and clearly visible from the shores of Higuey, soon attracted his eyes, and the Indians whom he questioned declared they were rich in gold.

That was enough. His own province, peaceful, fertile, and beautiful as it was, now lost all charm for him; and he petitioned Ovando, who was then governor of Hispaniola, for permission to explore this new region.

Ponce de Leon's eyes were here gladdened by a glittering ore which he believed to be gold. With samples of this he returned to Hayti, leaving several of his companions behind him.

Governor Ovando, to whom the ore was presented, tested it in a crucible, pronounced it gold, and decided immediately upon the conquest of the island. He sent Ponce de Leon back to complete the work.

But now other difficulties beset the Spanish adventurer, owing to the distance between Spain and her colonies, and to the jealousy existing between the king and his officers in the New World. Ponce de Leon was duly appointed governor of Boriquen (or Porto Rico) by Nicholas de Ovando.

But Ovando was recalled to Spain, and Don Diego Columbus, son of the discoverer, who succeeded him, gave the appointment to some one else. At last, when the matter was decided in Ponce de Leon's favor, the Indians had learned what it meant to have Spaniards for masters, and were no longer the submissive friends they had formerly shown themselves. They made no open protest, but they plotted vengeance.

Before venturing to attack the Spaniards they took the precaution to kill one of them to make sure that the men of this strange race were not immortal. The Indians offered to carry a Spaniard across a ford, and when half-way over they dropped him, and held him under water until he ceased to struggle. Then, having borne the body to the shore, they laid it down and began to wail and lament over it, declaring that the man had been drowned accidentally, and making the most abject apologies to the corpse for their carelessness. This was done lest by any chance the body should revive and take vengeance upon them. Even when it remained dumb and cold, they were not satisfied, but kept guard over it three days before being finally convinced that it was dead.

Spaniards could be killed then! The next thing was to kill more of them, — to kill them all!

Everything was at last arranged for a midnight massacre. The Spanish villages were to be simultaneously fired, and all the inhabitants slaughtered. But a sister of the chief, who was informed of the plan, went secretly to a Spaniard, Don Christoval de Satomayor, with whom she was in love, and gave him warning. Don Christoval then decided to convey the warning to Ponce de Leon.

While upon his way thither he was attacked. He and all his party were murdered with the exception of one man, who escaped and carried the news to the governor.

When, therefore, the savages reached Caparra, — a fortified place, — they found their enemies alert and ready for them. They could not carry the place by assault, but proceeded to besiege it, confident of success.

The Spaniards were, indeed, reduced to a desperate strait. All their villages were destroyed by the Indians, a hundred of their people were slain, and the remnant — less than a hundred, and many of them wounded — were shut up in this small fortress in the midst of a populous and hostile country. But Ponce de Leon was an old soldier, and he did not despair.

His men, divided into three little companies, fought bravely, and it required all his authority to keep them from being too venturesome.

One of his most valuable warriors during this extremity was a huge yellow and white dog named Berezillo. It is said that this animal could even distinguish between the Indians who were allies of the Spaniards and those who were hostile. It is certain that the creature rendered such good service that his master was allowed on his account the pay, allowances, and share of booty ordinarily assigned to a trained cross-bowman.

At length reinforcements arrived from Hispaniola; and Ponce de Leon, sallying forth at the head of these and his own troops, took the enemy by surprise, and inflicted on them a disastrous defeat. The natives, who had not observed the arrival of the fresh troops, were seized with panic, believing that those whom they had already slain must have come to life again to destroy them.

Ponce de Leon followed them in their flight through the forest, and came up to their camp, opposite which he erected a slight fortification. The savages rallied at sight of their foes, and just at nightfall they dashed forward, and made one last valiant effort to retrieve the fortunes of their race. They were repulsed, and their chief, Agueybana, fell dead from a bullet through his heart.

No sooner had Ponce de Leon completed his victory than he learned that he was no longer governor of Porto Rico. A former governor whom he, after a fierce quarrel, had sent back to Spain a prisoner, had now returned to take his place under a commission from the king.

Ponce accepted this reverse with a better grace than might have been expected, for he was already dreaming of the blest island of Bimini and the Fountain of Youth. He set sail in search of them, and found our beautiful Florida!

Soon after his return he went to Spain to report his expedition to the king. At court he was the object of many stinging witticisms from the nobles on account of his search for the fairy Fountain. When he returned to the West Indies, he bore the high-sounding title of Adelantado of Bimini and Florida. He was in command of a fleet of three ships, designed to punish the warlike Caribs for the injuries they had inflicted on Spanish settlers. This expedition failed disastrously.

He came back to Porto Rico disheartened and irritated. He was again made governor of the island, where he remained for several years. In 1521 he sailed once more for Florida, which he had now learned was a part of the mainland, with the intention of exploring and subjugating it. No sooner had he landed upon the coast than he was attacked by a large number of Indians; many of his men were killed, and he himself was wounded in the thigh by an arrow. He was carried back to his ship, and gave orders to make for Cuba. He had not the force to rally from his wound, and died a few days after his arrival.

Upon his tomb was placed this epitaph: —

MOLE SUB HAC FORTIS
REQUIESCUNT OSSA LEONIS
QUI VICIT FACTIS
NOMINA MAGNA SUIS.

"Beneath this mound rest the bones of a mighty Lion, who by his deeds surpassed the great names he bore."

Mrs. Laurens followed her husband in story-telling, and related an Indian romance of which the Lelands had incidentally heard.

THE INDIAN PROPHET.

A TALE OF ALABAMA.

"Econochaca!"

The name looks strange. Its history is more strange than the name. I have found in American history no events more weird and remarkable than those associated with this place.

It was a city of refuge, modelled after the Israelitish cities in form and government. It was a hidden city, and was built upon the left bank of the Alabama, in what is now Lowndes County. No path or trail led to it. The Indian who reached it, whatever may have been his danger, was safe. It was holy ground.

It was built by Weathersford, an Indian warrior, who was at one time the idol of his race. Tall, straight, and kingly, with dark eyes and electric glance, he seemed born to command. He was a savage, yet he possessed the heroic virtues of a Spartan, and a martyr's spirit that would have been noble in the early Christians.

When this wonderful man had built his hidden city, he prepared to dedicate it.

There lived among the Shawnees a brother of the great Tecumtha, who claimed to be a prophet.

His birth was wonderful. He was one of three children born of the same mother at the same time, and regarded with awe from their natal day.

One day in his early years, he fell upon the ground as one dead. His body was borne away for burial. As the Indians were preparing for the last rites, he suddenly started up.

"I have seen the Land of the Blessed," he exclaimed. "Call the people together that I may tell them what I have seen."

The nation was called to assemble. He rose up before them, told them of his celestial visions, and virtually announced himself to be a prophet.

He was believed to have performed miracles. Corn as big as meal-bags sprung from the earth at his bidding, and pumpkins as large as wigwams came into the maize-fields at his call.

His appearance at a council of the Creeks just before that nation declared war was terrible and awful.

"You shall see," he said, "the arm of Tecumtha, like a white fire, stretched forth in the sky."

A comet soon after appeared, and the Creeks believed it to be the spirit arm of their chief, pointing them to war.

"You do not believe that the Great Spirit has sent me forth," he said to a sceptical warrior. "You shall believe it. I go to Detroit. When I arrive there, I will stamp my foot upon the ground. You shall hear it in Alabama. When I stamp my foot, your houses shall fall."

The prophet went to Detroit. Strangely enough, at the time of his arrival, an earthquake shook Alabama, and the houses were seen to totter and reel to and fro.

"Tecumtha has arrived in Detroit! Tecumtha has arrived in Detroit!" said the affrighted Creeks.

The Prophet might have learned from the English the near approach of the comet, but that the earthquake should have fulfilled his prediction is one of the most curious and mysterious events of Indian history.

Weathersford sent for the Prophet to dedicate the hidden city of refuge.

It was summer. The blue Alabama rolled quietly along under the shadows of the green forests. In the open square of the Holy City smoked an altar, or altars; and the Prophet stood by them, dressed in royal attire, and offered up human sacrifices to the heavens.

What a scene it must have been when the fires died, and the moon arose, and feathery beings formed rings and danced to the barbarous music of their primitive instruments!

From these awful rites Weathersford prepared to go forth like a firebrand and exterminate the whites. He was surprised by the latter and defeated, but himself escaped alive.

One day at sunset there appeared at the American camp an Indian. He folded his arms in the presence of General Jackson, and said, —

"I am Weathersford. I have nothing to request for myself. Kill me if you wish. I have come to beg of you to rescue the Indian women and children who are now starving in the woods. Your people have driven them to the woods without an ear of corn. I have come to ask peace for my people, but not for myself."

Jackson was astonished at such Roman heroism.

"I am a soldier," continued the chief; "I have fought, and would fight now, but my people are gone. Once I could animate my warriors to battle, but I cannot animate the dead."

General Jackson could not order the execution of such a man, but set him free.

Weathersford became a respected citizen of Alabama. He married; and one of the generals with whom he had contended, Samuel Dale, acted as groomsman at his wedding.

What became of the Prophet?

He had so great faith in his powers that he at last announced that he would render the Creek warriors invulnerable. He assembled them, and went through fantastic incantations, and declared that no power on earth could harm them. Believing this, the Creeks went forth to battle.

One by one the invulnerable warriors exposed themselves to the enemy. One by one they fell. They thought that they had been changed into gods, but found that they were but men.

The Prophet became distrusted. His supernatural power over the Creeks diminished; and he at last fell in battle in Canada on the Thames, showing that he, like the others, could be wounded, and suffer death like a common man.

His history is worthy of a novel, a poem, or an opera. Among the dark mysteries of the past there is no dusky figure at once so inexplicable and poetic as that of the Prophet.

Henry Laurens followed his father and mother, and gave an account of a recent expedition in Florida that had greatly interested him.

THE MYSTERIOUS EVERGLADES.

The Everglades of Florida until 1884 were a land of mystery, — a reptile empire whose secrets were unknown.

In that year the New Orleans "Times Democrat" equipped an exploring party, and placed it under the command of Major Archie P. Williams, a son of one of the most able women-writers of stories, history, and poetry that the South has produced. I follow the narrative by this lady in this account. I can give only a few points of the series of adventures. But these incidents may give a view of the *terra incognita* of the Flowery Empire.

November 6, the explorers coasting the southern shore of Lake Okeechobee, in search of some outlet which would enable them to penetrate the dense jungle which borders the Everglades, came to the mouth of a river running in the direction of the Everglades. The stream was one hundred yards wide and eight feet deep, the water as clear as crystal; and it had no perceptible current.

IN THE EVERGLADES.

Hoping that this stream would take them some distance in the right direction, they entered it full of hope. The banks were beautiful, fringed with a dense tropical growth of trees and shrubs, which presented a wall of vivid green to the eye. Vines were interlaced with the foliage, with strange flowers; and among them a species of gourd, its fruit the size of billiard balls.

Two miles farther and the river narrowed. The walls of foliage almost met; large roots and low-lying branches forbade further movement in that stream. The line of alligators in their wake increased, and they found that the river ends in an impenetrable morass, or swamp.

The explorers returned to camp, and upon investigating the shore found the mouths of eight rivers, all running south and in the right direction. To six of these rivers boats were assigned, with instructions to follow them as far as possible. When the report was brought into camp that night, one sufficed for all. The rivers ran only one or two miles, and then ended suddenly in swamps.

They decided upon one of the rivers, Rita River, as the point of departure. It took them within half a mile of the marsh which bordered the Everglades, and which they now decided they had to penetrate by some means or other.

That night in camp was an awful one. They were bitten by hungry mosquitoes; worms of all kinds, shapes, and sizes crawled over them; and pouring rain drenched them to the skin. One of the colored men remarked, "I swar to gracious 'fore I'd lib on Lake Okeechobee, I'd burn myself up."

The next day the hard work began, and the compass was the only guide. The river had ended in a dense swamp of custard-apple. Axes and machetes were employed to cut away trees and vines; and about three o'clock in the afternoon of the 10th of November, the explorers found themselves in a marsh of yma grass, wampee, and scrub willows,—five inches of water and fifteen feet of mud.

Climbing a tree to take observations, they saw, south of them, only an interminable marsh. There was no use discussing the situation. Orders were given for every man to go overboard, and overboard they went; and the canoes were propelled inch by inch through the mud.

The difficulty of getting through the grass was so great that Major Williams decided to fire it, which was done. The men suffered terribly from their legs and feet coming in contact with the roots of the "wampee," or "warm pea," which produces a burning and stinging sensation, as if the skin had been rubbed off, and red pepper rubbed in.

In pursuit of scientific information, Major Williams tasted the wampee.

A thousand needles seemed pricking every nerve of his face for hours afterward, and the pain was maddening.

Two men who had been sent ahead to fire the saw grass found one foot of water about two miles and a half from camp, which was encouraging news, as the progress by pushing the canoes through the mud was painful and wearisome in the extreme.

But the explorers found their route to the desired water was beset with new difficulties. Not only the marsh grass had to be penetrated, but also a species of scrub willow, with small stems, but having roots as large as a man's leg, which reached several yards outward and lay a few inches below the surface of the water.

As the canoes were only a fifth of an inch thick, to snag a hole in one of them would mean its abandonment. The bateaux, with provisions, were unable to pass these obstructions; so the men went ahead with machetes to cut a way.

It was hard work, and the expedition on the 12th of November advanced only three quarters of a mile. In fact, on the fourth day from Lake Okeechobee, their progress had been so slow that they had never lost sight of a large cypress-tree standing at the point of their departure from the lake.

On the morning of the 13th a survey was taken from the high mast of the bateau. Not an encouraging prospect! One unlimited expanse of tall marsh grass! They were unable to distinguish where the marsh grass ended and the saw grass began, both being of the same color; and instead of ten miles of this grass, which they had anticipated, the field-glass showed a boundless extent of it.

By firing the grass in front, they made slow progress; but the men were discouraged. Moccasin snakes slipped between their legs as they crawled through the mud; alligator snouts were at their backs, though they never were attacked by them; the wampee stung them, and clouds of mosquitoes added to the general miseries.

The unbroken silence of these solitudes is depressing. Not a bird sings in the branches; not even the croak of a frog is heard. It is a world of reptiles, and unfit for the habitation of any but the lower forms of life.

On the 19th they saw two columns of smoke about ten miles to the southwest, which they understood were made by Indians. None of the explorers "hankered arter Injuns," as one of the colored crew expressed it. But their smokes that day were quickly answered to front and westward by similar smokes.

On the 23d they sighted the cypress timber which lines the western border of the Everglades. That day numerous flocks of ducks and curlews

SCENE ON THE ST JOHN'S RIVER.

flew overhead, and they killed a supply of them. The next day they entered a basin, and found on its banks five feet square of dry ground, the first seen after leaving Lake Okeechobee. On the 28th of November they sighted the first island of the Everglades, and entered the grassy waters which surrounded it.

The island is about three acres in extent, covered with wild fig and custard-apple trees, with about twenty feet of dry ground. From the top of a high tree they could see hundreds of little islands, divided from each other by grassy waters. There the weary explorers camped, to mend their boats and rest from the fatigue of their toilsome journey.

The men suffered, too, from leech bites, which pests had fastened upon their legs and feet in the mud. After that, the difficulties were over. There was plenty of water for the boats. The islands grew thicker as they traversed south, and the timber on them was larger. The signal smokes of the Indians were seen constantly, but none approached the expedition.

There is little dry land on any of the islands, and some are so infested by snakes that the men were not willing to risk even a landing. The bottom of the basin of the Everglades is solid rock; and as the men moved on they found this rock beginning to crop out above the surface, and they were obliged to lift their canoes over the ledges.

December 6, they reached Shark's River, and soon found themselves in Whitewater Bay, thus coming out in the Gulf of Mexico without diverging a mile to east or west from their due southern course.

The result of the expedition proved that the Everglades is an irreclaimable marsh, and for ages to come will remain so. It cannot be drained, the rocky barrier which surrounds it offering almost insurmountable obstacles. No telegraph line can be established or kept up in it; and it is safe to predict that few white men will again brave its perils.

At St. Augustine the Lelands visited the old Spanish fort, and went several times to the quaint cathedral to see the picture of the first Mass in America.

CHAPTER VIII.

STORY-TELLING AT ST. AUGUSTINE.

LORIDA, which is becoming the winter park of our Northern cities and the semi-tropical garden of the whole country, was the earliest discovered and settled part of America. It is an empire; from the Perdido River to Cape Sable it is seven hundred miles long. A large part of the State is a vast swamp of decayed trees, on which grow the mistletoe and gray Spanish moss.

Florida Highlands has one of the most beautiful climates in the world, especially the portions near Tampa Bay. Here it is eternal summer. The roses bloom and the mocking-birds sing every month in the year. The white sands are covered with oranges in midwinter. The air-currents of the Gulf Stream warm the coast in winter and fan it in summer. De Soto climbed these highlands, vainly looking for the golden domes of another Peru.

Jacksonville is the port of Florida, and St. Augustine stands like a porter's lodge to a park beside it. The great river-road is the St. John's, on which beautiful steamers run to Sanford, a distance of some two hundred miles. All the parks in the world could hardly equal in beauty the scenery of the St. John's,—the old river May of the Spanish and French colonists. The river is walled with palmettoes and with great trees, the latter of which are webbed with Spanish moss. Birds are everywhere to be seen. The river at night, under the electric light of the steamer, is a ghost land.

The lower parts of Florida, where the earth pours out flowers, fruits, and vegetation like a flood, is subject to malaria. The highlands of Florida must in time become the principal places of residence.

St. Augustine is not the only place in Florida that is full of old romance. Tampa and the region about Tampa Bay is a land of stories. De Soto landed here with his thousand cavaliers, and began the march that ended in the discovery of the Mississippi. Here were Indian romances which the pen of the historian has but lightly touched. Tampa Bay — the Santo Espiritu of old — is as beautiful as a vision or dream. Tampa is like a poet's dream, and the region around it will one day be a park.

The moral atmosphere of Florida is remarkable. The old Floridians were religious, as were the old slave people. The leading capitalists who are developing Florida are men of positive convictions, like Plant and De Land. The Sabbath is respected; temperance principles prevail; the poor people are self-respecting, and moral sense has gone into the hotel towns with the best Northern intelligence.

The old red settle was in constant use evening after evening. Stories, historical, provincial, and local, were related; and the name of the Assawamsett Club was here changed to the Old Red Settle Club.

Mr. Laurens related some touching but very beautiful tales of the Huguenots, the colonists of Admiral Coligny. Their devout and poetic character, transmitted to their numerous descendants in the South, seemed to meet Mr. Laurens's moods, as he himself was a descendant of a Huguenot family. One of these, although a mere character sketch, much interested Mr. Leland and Charlie, for it showed certain types of the two races in some of their picturesque and novel features.

THE YOUNG HUGUENOT, OR THE COUNTRY AUCTIONEER.

I remember the scene well.
"Going, going, going! Once, do I hear it? Twice, do I hear it? Three times, do I hear it? Gone!"

It was early June, — a shining morning, with dew and blossoms everywhere. The eaves of the stately old farm-house appeared through the trees. In the yard was a crowd of people, and on a bench in the yard stood a jolly old auctioneer.

I recall the curious dialogue. It was like this : —
"And here is the family cradle. Who bids? How much am I offered?"
"Fifty cents — one dollar — do I hear it?"
"Fifty, fifty!"
"One dollar — do I hear it? One dollar. Now a quarter."
"Do I hear the quarter? Going, going, at one dollar — do I hear the quarter? Going, going — are you all done? Going, once, do I hear it?"
"Going, twice, do I hear it?"
"Going, three times, do I hear it? (*In low tone*) Going, going, going, going, going, etc. (*lower and lower*).
"Gone, Judge Tapley's cradle for one dollar to — what's your name, stranger? Dessalines."

I had never attended a New England country auction, and curiosity led me into the yard. The old auctioneer's vocabulary was musical and rather poetical. The crowd consisted of orderly farmers in their working-clothes.

There was a pause in the sale. They were bringing down furniture from the old garret. I sat down on the bench of an old grindstone under a spreading elm-tree. The sunlight glimmered through the leaves as through a cathedral window. On the lower limbs of the trees hung scythes. Above, the Baltimore orioles were fluting and flaming. An old man sat on the other side of the bench of the grindstone, leaning on a crutch.

"Pleasant mornin', stranger. Be you one of Square Tapley's folks? No. I didn't know but you mought be. So the old Square's cradle has gone, before he is dead, — right before his own eyes, too. Sold for a dollar. To that young feller they call Dessalines. Curi's kind of a name."

"Who was Squire Tapley?" I asked.
"Who *was* he? He ain't *dead*, stranger. They generally have the funeral

first, and the auction afterwards, but this time they're havin' the auction first; but the funeral, in my opinion, will be pretty sure to follow. There is the Judge now — Square Tapley — by the chamber window there."

THE AUCTION.

An old man leaned out of the open window and looked at the auctioneer. A terrible look came into his thin face. His hair was white, scant, and uncombed; his mouth opened and shaped words without sound or any emotional expression. A young man came and stood beside him. He had a marked face and was elegantly dressed.

"That is Tinley Tapley, the broker, the Judge's son. I wonder how *he* feels to-day."

There was an anxious look in the young man's face, and I noticed that he bent his eye upon me suspiciously. I heard him ask some unseen person, "Who is that stranger?" And I wondered why the appearance of a stranger at a public auction should have excited his attention.

His face was what would be called handsome, but was heartless and unprincipled. I felt sure that character had moulded it the impression of the soul, and had written upon it the secrets of the inner life. The face of the soul always comes to the surface at last.

"School books and law books!" shouted the round-faced auctioneer; "Scott's novels; the works of Fletcher; Methodist hymn-book; Family Bible —

"Eh, Squire, shall I put in the family Bible?

"Yes, the old Bible, — Mrs. Tapley's old books, all good as new. The Squire always took good care of his things.

"How much am I offered? Start the lot, somebody. School books, law books, and religious books.

"Two dollars.

"Three, do I hear it?

"Two dollars — who says three?

"Going, once, do I hear it?

"Twice, do I hear it?

"Three times, do I hear it? (*In low voice*) Going, going, going, going, going, etc.

"Going — gone to what's your name again, stranger? Dessalines. Sold to Dessalines for two dollars."

There was a strange movement at the chamber window. The old Squire leaned out and shook his cane in an agitated way. His son laid his hand upon his arm firmly and drew it back. I never shall forget the look that came into the old man's face. It was bitter beyond anything I ever saw. His eyelids dropped and his lips curled.

Some of the people in the yard had noticed this mysterious episode. I heard the question passing from mouth to mouth, "Who is Dessalines?" No one seemed able to answer the question except in one way: "The old Squire knows who he is."

I could but notice that there was something remarkable about this young stranger, perhaps thirty or thirty-five years of age, who had given his name to the auctioneer as Dessalines. He was tall and well-formed, with a mild, dark eye; his face mirrored his emotions, and had grown into a picture of benevolence.

It was a face so beautiful in its beneficent expressions, so serenely spiritual, as to win confidence at once, and to assure you that some good angel of character lighted it from within. It presented a strong contrast to Tinley's.

I turned to the old man beside me, and asked, —

"Who is Dessalines?"

"I was just a-goin' to ask you that question myself. As you are a stranger, I did n't know but that he might have come along with you! You don't know him, then?"

"No. I have never been in this place before; I am spending a few days at the Kino House in the town. I was taking a walk, saw that an auction was going on here, stopped out of curiosity, and that is all I know except what I have seen. He does not seem to know any one here."

"It seems as though he does, too. I 've been watching him. He seems to be kind o' recognizin' people by his looks. He looked at me just now, and appeared to know me, though he said nothin'. Strange that he should be here buyin' a cradle, — old Squire Tapley's, too!"

"I should have thought the son, Tinley, would have bought *that* cradle."

"But hold, stranger! Don't you know? He 's bankrupted, — is n't worth a dollar. Failed. I thought everybody knew that, — Tinley, the New York broker. Why, it 's been in all the papers. Ruined the Square, too. Ye see, the Square endorsed Tinley's papers; that 's why this auction is here to-day."

I began to grow interested in the history of this family, hitherto as unknown to me as any people could be. The disappointed face of the excited old man at the window, the weak handsome face of the son beside him, and the mysterious figure of Dessalines made for me three contrasting pictures, — like open books, written in characters that I could easily outline and guess, but not quite translate or comprehend.

The sale went on. Noon came. The bread-cart men rode up with jingling bells, and the farmers bought gingerbread and buns, and ate them in the shade. The ospreys wheeled overhead in the open sky, and now and then sweet-scented winds came drifting through the apple-blossoms. The auctioneer was asked into the house to dine with the Squire and Tinley. Dessalines had disappeared.

"Have you found out who that young man was?" said the man with the crutch.

"No."

The neighbors, seeing the farmer questioning me, began to gather in a near circle around me.

"I'll tell you who he reminds me of," said the old man, addressing his neighbors. "Fletcher."

"Who is Fletcher?" I asked.

"You see that spire yonder?"

"Yes." A golden vane on a white pinnacle shone over the green sea of the tree-tops.

"Well, Fletcher first started the society out of which that church grew."

"But who was he?"

"He was the son of a French Huguenot who died young," continued the old man, "and the Square married the widow. So the Square was his step-father."

"Well?"

"Well, the Square he was a money-making kind of man, and he came to hate the boy. The Square used to say that he could never make anything of him; that there was no business in him.

"Well, Tinley was born. The Square set the world by him, and he used to treat the boy Fletcher shamefully.

"There was a great religious interest in the town about the time Fletcher was sixteen years old, and Fletcher joined the church and thought that he had a call to preach. The Square always hated anything of that kind, and one day he turned the poor boy out of doors, and forbade him to come back again, even to visit his own mother.

"His mother loved him; and she never saw a happy hour after that day. She began to droop and lie awake of nights, and at last her reason went out. She became violent, and they took her to an insane hospital.

"Everybody pitied Fletcher, and this sympathy made the Square hate him the more. He used to speak of him as 'that worthless French fellow.' Men always hate those whom they injure. The Selectmen offered the lad the district school; and although the Square opposed the appointment, he began to teach, and he put his mind and heart and conscience into his work. We never had a teacher like Fletcher.

"One day, after he began to teach, there came riding up to the schoolhouse on horseback a man from the hospital, with a message that made his face turn white. The man said to him leaning down from the horse and speaking through the open window, 'Your mother is dying, and wishes you to come.'

"Fletcher sank down into a chair as though smitten. The children began to cry. Then he dismissed the school, and hurried towards the Squire's and asked for the use of one of the horses to ride to the hospital.

"'I told you not to come here again,' said the Square. 'You have made me trouble enough. I can't gratify the whims of a crazy wife. If she'd been dying, she would have sent for me.'

"Fletcher walked to the hospital, a distance of seven miles. It was as the messenger had said; the poor woman's sufferings were almost over. The scene between the mother and her son made those who saw it shed tears like children.

"'Fletcher,' she said, 'my own boy, the darkness has gone; and the doctor said that when the darkness went, I would die. I've been praying for you, Fletcher.' The boy took his mother's hand.

"'I've been praying God would make your life a blessing, Fletcher. My boy, He has heard. I want you to make me a promise, Fletcher. 'T is about the Square. 'T is a hard promise, for he has not used you well. If ever sorrow comes upon him, I want you to promise to be to him a son.'"

"'Why?'

"'For Christ's sake. 'T is a hard thing; but he said, "Love your enemies,"—you know the rest. His words are so beautiful! And God has promised me in my spirit that He will bless you. Will you promise?'

"'O mother!'

"'Is it *yes*, Fletcher?'

"'Yes.'

"'Will you be to Tinley a brother, if trouble comes?'

"'Yes.'

"The peace of death came. Her crazed brain had entered the endless calm. They brought home her body, and buried it in the corner of the east meadow. It is a hay-field now. His mother's sorrow and death made a feeling man of Fletcher. He became unlike other people; he seemed never to think of himself. His mother's influence appeared to be with him always like an angel of good; people said, 'He has his mother's heart.'

"He taught school here three years. He began a Sunday-school in the school-house. It has changed into a church. The old school-house is gone, and a new one has taken its place, but his influence lives in the character of every scholar that it touched. He multiplied good in others. Every sufferer found in him a friend.

"Tinley,—do you want to know about Tinley? He never seemed to have but one purpose in life, and that was to gratify himself. But the Square used to say that he had business in him, and that he would be a rich man one day. He spent his Sundays in riding and his evenings at the billiard-saloon in the village, where there was a bar.

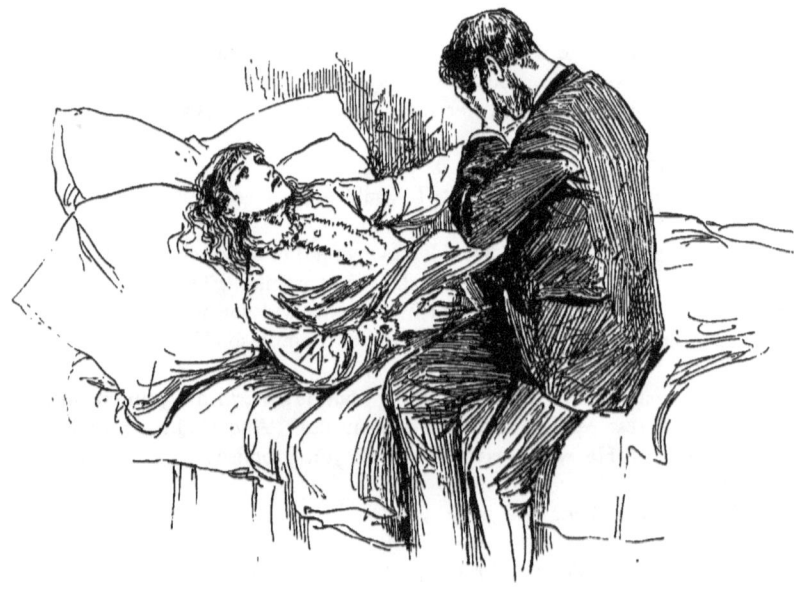

THE BOY PROMISES.

"The Square let him have money, and he went to New York. 'Tinley will open your eyes one day,' the Square used to say.

"He did open our eyes. He speculated. They said that he was rich. He spent his summers at Saratoga and at the watering-places. He came back here one summer, drove fast horses and entertained gay people. The old Square seemed delighted that his prophecy had proved true. Then he failed and opened our eyes again. What you see to-day is the end of it all."

The good farmer, seeing that I was greatly interested, went on:—

"Tinley gave to the town a billiard-saloon. That would have been well enough, but he put into it a bar. Tinley's old comrades are all ruined or dead, and his gilded saloon is turning out wrecks of character and paupers. His life has withered whatever it has touched. He has no true friends. He is lost to himself and to everybody.

"They tell two stories, — the lives of those two boys. One's acts of good are helps to others, and one's acts of wrong are injuries to others, for we all of us live in others' lives as well as our own. Ah, well, stranger," said the farmer in conclusion, "young folks cannot see things as older eyes see them. When the making up of life's account comes, it is less what we have gained of this world than what we have surrendered that will be the account that we shall most like to see."

The old auctioneer came out of the house. A carriage was driven into the yard, and two strangers alighted from it, hitched the horse, and stood silently apart by themselves. They were dressed differently from the townspeople. I was sure they came from the city. I suspected that they were officers of the law.

The auction went on. But the country-people seemed to lose all interest in the sale. They gathered together in little groups and talked in low tones. In the afternoon women came and filled the old house. I could see them whispering together here and there, and watching every movement of the four strangers on the premises, — the two officer-like looking men, Dessalines, and myself. There was an air of mystery everywhere.

Dessalines returned about the middle of the afternoon, and spoke to me.

"I have been walking over the farm," he said. "There is one place here that is more sacred to me than any other on earth, — a grave in the meadow. It was hard to find it."

And now the great sale of all is to be made, — the Tapley farm itself.

The men gathered around the auctioneer. Heads filled the windows. Dessalines and I stood outside the circle of men. The two strangers whom I had taken to be officers were passing about nervously from place to place.

The old Squire came out of the front door slowly, and stood upon the piazza. He was alone. No one cared to share his company in this critical hour of his life. His head was uncovered, and his hair was white and thin. The declining sun poured its light over the tree-tops. The green aisles of the old orchard back of the house grew shadowy. The martins came back to the bird-houses beneath the eaves, and the doves cooed in the dove-cotes. Nearly sunset.

"Are you ready?" asked the auctioneer.

The old Squire looked toward the open fields through the opening in the locust trees. The waving meadow where his father and mother and wife slept was there. The family graves were to go with the rest. Sunset.

"Are you ready?" The auctioneer now addressed the Squire.

"Wait — where is Tinley? I want him here."

There was a stay in the proceedings. Men inquired for Tinley; women looked for him in all the rooms.

But more anxious than the old man or the country-folks appeared the two strangers. The latter entered the house and went from room to room. A thrill of suspicion and excitement ran through the crowd of people. Presently the men appeared upon the piazza beside the old man, and one of them whispered in his ear. Every eye was turned from the impatient auctioneer upon the old Squire.

The Squire turned upon the strangers his cold gray eye. The look that came into his face cannot be pictured. It was as though hope — as though his very soul — had died then and there. He stood still, with motionless lips; only his thin fingers trembled.

I looked into the face of Dessalines. He laid his hand on my arm.

"Ready all," said the auctioneer.

"The Tapley farm and homestead, — the finest farm in Tolland. Buildings all in the best of order. You all know it, — how much am I offered?"

"Two thousand dollars," bid a farmer.

"Two thousand dollars. Worth five. Do I hear the three? Three, do I hear it?

"Two thousand dollars! Look out on the orchards and meadows; what more could any one wish? Two thousand dollars."

"Three."

"Three I am offered. Four? Four? Do I hear the four? Think how the old Squire has thriven here. Four? Do I hear it? Do I hear the four?"

"Four."

"Four thousand dollars. Five? Do I hear the five? Four, four; do I hear the five? Five, do I hear it? Are you all done? Are you ready?

"Going — one."

"Four, one hundred," bid one.

"Four, one. Four, one. Now, two."

"Two," bid another.

"Four?"

"Four."
"Nine?"
"Nine."
"Four thousand nine hundred dollars. Do I hear the five? Five, five? Do I hear the five?"
"Five thousand dollars."

The voice startled the people. It was a mild voice, a beautiful voice, — that of Dessalines.

I felt his hand tremble on my arm. There was a pause, — a painful silence, except that the birds were singing.

The old man stood as rigid as marble. He had not answered the question of the officer beside him. He never would now.

"Five thousand dollars. Five, one? Are you all ready? Five — once, do I hear it? Five — twice, do I hear it? Five thousand dollars — your third and last chance — going, going, gone for five thousand dollars, and sold to — "

He paused and repeated the old musical ditty —

> "Good people, all give ear
> To my 'Going, going, gone!'
> I 'm a country auctioneer,
> And my goods are going, gone.
> Prize well your blessings here,
> For they soon will disappear;
> For Life 's an auctioneer,
> And his goods are going, gone."

He added, amid an awful silence, "Are you all done bidding?"
"Going, going, once.
"Going, going, twice.
"Going, going, third and last chance — to Jean Dessalines Fletcher."

The white-haired old man stood like a figure of alabaster in the red light of the sunset. His figure then seemed to shrink, and his thin fingers clutched at the air. He tried to speak, but simply said, —
"Gone."

They bore him to his room paralyzed.

Dessalines moved slowly toward the house. His old neighbors pressed upon him. They tried to grasp his hands. He entered the house, and went to the chamber where lay the old Squire, breathing heavily. The room, the door, the stairs, were filled with people.

Presently the old Squire opened his eyes.

"Where is Tinley?" he asked in an apprehensive tone, like one awakened from a fearful dream.

"He has escaped," said the old housekeeper. Then she added in a low tone to Fletcher, "The two strange men accused him of forgery."

The Squire bent his eyes upon Fletcher.

"You will let me die here?"

"Yes, *father*, and live here."

"Then you forgive me?"

SCENE IN MARTINIQUE.

"As the All-Merciful has forgiven me."

"Did you say *father?*"

"Father."

The old man turned his face upon the pillow. He was a child again.

A year passed. I again visited the town, and passed the old Tapley estate. The church spire glimmered above the trees. Groups of children were playing about the beautiful school-house.

From a corner of a meadow near the fork of the road, and enclosed by an iron fence, a white shaft of marble rose. I stopped to read the inscription:—

>
> ERECTED
> BY TOWNSMEN OF TOLLAND
> TO THE MEMORY OF
> MARY FLETCHER TAPLEY,
> THE MOTHER OF THE
> REV. JEAN DESSALINES FLETCHER,
> MISSIONARY TO MARTINIQUE,
> WHOSE EARLY LIFE IN THIS TOWN
> WAS THAT OF A BENEFACTOR.

Beside the base of the shaft was a fresh grave. It was the Squire's.

The life of Dessalines bears its flowers and fruits in the Windward Islands, and his influence has lifted there a gold-crossed spire above the savannas, near the old provincial town of Port Royal. I count it among my blessings to have met the influence of his young life even there at that country auction, under the apple-boughs. A good life preaches wherever it may be. His has left an ideal in my memory, and has made me a better man.

Many years have passed since that day, but often the musical tones of the old auctioneer have come back to me with the haunting ditty, —

> "Good people, all give ear
> To my 'Going, going, gone!'
> I 'm a country auctioneer,
> And my goods are going, gone.
> Prize well your blessings here,
> For they soon will disappear;
> For Life 's an auctioneer,
> And his goods are going, gone."

They were a true-hearted and lovely people, the French Huguenots who came to our shores.

Mrs. Laurens followed this narrative with another provincial story.

"WHEN THE STARS BEGIN TO FALL."

I am about to give you as well as I can a picture of old slave life as it was, somewhat as my husband has aimed to give you a view of the devout and amiable character of a typical French Huguenot.

Well, first the scene, — I recall it vividly. It was like this : —

Aunty, within doors, was churning ; I, on the back steps, was shelling peas, — for the days of the old *régime* had gone by, and in our Southern home we had proved that white hands, though not so skilled as black ones, were apt enough in household work.

From the pantry came irregular strokes of the churn-dasher. Aunty had her own way of performing her task. There she sat, — an old sun-bonnet pulled over her eyes to keep out the light, and her head bent down over a well-worn copy of Bunyan. She would churn furiously for a moment ; then, as she reached some thrilling incident, the strokes were fewer, slower, until they would cease altogether, only to begin again faster than ever.

The gate-latch clicked, and little George, a copper-colored youngster of ten, came languidly up the walk.

"Gran'mamy's mighty sick," said he, as he shook hands affably. "She do say de angel Gabriel is callin' her at las'. She wants you chillen to come right away."

"Why did n't she send for us before?" cried I, springing up, forgetful of the peas, that scattered themselves far and wide to the delight of a motherly old hen and her family looking for grubworms near by.

Little George took a seat and munched a pea-pod.

"Well, she kep' a-thinkin' some of you would drop in," said he, reflectively. "An' Mammy could n't stop her washin', an' I'm pretty busy with my schoolin'." And he crossed his short legs with easy dignity.

Aunty's serious brown eyes were tender and troubled. Bunyan was thrown into a corner, and the churning recommenced vigorously.

"You girls must go at once," said she. "I will hurry with the butter, and send her a nice fresh pat. Ruth can beat up some sponge-cakes, and you can gather some figs for the poor old soul."

Ruth was in the coolest place in the house, — the front hall upstairs by an open window, — from which she could look past the long white streets to the gold-crowned hills in the distance. She was engaged in the prosaic work of darning stockings; but her thoughts were wandering wild and free, to judge from the song that gushed upon the air, —

> "I'll chase the antelope o'er the plain,
> The tiger's cub I'll bind with a chain,
> And the wild gazelle, with his silvery feet,
> I'll give thee for a playmate sweet."

"Ruth!" screamed I, as she paused for breath; and the next instant her flower-like face peeped over the baluster. "Come down, my dear, and Aunty will tell you what she wants you to do."

Then seizing my basket, I set out for a long row of fig trees that stretched half across the garden, their thick green leaves clustering close, and their tough branches crooked into cosey seats, where I had done my day-dreaming, safe from all intrusion save that of the impertinent sun, who peeped at me shyly and left his mark on face and hands.

I was soon up in one tree, and little George in another. While I dropped the luscious fruit in my basket, my thoughts turned lovingly to dear old Gran'mamy, and all she had been to us from the time we were babies in her arms.

She was all tenderness when we were wee toddlers, not more than able to catch at the great gold hoops in her ears, or cling to her gown as she bustled about; but she showed a sharper side as we grew older, and "bothered around the kitchen" with inquisitive eyes and fingers and tongues.

"I never seed sich chillen in all my born days," she groaned one day when Ruth interrupted her in the midst of custard-making, to beg leave to get in the kettle of boiling soap, that she might be boiled clean once for all, and never need another bath; while Sam on the other side entreated that she make three "points" of gravy with the fried chicken for dinner.

Sam always came out strong on pronunciation. His very errors leaned to virtue's side.

"I 'clare to gracious," said poor Gran'mamy, "you'll all drive de sense clean out o' my head. How Miss Mary expec's me to git a dinner fit for white folks to eat, wid you little onruly sinners under foot, is more dan I kin say. An' heah 's Leah an' Frances, my own gran'chillen, a' no more use dan two pieces o' yaller dirt."

Gran'mamy looked very threatening as she shook her rolling-pin at her delinquent grandchildren. They only grinned in an aggravating way; for to them as well as to us, the great wide kitchen was the pleasantest place in the world, with its roomy fireplace, where the back-logs glowed and the black kettle hung beneath the smoky rafters from which swung strings of bright peppers and bags of odorous sage.

As Gran'mamy grew older, her manners grew softer, her love less fluctuating. It was to her we ran to tell of triumphs and sorrows,— to get sympathy, ashcakes, and turnover pies in return. It was she who nursed us when sick, who told us stories more beautiful than we read in any books, who petted and loved us more with every month of our lives.

During the troubled four years that swept like the hot breath of the simoom over our country, she was true to the family. Her love, her courage, her faithful work, enabled us to bear up under our heavy trials. And when the gentle mother whose life had been set to sweet music,— when she died, it was in Gran'mamy's arms, and neither husband nor children mourned more tenderly for the beautiful life cut short.

After the war there came a change. Uncle Ned (Gran'mamy's husband) became possessed of a devil — of ambition. He was a dried-up old man, very wrinkled, with a bald head as shining as a polished cocoanut. For fifteen years he had done nothing but drive our carriage; but he now believed himself qualified to make a fortune. He had always in the past submitted as placidly as any of the children to Gran'mamy's rule, but freedom made a new man of him. For the first time in his life he asserted his will against hers.

"I dunno what to make o' Ned," groaned the subdued old woman; "I can't do no more wid him dan if he was a lightnin'-rod. He say 'de man is de head o' de woman,'—pervertin' Scripter at me, de blasphemous boy!"

His son-in-law, the father of little George, had offered him a share in his draying-business, and a home under his roof; and go he would, in spite of Gran'mamy's tears.

She was never well after making the change,—could not reconcile herself to her new home. The tables were strangely turned since our childish days. To see the once strong old woman cling to us, her tears and helplessness, her deep unchanging love, her joy at any little remembrance—for the pathos of all this I have no words. And we—of course we loved Gran'mamy; but our lives were just beginning to crowd with their own sorrows and joys. We were thoughtless, as young people will be before they know that thoughtlessness means cruelty.

"Never mind," thought I, remorsefully, as my long revery came to an end, and I jumped down out of the tree; "I'll do better hereafter. I'll see Gran'-mamy every day of my life."

Now for my story:—

Reaching the house, I found Ruth just taking the fragrant cakes out of the oven, and in a few moments we had started on our visit.

Aunt 'Lizabeth, Gran'mamy's daughter, lived a long way off. Past all the fine houses, among the red sand-hills were nestled half a dozen or more little wooden buildings, looking as if a strong wind would blow them away. They were unpainted and comfortless enough, except for the hollyhocks and sun-flowers that grew about them, and the cows and pigs that were lying around loose, that gave an element of sociability. In Aunt 'Lizabeth's yard her wash-tubs stood empty.

Uncle Ned's dray, too, was off duty.

Aunt Elizabeth met us at the door, her comely black face swollen with tears.

"I'm mighty glad you've come, honey," she cried. "It did 'pear like Mammy'd have no rest in mind or body till you got here."

"How is she now?"

"Well, directly arter little George left, she had a faintin' spell, ain't roused much since, excep' to say, 'Is de chillen come?' O my chile, I'm feared Mammy's mos' gone."

"I did not know she was so sick," cried I, bursting into tears.

Gran'mamy heard my voice, and called faintly. I sprang to her. She clasped her dear old arms about me, and sank back with a satisfied smile. There was a gray shade on the dark face, thrown into such strong relief against the white pillows, and under the pretty, many-colored turban that she always wore.

"It come on sudden-like, my chile," said she; "but don't you fret. I'll soon be well."

"Of course you will," said I, with ready hopefulness; "all you want is to gain your strength. Try and eat a little now, Gran'mamy. Ruth has made you some nice cakes."

"No, my chile," said she, with a loving but far-off smile in her eyes; "no more earthly food for me. The Lord has called me, an' I'm ready to go."

The cakes rolled unheeded to the floor. We looked in awe upon the glad old face. Uncle Ned, who was sitting in the corner, his head buried in an immense yellow handkerchief, gave a subdued groan and a pious "Bless the Lord!" But Aunt 'Lizabeth threw herself on her knees by her mother's bed, and burst into loud weeping.

"O Mammy! Mammy! how kin I give you up? You've been so patient an' long-sufferin' an' kind."

"No, 'Liz, no," said the weak voice. "In dis hour I know what I has been, — proud an' ongrateful, forever kickin' against de pricks. An' yit " — here her tone fell into one of solemn rapture, of strong yet wondering joy — "an' yit, for all my sins, in dis hour He is wid me. He has kept His promise; for in all my wanderin's I have loved His name.

"My chillen, I haven't done my duty by you. I've been fractious an' cross, an' I haven't shown you de *joy* o' de Redeemer's love. An' I can't die widout tellin' you His message once more. O my little ones, when you come to whar I am now, all de past life — no matter if it's been full to de brim o' worldly joy — it will all seem as small as a speck away off in de blue air. It's all nothin', *nothin'*, — eternity is openin' before you. God's love is all in all.

"It's so easy, my chillen; an' jest think what it means, — *de love o' God!* It's like plantin' a little spear o' cocoa-grass. 'Fore you know it's grown, it has run all over de gyardin. Jes' so once get de love o' God in your hearts, an' it'll strike so deep an' spread so fast dat de devil himself can't root it out. An' den, whatever you do or say — from de least to de greatest — has God in it."

Old Ned swayed to and fro, humming a cabin tune in a minor key. Aunt Elizabeth whispered low as if in prayer, —

"Dars de riber of gold,
And dar is de silver boat,
A-rockin' along de shinin' tide,
And my mother is sittin' at de side,
And away she float, she float.
We's a-gwine over de yellow sand,
And we's stop at de steps of de shinin' land,
For my Lord and Mars'er is on de shore,
We won't neber leave Him any more.
O de riber of gold,
O de silver boat,
And we'll neber die no more, no more.

"Oh, dars de riber of gold,
And dar is de silver boat,
A-rockin' along de shinin' tide,
An' my brudder is sittin' at de side,
And away he float, he float.
We's a-gwine over de yellow sand, etc."

"Sing," said Gran'mamy. "Have a consolation meetin' now, chillen. De chariot ob de Lord, it am on its way, chillen, to take one more redeemed one home."

"Consolation meetings" were not uncommon in the slave cabins in this part of the South. They were held when one of the race was very sick or dying. They consisted of prayers and singing. The hymns were usually full of sublime images of the judgment day, the beauties of Christ, and the glories of the celestial state. Several negroes came in from the near cabins, walking very softly, and seated themselves in the shadows of the room.

"Let us have a consolation meetin'," said Old Ned. "What shall we sing, 'Lizabeth?"

"Sing 'When the stars begin to fall,'" said Elizabeth, with a groan.

The negroes all bent over so as to rest their elbows on their knees and to cover their faces in their hands.

The hymn began. The prolonged sadness of the line, "When the stars begin to fall," I have never heard equalled in music, nor have I ever seen anywhere so weird a scene.

"De great day is at hand," said Gran'mamy. "Be silent, chillen."

She was silent a moment, and when she spoke again it was very cheerfully.

"I wish my boy was here. (Sam was in Kentucky at the Military Institute.)

"I've got a little keepsake for him and for all of you. 'Lizabeth, open de big chist."

When the Stars begin to Fall.

The great wooden box opened. Gran'mamy's treasures were in a state of odd confusion, but she seemed to know where everything was.

"Fust my burial close," said she. "Lay 'em out keerfully, 'Lizabeth, and let de chillen see how nice dey are."

They were fresh and white and fragrant. How long they had been folded away I could not ask; but the rose-leaves shaken out of them were scentless and dry.

IN THE HEART OF GEORGIA.

"You see, chillen," said Gran'mamy, brightly, "I've been worryin' in my mind about Sam, away off at de milintary school. Mars' Charles ain't got de money he once had, an' boys at school needs a heap. So I've jes' been savin' along, an' a month ago I took my little pile to de bank, an' got two bright gold pieces for it. Dar dey is, 'Lizabeth, right under your han', in de little pine box your daddy made. Now, Miss Kath'rine, honey, you jes' send 'em to my boy, and tell him to buy a nice fat turkey every Sunday as long as de money holds out. I know how school-boys is starved an' put upon."

I took the little box. Not for worlds would I have pained her by refusing it!
"Now, 'Lizabeth, look a little lower down, — dat passel wrapped in brown paper."

The parcel was handed her; and taking off the outer covering, a white one was revealed, then a third wrapper of silver paper. Slowly, reverently, she unwound this; and there were two tiny, high-heeled satin slippers, yellow with age, but dainty enough for fairy feet.

"De night your mother was married, honey," said Gran'mamy, proudly, "nobody waited on her but me. I unlaced de fine weddin' dress, — all lace an' satin, — an' I put de white nightgown over her head. An' when I took de slippers off her slim, pretty feet, she flung her white arms aroun' my neck an' she says, 'Keep 'em, Gran'mamy, in memory o' dis night.' An' now, my chile, arter all dese years, I gives 'em to you, de fust-born, — your dead mother's weddin' slippers."

I could not speak for my tears. Was there ever a gift so delicately bestowed? I pressed the slippers to my heart, kissing them and the faithful black hands that had taken them from the little feet so many years ago.

"Now, my little singin' bird," said Gran'mamy to Ruth, "I was boun' you should remember me. So I jes' went to de picture-man, and here's my ole black face for you to keep."

The likeness was perfect; and as Ruth warmly thanked her, she sank back wearily on the pillows.

"I'm tired now," she said. "Miss Ruthy, I'd like to hear you sing once more — before I hear de angels on de other side."

Ruth hushed her sobs, and her exquisite voice rolled out in those quaint words, —

"Swing low, sweet chariot."

The negroes joined in the chorus, not singing the words but humming like minor tones on a reed organ.

Then Old Ned prayed, — a prayer full of the images of Ezekiel and the Revelation, which he had learned in some mysterious way.

"Only waitin'," murmured the dying voice. "O my chillen," — and she spoke with sudden energy, — "in your hearts you are pityin' your poor ole Gran'-mamy; you are thinkin' o' de sun shinin' outside, an' de flowers, an' home, an' love. You see me lyin' here, ole an' black, an' racked wi' pain. But, oh! what's de sunlight of earth to de glory roun' de throne of God? What's de flowers here to de flowers in de gyardin yonder? An' what's de love of earth to dat waitin' for me, sinful an' onworthy though I am?

ANCIENT NEGRO BURIAL-PLACES.

"Shinin' ones," she whispered softly; "how dey hold der hands to welcome me! Ned, you remember Willy — our crippled boy?"

"Remember him?" said Uncle, with a start. "Yes, Molly, but it's mighty long ago; nigh on to forty year, Molly, sence we put him in de coffin."

"He is waitin' for me," said she, gently; "Willie an' my young mistis — side by side."

Then stretching her hands to mine, "O my chile!" cried she in a yearning voice; "what word shall I take to your mother from you? Try an' bring it to your mind, honey — I'm gwine to see her — your own sweet mother! Don't you mind how she prayed for you on her dyin' bed, — that you might meet her in de heavenly land? Must I tell her you're travellin' in de right road?"

Alas! alas! I had no answer to give.

"My strength is goin'," said she; "raise me up once more."

We raised her with her face to the window. The sun was sinking in a peace as calm and majestic as that of the dying bed by which we stood. Its last lines of light shone softly into the room. Soon Gran'mamy sunk into a slumber, from which she only roused for a moment when Aunty came in.

"Good-by, Miss Martha," said she, pleasantly. "Take good keer o' Miss Mary's chillen."

It was a strange night. The neighbors gathered in the next room, and through the long hours crooned strange, wild hymns, the mellow voices rising and falling in sweet, weird, haunting cadences, that once heard can never be forgotten. Uncle Ned wandered forlornly from one room to another. Little George abstractedly swallowed sponge-cake in the corner. Ruth fell asleep, while Aunty and I, with the stricken daughter, watched by the dying bed.

Towards morning Gran'mamy spoke.

"De love o' God," she murmured softly.

Her eyes opened wide with a look of rapturous joy, — another moment, and the spirit had gone home. Then all the negroes knelt down in the room around the bed and sang, —

"My Lord, what a morning."

This was followed by a hymn more tender and comforting, —

"Angels waiting at the door."

I shall never forget that night, — its solemn lessons and poetic glooms; and whenever I recall it I shall seem to hear again that strain of rude but sublime music, —

"My Lord, what a morning,
My Lord, what a morning,
My Lord, what a morning,
When the stars begin to fall!"

2. She has laid down her cross and gone home, etc.
3. She has taken up her crown and gone home, etc.

CHAPTER IX.

FUNNY TALES OF THE NEGRO CABINS. — THE ST. JOHN'S RIVER.

THE last story greatly interested the Lelands.

"What shall be our thought to-night?" asked Mrs. Laurens on the following evening, as she again took her place on the old red settle.

"Tell us some more stories of the negro cabins," said Charlie.

"And something more about plantation songs," added Mr. Leland. "I enjoy these stories of simple life, — they seem so near to true human nature. I cannot tell why, but stories of the religious life and even of the superstitions of the negroes have an intense interest to me."

But here an unexpected story-teller appeared.

After tea was over at Mr. Laurens's, Aunt Parthenia, high-priestess of the mysteries of the kitchen, had put everything in her department in prime order, as she always did after each meal.

She was now adding the finishing touch, which was to scour the tin coffee-pot so bright that she could almost see her own black face in it. She was carrying this much-respected coffee-pot to the kitchen door, where she could get the last evening light to the best advantage, when that light was suddenly obscured by the tall form of an ancient "cullud gem'man," — Uncle Romulus, or, as she called him, "Mr. Grievous."

"Why, Mr. Grievous, you skeered me!" cried Aunt Parthenia. "Come in an' take a cheer. How's yo' health? An' how's Mrs. Grievous?"

"I is po'ly, po'ly, Mrs. Waters," answered Uncle Romulus. "What wid de pluralisis an' wid de scianticus an' de plumbago, I isn't much. An' dere's Queen, she's only tol'able. Las' night she was all but skeered to def at de consolation meetin'. I seed you was not dar, Mrs. Waters; an' dat was my princerpal objec' in callin' dis ev'nin', — for to 'scribe to you dat meetin' ober at John Bug's cabin."

Mrs. Laurens had overheard the conversation.

"Come up here on the piazza, Uncle Romulus," she said, "and you, Auntie. Sit down on the settle here, and tell us about the meeting too."

Uncle Romulus and Aunt Parthenia came, and the former proceeded: —

MR. GRIEVOUS'S REMARKABLE STORY.

"You is awar' dat Cath'n Bug has a fever, — had ben lyin' at de p'int ob def for mor' 'n a week; an' as she was his onliest darter, nothin' would do but all de neighbors mus' 'semble an' kind o' comfort him up a little."

"Yes," said Aunt Parthenia, "so I heerd. In truf I got a invite myself, but I hadn't never visited none o' John Bug's family, an' 'sides dat I was sufferin' sech a misery, I wasn't studyin' 'bout goin' nowhar, nohow."

"Dat was my fix persizely," responded Uncle Romulus, "I hadn't never had nuffin' to do wid John Bug, nor wid his family. I has always maintained my verlocity, an' I never did keer to 'sociate wid nobody outsiden de fust quality. I 'se allers ben foun' in de bes' s'ciety, — cullud an' white.

"But, as I was a-sayin', sickness is de gret equalifier ob all 'stinctions; an' when I come home yistiddy, Queen she was all on aidge fer ter go to de meetin', to sorter console up John Bug.

"'What does yer want ter go for?' sez I, 'to a place whar you never does go, an' whar I never keers to go?'

"'Why,' she sez, 'dat po' gal Cath'n is sick, an' dey done sont fer me, an' I can hardly 'fuse at 'sich a 'mergency.'

"Well, I argified right smart, but fin'ly I giv' in ter my ole 'oman!

MOUTH OF THE ST. JOHN'S.

"'Cordin'ly we 'rayed ourselves to walk 'cross lots dat ebenin' to John Bug's cab'n, dough my rheumatiz was bery onwillin'. I reely b'lieve I trabbled all ober de worl' wid my ole Marster wid mo' qualification an' less fatigue dan I trabbled 'cross dem few lots an' parstures.

"When we come to de fiel' whar de cab'n is, — you know 't is a big grass fiel', — I see Mars' William's ole blin' mar' in de lot. Mars' William 's jes' kep' her kase she was ole Mis' ridin' mar' in ole times.

"'Sho 's you born, Queen,' I sez, 'some dose triflin', no-'count folks done lef' de bars down, an' in gropin' aroun', dat po' ole mar's grup fru 'em ober to dis yer'.'

"'You bes' turn her back 'gin,' sez Queen.

"But I sez, 'I ain't gwine ter. Not seein' whar to go she is difficle ter dribe, an' I ain't a-gwine to sile my Sund'y shoes trompin' round in de mud after her. Dar ain't no place she kin hurt herself, so I'se gwine to lef' her be till I comes back.'

"As we 'proached the cab'n we could hear de voices of dose dat was consolin' an' comfortin' an' edrifyin' de fam'ly, — all talkin' to onct, — an' chief above all de bellifluous voice ob Jeems Lytle.

"I 'marked I did n't understan' how *he* come dar, kase he 'siders hisself de top ob de pot, an' none ob de Bug fam'ly dast hole a can'le to him. But Queen say he done come same as we did, to comfort de bereaved fam'ly widout 'stinctions ob rank.

"When we got dar, John Bug come to de do' hisself. Cath'n was layin' on de bed in de middle ob de room, 'pearantly takin' no interus', 'ceptin' a groan onct in a while ; Mrs. Bug, de b'reaved parent, was a-settin' at de head on de right han'-side, wid a pocket-hankerchen to her eyes, — a s'iled one at dat, dar ain't no 'countin' for de ways ob po'-white-folks' niggahs, — an' wid a great black cap on her head.

"On de lef' was settin' Lon, de brudder of Cath'n, cryin' widout any hankerchen ; he better ben cryin' 'bout dat shote he done stole. All roun' ag'in' de walls was settin' de frien's of de 'ceased.

"Dey sot me an' Queen cheers, but it 'peared like I felt stranger 'n I did when I crossed de seas wid ole Marster, an' landed at Rome long years ago, — only we did n't 'xactly *lan*' at Rome, but at de po't o' Rome, which am Chippity Wiggity, — a matter o' ten mile or so from Rome.

"Den Mr. Lytle he began again his shoutifications, an' hoped dey all had de courage he felt in his soul at all times of trial.

"Den dey all shouts ag'in, 'Dat's so. We 's all bold like de lion now.'

"Well ! ef you b'lieve me, jest at dat bery p'int whar dey 's hollerin' loudes' 'bout der courage, dar was de greatis' rumpus of stompin' outside de do' you eber heerd.

"De bucket ob water was frowed from de shelf a-side de do', an' we heerd it roll cl'ar down to de bottom ob de hill wid a tremendous racket, an' lan', ker splash! in de branch, ag'in a big rock. Dat consolation meetin' were stiller 'n def itself, an' all we was de color ob de ashes when de fire 's all gone out.

"Den come a awful shakin' an' poundin' at de do', an' hard breavin'. Den anodder clashin' of iron, an' anodder shakin' at de do'. Heerd de skillet fall an' a whole lot odder tings. Did n't one dem folks say nothin' 'bout courage, den. Dose folks done forgot all 'bout der braggin'.

"De nex' stroke on de do' it c'menced ter come open; an' you never see sich a scatterin' sence you was born. Ebery one dem tarrified folks run an' clim' outen de winder; an' dat little ole winder was n' much bigger 'n de top of dat ar coffee-pot.

"I was n't skeered, you understan', kase I knowed better; but I was disabfusticated, an' what wid my rheumatiz, an' de pressin' an' jammin' of dose or'nary folks behin' me, dey done manage to scrouge me thru dat winder, too. I nebber knowed how dey done it.

"When I come to look for Queen, she was so tarrified she 'd done fell right down on de groun', onspeechless an' onsensible.

"I tell you dar was a mos' tremendous rumpus in dat ole cab'n. Heerd de ole cheers smashin' right an' lef', an' de chaney, — what little dar was of it, an' fru all dat a voice callin' from outen de cloud, it 'peared like, 'For mercy's sake, Uncle Romulus, doan' leave me! for mercy's sake, help me down frum heah.'

"I could n't see nothin', an' I could n't get no adsistance.

"Thar wan't no John Bug, nor none er his fam'ly anywhar roun'. I sez, —

"'Queen, doan' you be skeered; dat ar' noise ain't nothin' but Mars' William's ole blin' mar'! She 's done groped aroun' de lot tell she 's grup her way inter de cab'n. Dem no-'count folks is 'bandoned eberyting; but I 'se gwine to look in, an' I 'spect Cath'n 's dead now, for sho', for all dem triflin' folks done gone an' lef' her right in de berry jaws ob 'struction.'

"De inside ob dat cab'n looked like de lightnin' done struck it for sartain.

"Dar wan't no Cath'n! I searched faithful.

"Well, whar was Cath'n? Ef opportunity would submit I could make a mighty good tale outen dat ar; but my bref 's gettin' powerful short, so I 'se jest gwine to gib yo' de simple splanification of de 'sterious disappearance of Cath'n. Whar do you s'pose she was?"

"Under de bed?" asked Aunt Parthenia.

"Dat bed was flat on de flo' whar de ole mar' tromped on it. She wan't dar."
"Behin' de do'?"
"No. De mar' had kicked it over against de wall, an' crouchin' behin' it war Brudder Jeemes Lytle, wid his courage all done gone!"

"SHE DONE CLOMB UP DE CHIMNEY!"

"Den I can't never guess whar she was."
"Wall," said Uncle Romulus, solemnly, "she done clomb up de chimney! An' dar she sot. Dat's de naked truf.
"Well, good-evenin', Mrs. Waters, I must be a-gwine; good-evenin', all."

And Uncle Romulus took up his hat and stick, and shuffled off.

Mrs. Laurens followed Mr. Grievous, and in the same course of thought.

A STORY OF OLD PLANTATION HYMNS AND SONGS.

The organ specially developed in the African race is music. They imported their "tomtoms," a species of banjo, from Africa; and there was a rhythmical cadence even in the barbarous, monotonous chant with which they accompanied these rude instruments. These chants had some resemblance, in their limited number of notes, to those of the American Indians; but the musical voice of the African, and his fervid action, gave them a life and harmony in which the music of the other race is totally deficient. In a very short time the quick ear of the African caught not only the intonations of the voices of civilized people, but their melodies. Yet the songs of the negro race have a special character of their own.

In some of their hymns are memories of old African war-chants and dance-songs that I used to hear in childhood from an old Congo on my grandmother's plantation. His speech was almost incomprehensible, but his music was very effective to inspire either fear or compassion. Probably his grandchildren or great-grandchildren have introduced these wild melodies into the Christian hymns they sing, as no other race under the sun can do. The words of these hymns with their reiterations are often absurd to the last degree, but I would defy any one to hear a whole plantation singing them, without feeling the heart moved, and the eyes filled with tears at the profound pathos of the tones. Pathos is a distinctive feature in their melodies; but some of their hymns are as wild and rollicking as a German "Trinklied" (drinking-song).

I once collected a number of these songs, and I have them now. I went to the very fountain-head — old plantation negroes — for them. Perhaps you think it was an easy task; a piece of paper, a pencil, and a willing colored brother or sister sitting opposite, only too glad to pour forth a stream of melody. Well, you shall have the benefit of my experience.

Old Aunt Almiry Jane, one of our servants at the time, was called a "knowledgeable ooman," — that is, she had an unlimited repertoire of hymns and melodies. She was an old friend of mine; and I went to her house to enlist her services.

"You wants ole plantation hymns, does you, honey, — why, bless your soul, I dunno no oders, an' wot's more I don't want um. De ole ones is plenty good fur me. But, honey, I can't sing a mite ter-day, fur I 'm powerful hoarse."

"But you need n't sing, Aunty. Just repeat me the words."
"Why, chile," — laughing heartily, — "I could n't' member a single word ef I did n't sing it. But here's my little granddarter Ellen. She kin sing fust-rate. Now, Ellen, wot kin you sing for Missus?"

"I FOUND TREE GEESE."

"I knows 'De Willerness,'" spoke up Ellen, in a conceited manner.
"Very well, let's have "The Wilderness," I said.
"I found tree geese in de willerness —"
"Wot's dat you're singin', you sassy no-'count ting," cried her grandmother, angrily. "Who teached you to say 'tree geese'? Whar's any geese in dat hymn? Why don't you sing it right?" And then, like a hoarse raven, the old woman lifted up her voice and sang, —
"I found free grease in de willerness —"

"Just stop a minute, Aunty," I cried desperately ; for between the absurdities of " tree geese " and " free grease " I could see little difference. " I could n't have understood you. Did you say *free grease ?*"

" Yes, honey, dem 's de 'dentical words."

" But what does it mean ? " I asked bewildered. I did n't relish the idea of having my collection more utterly absurd than that of anybody else.

" Well, honey, I ain't nebber studied de meanin'. I reckon it means de Gospel makes you stick like grease. Oh, ef dar ain't Brudder Gardner passin'. He kin sing beautiful, an' he knows more hymns dan I does. Here, Ellen, lope arter him, an' tell him to come right off."

" Brudder Gardner" was a venerable old man, and as soon as he understood what I wanted, expressed himself willing to oblige. Oh, yes, he knew " De Wilderness."

" I found free grace in de wilderness,
In de wilderness, in de wilderness,
I found free grace in de wilderness.
Shout! shout! I 'm gwine home.

CHORUS.

So git you ready, sister, git you ready,
Put your golden slipper on your feet ;
For I 'm a-gwine home to-morrer,
I 'm a-gwine home.

" Wot did I see in de wilderness,
In de wilderness, in de wilderness ?
I found a lamb in de wilderness.
Shout! shout! I 'm gwine home.
So git you ready, brudder," etc.

The old man's voice was magnificent, deep, sonorous, and untouched by time. If Aunt Almiry Jane noticed any difference in his version, she did not say a word ; but she rocked her body, waved her hands, and joined hoarsely in the chorus. I found, however, that I could get the words of none of their songs unless they sang them. To repeat a line without the tune was impossible. Old Gardner said apologetically, —

"You see, ma'am, we can't read in books, an' we larns de words an' tune togedder, so somehow we can't git at 'em apart. I'm gwine to sing ' De Social Band.' "

"I'll jine de social Band,
I'll jine de social Band,
I'll jine de happy company,
Dat's gone along before.

CHORUS.

Don't git weary, mudder,
Don't git weary, —
Fur Jesus true has promised me
To come bimeby.

"I'll jine de Band bimeby,
I'll jine de Band bimeby;
My way is dark and cloudy, Lord,
But you will come bimeby.
Don't git weary, brudder," etc.

Unless you heard this hymn sung as I heard it, you could not realize the heart-yearning, the pathos, that could be thrown into these rude words. It must certainly have been composed at a time when the slave's heart went out in intense longing for the "bimeby" of a heavenly and eternal freedom. I asked Gardner if they sang those hymns often now.

"We sings 'em 'mong ourselves, ma'am, we ole folks, but dey don't sing 'em at meetin' no more. We's got pow'ful fine preachers, but dey sings mostly outer pra'r-books, new hymns; an' de young folks, dey follers 'em. Dey says as how our ole hymns ain't got no sense in 'em; but, bless you, dey's got a heap ob sense to us. Dey kin lift us up high as de golden chariot, an' dat's 'nuff fur me, I reckon. Did you eber hear 'De Gospel Boat'? We used to lib on a big plantation on de Massissippi, an' seein' boats a-passin' up an' down put de words in our heads.

"De Gospel Boat am comin',
I hears it jest at hand;
I hear de steam a-puffin'
And a-roarin' troo de land.

CHORUS.

Git aboard, chilluns,
Git aboard, chilluns;
Dar's room fur a-many more

"I tinks she'll make a little halt
And wood up on de shore,
And gib you all a chance to go, —
You, and a tousand more.
Git aboard, etc.

"Dar's John and Mark and Abraham,
And all de 'postles too;
And Christ hisself is gone aboard,
To pay your passage troo.
Git aboard," etc.

"I knows a heap more hymns," the old man said; "but you see, Mistiss, I'se in a powerful hurry dis mornin'. Ef you'll come round here Saturday night, we'll all meet. We'se got some fine singers 'mong us old plantation niggers, and we likes to hab a real 'ligious time. You see de new preacher he don't like shoutin', an' some ob dem hymns brings de shout to your mouf 'fore you know wot you're 'bout."

Of course I was only too glad to promise, and Saturday night found me in a corner at Almiry Jane's. The meeting had begun some time before I reached there, and they were singing at the top of their voices, —

"O brudder, ef you falls ter-day,
Don't weary long,
But rise and come 'fore Jedgment Day,
Don't weary long.
From cherry tree to Galilee,
Honor de Lord;
And shout, and clap, and do your best,
Jest for de Lord.

CHORUS.

I'm a-climbin' Jacob's ladder,
Don't you grieve arter me;
When I am dead and buried,
Don't you grieve arter me."

Gardner was the master of ceremonies, and he rose in his place. "My sisters and brudders," he said, "dat ar lady is comed here to take down some ob our old plantation hymns, wen we wos in de house ob bondage. Wot does you tink is de best ones?" One of the old sisters spoke up, —

"I tinks 'Mary and Martha' is a right peart hymn. Let's sing dat furst."

"'Sister Mary, whar wos you
When our good Lord was here?'
'I was in de garding a-prayin' to de Lord,
And a-drappin' many a tear.'

CHORUS.

Ho! ho! prayin' is de best.
I looks to de east, and I looks to de west,
Fur my good Lord is dar.

"'Sister Marthy, whar wos you
When our good Lord was here?'
'I wos in de kitchin a-cookin' fur my Lord,
And a-takin' work and care.'
Ho! ho! prayin' is de best, etc.

"Sister Mary she sot her down,
When my good Lord wos here;
But Sister Marthy she ups and frets,
And nebber stops to hear.
Ho! ho! prayin' is de best," etc.

"Decidedly," I thought to myself, "they've got the right version of the Bible story, if it is told queerly." They sang well, too, some of them exquisitely. But there was one old woman, with a voice like a screech-owl, whom they seemed to try to hustle aside, but she was determined to be heard.

"Look a here, Brudder Gardner, don't none on you know ' Mary's Blessin's'? I reckon dat would please de lady."

"I clean disremember it," Gardner said, with an appealing look around the circle. They seemed to understand it, for they all said they did n't remember more than a verse or two. "You see, Sister Marier," Gardner said, "it's a mi'ty long time sence I heerd it.'

"Sister Marier" gave a shrill cackle, and said she reckoned she could tackle it alone. She did tackle it until I thought my head would split with her sharp high notes, and the others groaned audibly.

"Sister Marier" started the hymn, but broke down at the first line. Nowise discouraged, she cleared her throat, and in a higher and shriller key began. My teeth were on edge, and it seemed to me Almira's plates and dishes rattled on their shelves; but the undaunted old woman sang on.

"De very furst blessin' dat Mary had,
She had de blessin' ob one,
To tink dat her son Jesus
Nussed at her breast so young.

"De very next blessin' dat Mary had,
She had de blessin' ob two;
To tink dat her son Jesus
Could read de Bible through.

"De very next blessin' dat Mary had,
She had de blessin' ob tree,
To tink dat her son Jesus
Could make de blin' ter see.

" De very next blessin' dat Mary had,
    She had de blessin' ob four,
    To tink dat her son Jesus
    Could bring de rich to poor."

During the last verse I whispered to Almira, who was near me, " How long is she going to sing? I can't stand it much longer."

The old woman laughed until her fat sides shook. "Why, honey, she kin run up to twenty blessin's. She can't sing a mite, but she's a good pious woman, and sometimes we lets her hab her way; but I'll stop it now. — Sister Marier," she called out when the singer had paused to recover voice for her fifth verse, " we ain't got time fur de rest ob de blessin's ter-night."

" No, we has n't," Gardner said quickly. " Sisters and brudders, let's sing 'I'll nebber turn back no more.'"

" De world is burnin' wid fire and flame,
    De angels mourn and de Christians groan;
    De angels mourn all round de trone,
    Hallelujah! ho! no more!

CHORUS.

No more, no more, no more, tank God,
I'll nebber turn back no more;
I'll gib you my heart, I'll gib you my hand,
I'll nebber turn back no more!

" I'll shout fur help till de Lord he hears;
    I'll shout and cry, ' Lord, you has said,
    De fire shan't burn de mourner's head.'
    Hallelujah! ho! no more!
    No more, etc.

" Oh, de golden gates fly open wide!
    Make room, make room fur de Lamb and bride.
    O brudder, sister, you 'se by my side,
    Hallelujah! ho! no more!
    No more," etc.

What words could give an idea of the *élan* with which this was sung! Hands were clasped, eyes streaming tears, and the sonorous voices seemed to burst through the roof of the little cabin and soar into space. At the chorus the circle clasped each other's hands, and the " Hallelujah!" was a shout of ecstasy. I understood now what Gardner meant when he said some of their hymns brought " de shout to de mouf."

Reading the rude words, people may wonder at the impression made upon me ; but all musicians or lovers of music understand that it is quite independent of words to convey ideas or sensations. If they could have heard the hymns as I did, sung by fine voices, thrilling with pathos, soaring with triumph, the simple words would have seemed grander than the most finished poem.

I did not want the impression weakened, so I took leave at once, Gardner promising to come to my house the next day with two or three of his friends who had fine voices, and sing "the cotton-picking song."

"You must have heerd it often, Mistiss," Gardner said, when, true to his appointment, he came with his friends. "You always libed on a plantation 'fore de war, and you must have knowed all dem ole songs."

"I know a good many of them, Gardner; but on the Ashton Place our people used to change their cotton-picking song whenever they changed the captain, or foreman, of the gang. You know, they make up verses as they sing them."

"Yes, 'm, but I wos captain ob de pickers on de ole Linwood Plantation, and most ginerally we used to have one 'ticklar one. I s'pose it was a favorite wid um. Now, boys, is you ready?"

"Oh, de cotton fields am white, and de pickers is but few,
    Save me, Lord, from sinkin' down ;
If your fingers is n't nimble, sure you nebber will git troo.
    Save me, Lord, from sinkin' down ;
If your bags is very light, den de overseer's lash,
    Save me, Lord, from sinkin' down ;
If you 're laffin' in de mornin', den at night your teef will gnash,
    Save me, Lord, from sinkin' down.

" Pick your cotton bolls so cl'ar dat dar 's noting left to waste,
    Save me, Lord, from sinkin' down ;
You Sister Ann Jerusha Brown, you better now make haste,
    Save me, Lord, from sinkin' down ;
De sun is gittin' low, and my fingers gittin' numb,
    Save me, Lord, from sinkin' down ;
Oh, I wish ter-night de Lord would say, ' Come up, poor sinner, come.'
    Save me, Lord, from sinkin' down.

"Ef I had died when I was young, I would n't cry ter-day,
    Save me, Lord, from sinkin' down ;
My soul would be like cotton white, my sins all washed away,
    Save me, Lord, from sinkin' down ;
Now it 's trompled in sin's dirt till de white is turned to black,
    Save me, Lord, from sinkin' down ;
But I 'll work de Hebenly gin till I gits its whiteness back,
    Save me, Lord, from sinkin' down."

"Let us make memoranda of the stories we have told and heard," said Charlie. "Let us cut the names of them on the back of the settle."

Henry took out his knife and made on the back of the old settle a list of the stories that had been told in the region of old Plymouth.

NEGRO VILLAGE IN GEORGIA.

Charlie added to this those that he had heard in Washington, and promised to relate these to the Laurenses as his father had given them to him, particularly those of Spotswood, Lord Fairfax, and Washington. He also added to the list the stories already told at St. Augustine.

"We ought to take the old settle with us," said Mrs. Laurens. "when we go to Nassau."

THE ST. JOHN'S RIVER.

ASCENDING THE RIVER.

"How?" asked Charlie. "It would be an unhandy thing to carry."

"I think not. We have engaged a steam yacht to take us from here to Nassau and among the islands of the old navigators."

"From St. Augustine! How generous you have been! Then the old settle can go too. I thought that we were to start from Tampa Bay."

In the mean time, before the journey to the Isle of June, Santiago de Cuba, and the tomb of Columbus in Havana, Henry took Charlie on a long boat excursion up the famous St. John's River, to the places associated with early Spanish settlements.

The boys left Jacksonville in a canoe for Palatka, a distance of fifty-six miles. Jacksonville was so named in honor of Andrew Jackson, who was an early military governor of the State. The city has leaped into life. Its docks are full of ships and piles of yellow pine lumber. In 1881 Jacksonville had but one railway; it is now the terminus of six railways.

The St. John's River is the natural avenue of Florida, although since the year 1881 more than a thousand miles of railroad have been built in the State. The mouth of the river for a distance of many miles, or to Jacksonville, forms a beautiful harbor, of which Jacksonville, some fifteen miles distant from the sea, is the port town. It is a river of swamps, palmettoes, and orange groves.

The river is lazy and calm. The fruits of the tropics and of almost all zones wave in the air when a breeze breaks the silence and sleep of Nature. Great alligators sleep amid the tall reeds and white lilies, and are sometimes seen; birds of gorgeous plumage doze among the eternal green of swamps and savannas; the air is languid, and the boatman's oars slowly rise and fall.

The St. John's is a water-street. There are little towns everywhere, and airy balconies. Magnolia, with its red towers, comes into view, — a city or town partly sunk in a green sea of magnolias and live-oaks. Three quarters of a mile or so from Magnolia are the Green Cove Sulphur Springs.

Palatka is situated about half-way in the usual steamer route of the St. John's. It is built on a high bluff, known as Palatka Heights. Palatka is in the orange-grove section, and is the usual starting-point for the Ocklawaha, one of the most beautiful of tropical rivers, that branches from the St. John's some miles above. The boys rested at Palatka, and leaving their canoe, went to Sanford by steamer, and thence by rail to Tampa, near which De Soto landed, and began his famous march that ended in the discovery of the Mississippi. On their return to St. Augustine, they stopped at Mandarin, the residence of Mrs. Harriet Beecher Stowe.

TAMPA.

And this is Tampa; yonder lies the Bay
    That Spanish cavaliers,
Enchanted, saw upon their unknown way,
    In far and faded years, —

That to their eyes so calm and placid seemed,
    So bright and wondrous fair.
They drifted on with silent lips, and dreamed
    The Holy Ghost was there.

Here lies a fortress old, a field of death;
    And here, as years increase,
The useless cannon hide their heads beneath
    The snow-white sands of peace.

The Gulf winds warm the orange orchards stir,
    And from dark trees like walls,
In long festoons and threads of gossamer,
    The trailing gray moss falls.

And ships come in from tropic seas, and go,
    And sails the Gulf winds fan;
And few do know, or seem to care to know,
    That here that march began

That set the crown of empires in the West,
    And gave the nations birth,
That stand like gracious queens, above the rest,
    Upon the thrones of earth.

A ZIGZAG JOURNEY IN THE SUNNY SOUTH.

The town is fair, and fairer yet the Bay,
   And warm the trade-winds blow,
Where lateen sails moved on their lonely way,
   Three centuries ago.

De Soto's hands lie deep beneath the wave ;
   Dust are his cavaliers.
The cypressed waters murmuring o'er his grave,
   The silent pilot hears

In that far river where they laid him down,
   Where low the ring-doves sigh,
And oft the full moon drops her silver crown,
   From night's meridian sky.

And here, where first his banners caught the breeze,
   The peopled towns arise ;
And his great faith that piloted the seas
   Beneath uncertain skies,

And dared the wilds by Christian feet untrod,
   Is strong with hope to man ;
And here, where touched the new world's ark of God,
   Fair skies the rainbows span.

O Tampa, Tampa, near the Gulf's warm tide !
   Who would not linger here,
Where on the homes the orange-gardens hide,
   June smileth all the year?

Where never comes the autumn nor the spring.
   Nor summer's fiercer glow ;
Where never cease the mocking-birds to sing,
   Nor roses new to blow.

CHAPTER X.

THE ISLE OF JUNE.

"SHIP whose keel is of palm beneath,
  Whose ribs of palm have a palm-back sheath,
  And a rudder of palm it steereth with.

" Branches of palm are its spars and rails,
  Fibres of palm are its woven sails,
  And the rope is of palm that idly trails !

" What does the good ship bear so well?
  The cocoanut with its stony shell,
  And the milky sap of its inner cell.

" What are its jars so smooth and fine,
  But hollowed nuts filled with oil and wine,
  And the cabbage that ripens under the lime ?

" Who smokes his nargileh cool and calm ?
  The master, whose cunning and skill could charm
  Cargo and ship from the bounteous palm."
                                        Whittier.

So the steam yacht glided out of the harbor of St. Augustine with the old red settle on board.

"We sail from the oldest town in the United States," said Mr. Laurens, "and I hope that we may visit the oldest standing European town in the Americas."

"Nassau is not the oldest standing European town in the Americas," said Charlie.

"No."

"Is Havana?"

"What then is the oldest?"

"Santiago de Cuba," said Mr. Laurens, "the ancient Spanish capital of Cuba, although Santo Domingo is older historically."

NASSAU.

The sea was calm, the air moist and warm, and two days' sail brought the party in sight of the cocoanut palms of the Isle of June. Then Nassau appeared in the garden of the sea, — a garden unlike any other, for here grow in winter the products of almost every zone.

The water of the harbor was a wonder, — in places blue as a robin's egg, in places like liquid amethyst, with rose tints here and there in shading light. The great hotel seems to stand above the island and to crown it.

The party was welcomed by the American Consul, a friend of Mr. Laurens. After an introduction to the Consul, Mr. Leland asked, by way of making conversation, —

"What are some of the fruits and other productions of the island?"

"Fruits?" said the Consul, thoughtfully. "Well, we have cocoa-nuts, bananas, oranges and lemons, pineapples, mangoes, the sapidilla, cashew, sweet sop and sour sop," —

(Henry and Charlie began to be very much interested.)

"The papaw, the mammee, star apples," —

(The boys' eyes grew with the list.)

"The sea-side grape, scarlet plums, guava, love in a mist, custard apple, tamarind, peanuts, breadfruit, citron, mandarin, rose apples, figs, dates, pomegranates, mulberries, almonds, jujube, and — "

"Are these all?" asked Mr. Leland.

"Oh no, I was about to add — "

"Thanks," said Mr. Leland, "these will do."

"Let us go on," said Henry.

"I should think so," said Charlie. "I wish to go on as fast as possible, and see the island for myself."

"Good-day," said the pleasant Consul; "I hope you will all have a pleasant visit."

"Was the Consul joking?" asked Charlie.

The Consul was not joking. The winter, marked at Nassau for the variety of its vegetable productions, has no equal in the world.

THE ISLE OF JUNE.

The Isle of June, — an island where every month in the year is June, and where January is the June of the North! It lies on the line of the tropic sea, some two days from St. Augustine, and some three days from New York. The passengers who leave New York in the Ward line of steamers on Thursday afternoon for the Isle of June may dine on Sunday amid the groves of cocoanuts and farms of pineapples. These steamers go some one hundred and fifty miles south of the dreaded Cape Hatteras, and five hundred miles south of Savannah. It is not long after they leave New York on this southern course before they begin to feel the influence of the warm tides of

ROYAL VICTORIA HOTEL, NASSAU.

the Gulf Stream. The distance from midwinter to midsummer is very short on such an excursion to the Isle of June.

It rises from the warm sea,—an elevation crowned with palms, and wearing the English flag in its fronded crown. Columbus is said to have visited this palm garden of eternal June on his first voyage. This is doubted; but the first island that he discovered, whether or

THE NATIVES.

not it be Guanahani, lies not a long distance south. The island is some twenty or more miles long, and some six or seven wide.

In Florida cold is felt sometimes, and sometimes in the month of June in the North; but in this Eden of the Bahama Island gardens cold is never felt. The trees are green continually; the flowers bloom always; the orange-trees are never smitten by frost.

For Cuba and the Spanish isles, one has much trouble about passports and landings, and trouble again comes through the language and habits of the people when one has passed the custom-houses. But the English flag floats free over the sea here, and one is as free to come and go as in the States. The government is an easy one for all good people; the good queen appoints her good governor and pays him, and apart from this the pacific and contented people govern themselves.

The Isle of June is the capital of the Bahamas. San Salvador, a sister island, is popularly supposed to be the first land seen by Columbus; but Watling Island was in fact the first discovery, — San Salvador in poetry, but Watling Island in fact.

One lands here in a park. No cabman importunes him; he may take up his baggage in peace, and go straight to the Victoria or other hotel.

One will be astonished to be recognized here by every passer-by, and will be apt to wonder if his reputation has thus preceded him. The easy-going negroes will all seem to know him and take off their hats. The climate in an hour will put him into the same democratic good-humor; he will feel easy, and be respectful to all the little world around him, and will return the bow of the little negro whose wardrobe consists of a single short garment.

One will be apt to find the windows of the Grand Victoria Hotel all open to catch the cool breezes of the sea, and the band playing upon the lawn. After a dinner unlike anything found elsewhere, one will be apt to saunter out to see the wonders of the island. Wherever one may go, he will feel quite at home.

Here may be found oranges, lemons, pineapples, bananas, cocoanuts, and limes, all struggling to outdo each other in prodigal productiveness. The trees, although loaded with fruit, seem to grow out of the rocks. Here are orange groves and pineapple fields and cocoanut plantations. Here one may drink the milk or water of green cocoanuts for a beverage, and a most delicious beverage it will be found. The milk is very fattening.

Grantstown is a curious suburb, where the poorer people live in cabins that are shaded by trees and circled by flowers. It is quite unlike other poor quarters of cities. At a distance it looks like a grove of cocoanut and almond trees, with brown dots of roofs like swamp-hay-stacks.

The island has a very ancient history, and abounds in curiosities. Among these is old Fort Fincastle, which looks like an immense ocean steamer aground. Here may be seen the banyan tree of India, or its like, and the silk cotton tree, of immense dimensions. How old it may be one cannot tell; it may have shaded the famous Bahama pirates, or even the Spanish explorers.

Nassau is a paradise of churches. The Episcopal Church, with my Lord Bishop, is the church of the island. Then follow the Methodist, Baptist, Presbyterian, Catholic, and others. There is no regular theatre, but a circus company sometimes excites the colored population in the tourist's "winter" season. The market days are the social days of the place.

The island has been under the flags of the Spanish, the pirates, the British, and once under the Stars and Stripes. The Spanish voyagers removed the entire population to Spain. For a century the island was without inhabitants. In 1607 an English sea-captain gave the island the name of New Providence (N. P.); then it became familiar as Nassau; then poetical tourists began to call it the Isle of June; and such it bids fair to remain to tourists always, whatever it may be to the business world.

A PLANTER'S HOUSE.

The famous pirate Blackbeard made the island his treasure-house. Here grew up a colony of sea-robbers. "Expulsis Piratis, Restitutia Commercia," was the motto on the old Bahama coat of arms. After the expulsion of the pirates the city of Nassau was begun, in 1694.

It is an isle of the palm, — not the date, but the cocoanut palm.

The cocoanut palm loves the sea, and the cocoanut is a great sailor. Falling into the ocean, the nut has drifted from island to island, and has planted itself. Its green crowns shine above the golden sands of all the tropic islands. To the traveller in the hot sun blessed is the shade of the palm, and delicious and cool the drink of its green fruit. It attains a height of almost a hundred feet, and the age of a hundred years. It blooms every month in the year, and blooms and nuts grow on the same bough.

Nothing can be more amusing than a free talk with the colored people of the Isle of June. The twenty-mile island to them is the world. They have as little comprehension of the world beyond the sea as they have of the magnitude and distances of the stars. They make no provision for anything. Why should they? The sea gardens are full of green turtles that can be had by turning them over; the sea is full of fish; the air, of cocoanuts; and the ground, of sweet potatoes, some of the latter being as large as melons. The children wear little or no clothing, and adults only such as is essential to modesty and decency. The atmosphere clothes the people in the same prodigal way that the earth feeds them.

The evening after the arrival of the yachting party was clear and beautiful. The sun went down in a crimson sky, and the moon arose like a spectral world. The party went to the cupola of the hotel to see the Southern Cross. On returning to the park, the boys attracted the attention of a company of negro children, and delighted some of them by making them presents of English shillings that they had just received in exchange for American greenbacks and gold. The wonder of the older negro boys on receiving these gifts repaid the generosity.

"Please God, I never did have so much money as this befo'," said the oldest boy of the group. "Dad did once, bless God!"

A shilling to the lad was a fortune, and the lad's conception of the greatness and wealth of the people whose sons could spare such gifts grew.

"Is the town where you come fro' bigger 'n here?" asked the lad who was called Bo.

"Boston? yes, there are a hundred people there to one here," said Charlie. "You have some fifteen thousand people here; New York has a million!"

"Sho', and how many is that?" asked Bo.

It was a hard question to answer.

"An' Americ', — how big is Americ'?"

"As big as a hundred thousand islands like this."

"Sho! what made you come here for then?"

"It is cold," said Charlie.

"What *is* cold?" asked Bo.

This question was also hard to answer. The negro boy had no conception of cold.

"Please God, what is cold, boss?" continued Bo.

"It is not to be warm," said Henry.

But there had never been a time when the little negro Bo had not been warm.

"You wait a minute," said Charlie, "and I will show you cold."

"Bless God, boss, I kin wait," said Bo. He certainly could, — he had done nothing else all his sunny life.

Charlie went to his room, and brought from it a piece of ice.

"This is cold," said Charlie, breaking the ice. "Let me drop this down your back, and then you will know all about it. That is the way."

Bo had but one garment, and this hung loosely around him.

"Pull your dress around you close," said Charlie, "and stand straight, and I will show you what cold is. Now, then —" Charlie dropped a handful of ice down Bo's back.

"Christifo' Columbus!"

The effect was electrical, almost as much so as a shovelful of hot coals employed in the same way might have been. Bo forgot his usual pious ejaculations, and appealed to history. He released his tightened garment instantly, and thus got rid of the broken ice.

"Snakes!" he cried. "Ki, hi!— snakes, you — Christifo' Columbus — you! I'll be up with you, putting snakes down my back. Ki, hi!"

One of the dusky children picked up a piece of the ice, but immediately dropped it as though it had been a coal.

"I'll show you *cold;* you'll see," said Bo. "I can feel 'um wiggle now all over my back. Christifo'!"

He tore off the only garment that he owned, bobbing up and down and swaying hither and thither during the sudden undressing. He dropped the garment and ran, throwing his feet high into the air!

The next day, as Charlie and Henry were walking through Grantstown, they heard a patter of feet, and looking around saw a crowd of children following them. At their head was Bo.

At the end of a pine pole Bo held out an ugly-looking creature that wiggled in a very excited way.

"Alabama! I'll pay you now," said Bo. "I'll give you Christifo' Columbus! Let me get this on to you just once, and your millyon islands won't be worth a cocoanut. He'll give you fits! Alabama!"

Bo bobbed the wiggler, whatsoever it might be, up and down with savage delight, singing an odd ditty, that sounded like —

"On the Isle of June you shall rest your weary bones,
Alabama, Alabama!"

The children joined in the refrain, "Alabama," that followed a very hostile-sounding song.

"Ki, hi! just look at 'im now! Ki, hi! he'll fix ye — hot!"

Charlie and Henry began to run. They had no means of defence against such a weapon. Negroes, even children, are not apt to run for a long distance in this enervating climate, and the day was very hot; so Charlie and Henry soon escaped their pursuers. Whether the awful bug or insect was a tarantula or centipede or scorpion, they never knew.

They did not attempt object-teaching among the native children again. They had a new kind of awe for the name of Christifo' Columbus, and a mysterious terror for the strangely used words, "Alabama, Alabama."

"The Isle of June is the most beautiful spot on earth," said an old English traveller, whose health had been broken by naval service, and who had come here to rest. "I have travelled everywhere; I have been among scenes of more striking features, but never among those that so nearly realized the old-time idea of paradise. I do not wonder that Ponce de Leon thought that the earthly paradise might be found here."

The English Government have shown their appreciation of the value of the island as a sanatarium, by often sending disabled officers here in preference to all other places.

The island is graced by a statue of Columbus. The great Admiral is said to have called it Fernandina.

Mr. Laurens here began to introduce a new method of story-telling. It was by reading stories selected from Columbus's own letters and narratives, as translated from the Spanish or Latin.

COLUMBUS'S OWN STORY OF THE BAHAMAS AND THE WESTERN ISLES.

A letter addressed to the noble Lord Raphael Sanchez, Treasurer to their most invincible Majesties, Ferdinand and Isabella, King and Queen of Spain, by Christopher Columbus, to whom our age is greatly indebted, treating of the islands of India recently discovered beyond the Ganges, to explore which he had been sent eight months before under the auspices an t at the expense of their said Majesties.

Knowing that it will afford you pleasure to learn that I have brought my undertaking to a successful termination, I have decided upon writing you this letter to acquaint you with all the events which have occurred in my voyage, and the discoveries which have resulted from it. Thirty-three days after my departure from Cadiz, I reached the Indian Sea, where I discovered many islands, thickly peopled, of which I took possession without resistance in the name of our most illustrious Monarch, by public proclamation and with unfurled banners. To the first of these islands, which is called by the Indians Guanahani, I gave the name of the Blessed Saviour (San Salvador), relying upon whose protection I had reached this as well as the other islands; to each of these I also gave a name, ordering that one should be called Santa Maria de la Concepcion, another Fernandina, the third Isabella, the fourth Juana, and so with all the rest respectively.

As soon as we arrived at that, which as I have said was named Juana, I proceeded along its coast a short distance westward, and found it to be so large and apparently without termination, that I could not suppose it to be an island, but the continental province of Cathay. Seeing, however, no towns or populous places on the sea-coast, but only a few detached houses and cottages, with whose inhabitants I was unable to communicate, because they fled as soon as they saw us, I went farther on, thinking that in my progress I should certainly find some city or village.

At length, after proceeding a great way and finding that nothing new presented itself, and that the line of coast was leading us northwards (which I wished to avoid, because it was winter, and it was my intention to move southwards; and because, moreover, the winds were contrary), I resolved not to attempt any further progress, but rather to turn back and retrace my course to a certain bay that I had observed, and from which I afterward despatched two of our men to ascertain whether there were a king or any cities in that province. These men reconnoitred the country for three days, and found a most numerous population, and great numbers of houses, though small and built without any regard to order, — with which information they returned to us.

In the mean time I had learned from some Indians whom I had seized, that that country was certainly an island, and therefore I sailed towards the east, coasting to the distance of three hundred and twenty-two miles, which brought us to the extremity of it; from this point I saw lying eastwards another island, fifty-four miles distant from Juana, to which I gave the name of Española; I went thither, and steered my course eastward as I had done at Juana, even to the distance of five hundred and sixty-four miles along the coast. This said island of Juana is exceedingly fertile, as indeed are all the others; it is surrounded with many bays, spacious, very secure, and surpassing any that I have ever seen; numerous large and healthful rivers intersect it, and it also contains many very lofty mountains.

All these islands are very beautiful, and distinguished by a diversity of scenery; they are filled with a great variety of trees of immense height, and which I believe to retain their foliage in all seasons; for when I saw them they were as verdant and luxuriant as they usually are in Spain in the month of May, — some of them were blossoming, some bearing fruit, and all flourishing in the greatest perfection, according to their respective stages of growth, and the nature and quality of each; yet the islands are not so thickly wooded as to be impassable. The nightingale and various birds were singing in countless numbers, and that in November, the month in which I arrived there. There are besides, in the same island of Juana, seven or eight kinds of palm-trees, which, like all the other trees, herbs, and fruits, considerably surpass ours in height and beauty. The pines also are very handsome, and there are very extensive fields and meadows, a variety of birds, different kinds of honey, and many sorts of metals, but no iron. In that island also which I have before said we named Española, there are mountains of very great size and beauty, vast plains, groves, and very fruitful fields, admirably adapted for tillage, pasture, and habitation. The convenience and excellence of the harbors in this island, and the abundance of the rivers, so indispensable to the health of man, surpass anything that would be believed by one who had not seen it.

The trees, herbage, and fruits of Española are very different from those of Juana, and moreover it abounds in various kinds of spices, gold, and other metals. The inhabitants of both sexes in this island and in all the others which I have seen, or of which I have received information, go always naked as they were born, with the exception of some of the women, who use the covering of a leaf, or small bough, or an apron of cotton which they prepare for that purpose. None of them, as I have already said, are possessed of any iron; neither have

FRIENDLY INDIANS DEALING WITH THE VOYAGERS.

they weapons, being unacquainted with, and indeed incompetent to use them, not from any deformity of body (for they are well formed), but because they are timid and full of fear. They carry, however, in lieu of arms, canes dried in the sun, on the ends of which they fix heads of dried wood sharpened to a point; and even these they dare not use habitually, for it has often occurred, when I have sent two or three of my men to any of the villages to speak with the natives, that they have come out in a disorderly troop, and have fled in such haste at the approach of our men that the fathers forsook their children and the children their fathers. This timidity did not arise from any loss or injury that they had received from us; for, on the contrary, I gave to all I approached whatever articles I had about me, such as cloth and many other things, taking nothing of theirs in return: but they are naturally timid and fearful.

As soon, however, as they see that they are safe, and have laid aside all fear, they are very simple and honest, and exceedingly liberal with all they have; none of them refusing anything he may possess when he is asked for it, but on the contrary inviting us to ask them. They exhibit great love towards all others in preference to themselves; they also give objects of great value for trifles, and content themselves with very little or nothing in return. I however forbade that these trifles and articles of no value (such as pieces of dishes, plates, and glass, keys, and leather straps) should be given to them, although, if they could obtain them, they imagined themselves to be possessed of the most beautiful trinkets in the world.

It even happened that a sailor received for a leather strap as much gold as was worth three golden nobles, and for things of more trifling value offered by our men, especially newly coined blancas, or any gold coins, the Indians would give whatever the seller required; as, for instance, an ounce and a half or two ounces of gold, or thirty or forty pounds of cotton, with which commodity they were already acquainted.

Thus they bartered, like idiots, cotton and gold for fragments of bows, glasses, bottles, and jars; which I forbade as being unjust, and myself gave them many beautiful and acceptable articles which I had brought with me, taking nothing from them in return. I did this in order that I might the more easily conciliate them, that they might be led to become Christians, and be inclined to entertain a regard for the King and Queen, our princes and all Spaniards, and that I might induce them to take an interest in seeking out and collecting and delivering to us such things as they possessed in abundance, but which we greatly needed.

They practise no kind of idolatry, but have a firm belief that all strength and power, and indeed all good things, are in heaven, and that I had descended from thence with these ships and sailors; and under this impression was I received after they had thrown aside their fears. Nor are they slow or stupid, but of very clear understanding; and those men who have crossed to the neighboring islands give an admirable description of everything they observed: but they never saw any people clothed, nor any ships like ours. On my arrival at that sea, I had taken some Indians by force from the first island that I came to, in order that they might learn our language, and communicate to us what they knew respecting the country; which plan succeeded excellently, and was a great advantage to us, for in a short time, either by gestures or signs or by words, we were enabled to understand each other.

These men are still travelling with me, and although they have been with us now a long time they continue to entertain the idea that I have descended from heaven; and on our arrival at any new place they published this, crying out immediately with a loud voice to the other Indians, "Come, come and look upon beings of a celestial race:" upon which both women and men, children and adults, young men and old, when they got rid of the fear they at first entertained, would come out in throngs, crowding the roads to see us, some bringing food, others drink, with astonishing affection and kindness.

Each of these islands has a great number of canoes, built of solid wood, narrow and not unlike our double-banked boats in length and shape, but swifter in their motion: they steer them only by the oar. These canoes are of various sizes, but the greater number are constructed with eighteen banks of oars; and with these they cross to the other islands, which are of countless number, to carry on traffic with the people. I saw some of these canoes that held as many as seventy-eight rowers. In all these islands there is no difference of physiognomy, of manners, or of language, but they all clearly understand each other, — a circumstance very propitious for the realization of what I conceive to be the principal wish of our most serene King; namely, the conversion of these people to the holy faith of Christ, to which indeed, as far as I can judge, they are favorable and well disposed. I said before that I went three hundred and twenty-two miles in a direct line from west to east, along the coast of the island of Juana; judging by which voyage, and the length of the passage, I can assert that it is larger than England and Scotland united; for independent of the said three hundred and twenty-two miles, there are in the western part of the island two provinces which I did not visit: one of these is called by the Indians Anam, and its inhabitants are born with tails.

These provinces extend to a hundred and fifty-three miles in length, as I have learnt from the Indians whom I have brought with me, and who are well acquainted with the country. But the extent of Española is greater than all

Spain from Catalonia to Fontarabia ; which is easily proved, because one of its four sides, which I myself coasted in a direct line, from west to east, measures five hundred and forty miles. This island is to be regarded with especial interest, and not to be slighted ; for although, as I have said, I took possession of all these islands in the name of our invincible King, and the government of them is unreservedly committed to his said Majesty, yet there was one large town in Española of which especially I took possession, situated in a remarkably favorable spot, and in every way convenient for the purposes of gain and commerce.

To this town I gave the name of Navidad del Señor, and ordered a fortress to be built there, which must by this time be completed, in which I left as many men as I thought necessary, with all sorts of arms, and enough provisions for more than a year.

I also left them one caravel, and skilful workmen both in ship-building and other arts, and engaged the favor and friendship of the king of the island in their behalf to a degree that would not be believed ; for these people are so amiable and friendly that even the king took a pride in calling me his brother. But supposing their feelings should become changed, and they should wish to injure those who have remained in the fortress, they could not do so, for they have no arms, they go naked, and are, moreover, too cowardly ; so that those who hold the said fortress can easily keep the whole island in check, without any pressing danger to themselves, provided they do not transgress the directions and regulations which I have given them.

As far as I have learned, every man throughout these islands is united to but one wife, with the exceptions of the kings and princes, who are allowed to have twenty ; the women seem to work more than the men. I could not clearly understand whether the people possess any private property ; for I observed that one man had the charge of distributing various things to the rest, but especially meat and provisions and the like. I did not find, as some of us expected, any cannibals amongst them, but on the contrary men of great deference and kindness. Neither are they black, like the Ethiopians ; their hair is smooth and straight : for they do not dwell where the rays of the sun strike most vividly ; and the sun has intense power there, the distance from the equinoctial line being, it appears, but six and twenty degrees. On the tops of the mountains the cold is very great; but the effect of this upon the Indians is lessened by their being accustomed to the climate, and by their frequently indulging in the use of very hot meats and drinks. Thus, as I have already said, I saw no cannibals, nor did I hear of any, except in a certain island called Charis, which is the second from Española, on the side towards India, where dwell a people who are considered by the neighboring islanders as most ferocious ; and these feed upon human flesh. The same people have many kinds of canoes, in which they cross to all the surrounding islands and rob and plunder wherever they can ; they are not different from the other islanders, except that they wear their hair long, like women, and make use of the bows and javelins of cane, with sharpened spear-points fixed on the thickest end, which I have before described, and therefore they are looked upon as ferocious, and regarded by the other Indians with unbounded fear ; but I think no more of them than of the rest. These are the men who form unions with certain women who dwell alone in the island Matenin, which lies next to Española on the side towards India ; these latter employ themselves in no labor suitable to their own sex, for they use bows and javelins as I have already described their paramours as doing, and for defensive armor have plates of brass, of which metal they possess great abundance.

They assure me that there is another island larger than Española, whose inhabitants have no hair, and which abounds in gold more than any of the rest. I bring with me individuals of this island and of the others that I have seen, who are proofs of the facts which I state. Finally, to compress into few words the entire summary of my voyage and speedy return, and of the advantages derivable therefrom, I promise that with a little assistance afforded me by our most invincible Sovereigns, I will procure them as much gold as they need, as great a quantity of spices, of cotton, and of mastic (which is only found in Chios), and as many men for the service of the navy as their Majesties may require. I promise also rhubarb and other sorts of drugs, which I am persuaded the men whom I have left in the aforesaid fortress have found already, and will continue to find ; for I myself have tarried nowhere longer than I was compelled to do by the winds, except in the city of Navidad, while I provided for the building of the fortress, and took the necessary precautions for the perfect security of the men I left there.

Although all I have related may appear to be wonderful and unheard of, yet the results of my voyage would have been more astonishing if I had had at my disposal such ships as I required. But these great and marvellous results are not to be attributed to any merit of mine, but to the holy Christian faith, and to the piety and religion of our Sovereigns; for that which the unaided intellect of man could not compass, the Spirit of God has granted to human exertions, for God is wont to hear the prayers of his servants who love his precepts even to the performance of apparent impossibilities. Thus it has happened to me in the present instance, who have accomplished a task to which the powers of mortal man had never hitherto attained ; for if there have been those who have anywhere written or spoken of these islands, they have done so with doubts and conjectures, and no one has ever asserted that he has seen them, on which account their writings have been looked upon as little else than fables. Therefore let the King and Queen, our princes and their most happy kingdoms, and all the other provinces of Christendom, render thanks to our Lord and Saviour Jesus Christ, who has granted us so great a victory and such prosperity. Let processions be made, and sacred feasts be held, and the temples be adorned with festive boughs. Let Christ rejoice on earth, as he rejoices in heaven, in the prospect of the salvation of the souls of so many nations hitherto lost. Let us also rejoice, as well on account of the exaltation of our faith as on account of the increase of our temporal prosperity, of which not only Spain, but all Christendom, will be partakers.

Such are the events which I have briefly described. Farewell.

CHRISTOPHER COLUMBUS,
Admiral of the Fleet of the Ocean.

LISBON, the 14th of March.

CHAPTER XI.

OLD HISPANIOLA.

THE old red settle was steamed away from the garden of eternal June one clear morning in March. The sea was as calm as a lake in the hill regions on a June day. The route of the yacht now lay among the palmy Bahamas. The Bahamas, including the raised little rocky sea-beds, number some three thousand islands, and make a procession of islands some five hundred miles long. Only the larger islands are inhabited, and the whole confederacy has a population of about forty thousand people. The islands form a curve from old Hispaniola to the reefs of Florida.

The sun went down blazing on the mirroring sea, and filling the sea and sky with splendor. The crimson melted away like an illusion, and the world went with it. Night came, and the Southern cross flamed through the dusk. Under the stars a long shadow appeared like a cloud, and the pilot pointed to it and said, —

"San Salvador."

The party gathered on the old red settle, and saw the shadow pass, and dreamed of that wonderful night of October nearly four hundred years ago, and of that equally memorable morning when on this island the banner of Aragon and Castile was unfurled, with its cross and double crowns, and the first Te Deums arose into the atmosphere of the New World.

Or was it Watling Island where this most picturesque and dramatic scene was enacted?

AVENUE OF PALMS.

Historians differ.

But in the pink fringes of the morning Watling Island, with its white rocks and lofty palms and cabins, lay in view.

In the forenoon the party again sought the old settle; and Mr. Laurens read the original account by Columbus of the settlement of these islands, then supposed to be a part of the borders of the golden kingdom of Far Cathay.

The old red settle was now near Cape Maysi, and the high mountains of Cuba, that so filled Columbus with admiration and wonder, were in full view. Turquino shone majestic in the sky, nearly eleven thousand feet above the sea.

The yacht passed into what has been called the most beautiful harbor in the world, guarded by an ancient, Moorish-like castle. Santiago de Cuba was now full in view, in appearance a veritable African coast city.

Santiago! What a history it had ere old Plymouth was born! It was founded by Velasquez in 1514. It is the oldest standing city on the continent. It is so ancient and Spanish that the crews of Columbus might recognize it were they to make some ghostly voyage to it to-day.

In 1518 Juan de Grifalva started from here for the conquest of Yucatan.

Hence sailed Cortes.

Hence, in 1528, Narvaez, for the conquest of Florida.

Here, in 1528, came the expedition of De Soto.

Here was the old Spanish capital; here the banners of Spain were raised for the conquest of the two Americas.

The party, during the visit to the city, continued to board on the yacht. One evening after an inland excursion, Charlie Leland asked of Mr. Laurens, —

"Where do we go next?"

" To Cienfuegos."

"And then?"

"To Havana."

"I have been thinking," said Charlie, "that Santiago is not historically the oldest place on the continent—"

"No. Well?"

"But Hispaniola."

SANTIAGO DE CUBA.

"Yes."

"I wish—pardon me if the suggestion seem impertinent—I wish—"

"You wish that the old red settle might go on to Hispaniola? Well, Charlie, so do I. It would make our Zigzag in early America wellnigh perfect."

"I have been thinking of the same thing," said Mrs. Laurens.

"So have I," said Mr. Leland; "but I should not have had the face to make the suggestion."

"Father," said Henry, "may I not tell the captain and pilot that we are to go on to San Domingo? We may never be so near it again."

"Yes," said Mr. Laurens, "you have all voted in the affirmative. We will take the old Puritan settle to Hispaniola, then to Havana, and we will end our historic journey at the tomb of Columbus after a visit to New Spain."

It was a story-telling tour, even among the splendors of the tropics.

The party took on board a new passenger at Santiago, and gave her a place on the back of the old red settle, with a chain around her leg. She was a parrot of most brilliant plumage and accomplishments. Charlie Leland was very fond of birds, and seeing this splendid specimen of tropical plumage for sale, had purchased her. She was said to be a wonderful talker; but as she spoke in Spanish her gifts were not fully appreciated.

Mr. Leland took as great an interest in the gorgeous bird as Charlie. "Let me recite to you a ballad I learned when a boy," he said, as he sat on the old settle beside Polly one evening with the party, enjoying the land breeze that mingled with the air of the sea. "It was written by Campbell."

"'The deep affections of the breast,
That heaven to living things imparts,
Are not exclusively possessed
By human hearts.

"'A parrot from the Spanish main,
Full young, and early caged, came o'er,
With bright wings, to the bleak domain
Of Mulla's shore.

"'To spicy groves, where he had won
His plumage of resplendent hue,
His native fruits and skies and sun,
He bade adieu.

"' For these he changed the smoke of turf,
A heathery land and misty sky,
And turned on rocks and raging surf
    His golden eye.

"' But petted in our climate cold
He lived and chattered many a day,
Until with age, from green and gold
    His wings grew gray.

"' At last when, blind and seeming dumb,
He scolded, laughed, and spoke no more,
A Spanish stranger chanced to come
    To Mulla's shore.

"' He hailed the bird in Spanish speech;
The bird in Spanish speech replied,
Flapped round the cage with joyous screech,
    Dropped down and died.'"

The company related stories of parrots; and one by Mr. Leland was both amusing and pathetic.

A PARROT THAT SPOKE IN MEETING.

"In an old farm-house in Swansea, Mass., there once lived an excellent deacon by the name of Cole. He had a son named Stanton, who followed the sea. On one of his voyages he obtained a parrot which proved such a wonderful talker that he brought it home as a present to his parents. Among its many accomplishments the bird could sing.

"The good deacon used to hold conference and prayer meetings at his house in the long winter evenings. At one of these social meetings Polly chanced to be left in the room. The good people commenced singing, —

"When I can read my title clear,"

to which pious strain Polly seemed to listen with wonder and delight.

"She seemed very thoughtful, as was proper at such a time, and began to talk to herself in a low tone; soliloquizing, I suppose. She kept repeating the word, 'Hey.' She seemed to have something important on her mind, but to hesitate to say it.

" After each brother spoke, she would ruffle her wings and preen her neck, with ' Hey.'

" At last the good deacon himself spoke, greatly to Polly's delight.

"' Hey —'

" Then the deacon's wife spoke, and sung an old hymn; to the latter Polly listened with deep interest.

" She at last seemed to think that it would be a good thing for her to improve her gifts, and not be backward in showing her approval of a cause that made people happy. The hymn ended, and Polly began, —

"' Hey, Betty Martin!'

" Could it be possible? The good deacon looked amazed; the young giggled, and the old found it difficult to retain their wonted soberness. Presently Polly began again, —

"' Hey, Betty Martin,
Tip, toe, tip, toe!
Hey, Betty Martin,
Tip, toe, fine!
Could n't get a husband
To please her, please *her*, —
Could n't get a husband
To please her MIND!

"' There now,' said Polly, 'what do you think of that, Granthur?'

"' Granthur' was Polly's word for 'grandfather,' — a provincialism that she had learned. The good people were greatly shocked.

"' There now, what you think, what you think, what you think?

"' Hey, Betty Martin,
Tip, toe —'

" The deacon put an end to Polly's voluntary by removing the cage at once, the poor bird not being able to comprehend why her well-intended efforts failed to be appreciated.

" The young man, Stanton, who brought home this bird, went again to sea. Eight years passed; and as nothing was heard from him during the latter part of this period, it was supposed that he was dead.

" The old folks in the retired farm-house loved and valued Polly more highly as it became probable that their son would never come back.

" One day Polly, looking out on the lane that led to the dwelling, seemed filled with a sudden delight. She at last flapped her wings and cried, —

"' Stanton! Stanton!'

"The old people started up, went to the window, and saw their son approaching the house.

"'Stanton! Stanton!'

"The old man wept. 'You dear bird,' he said, 'I am glad I kept you, Polly.'

"This parrot lived to be very old, and came to be considered almost as one of the family at last. In her last years she grew comparatively silent, but used to say mournfully, —

VIEW OF CIENFUEGOS.

"'Polly wants to go home, Polly wants to go home.'

"She was brought from the Windward Islands, and her memory seemed to reach back to the past. One day she repeated constantly, 'Polly wants to go home,' and the next morning she was found dead in her cage. The bird seemed almost human; and the day after she spoke in meeting, one of the neighbors said to the old deacon, —

"'Do you think that bird has a soul?'

"The deacon could not answer in regard to *that* bird."

THE STORY OF THE GOLDEN FLOWER.

"You will recall Ovando?" said the dying Queen Isabella.

"Yes," was the promise virtually made by King Ferdinand.

"As a punishment for the slaughter of my poor Indian subjects at Xaraqua, and the execution of Anacaona."

Ovando was the governor of Hispaniola, or New Spain; and Anacaona, or Golden Flower, had been the beloved and admired queen, or cacique, of the native inhabitants of that island which Columbus had thought to be the earthly paradise.

While Columbus himself was almost divine in the nobleness of his heart and character, his great discovery had been taken advantage of by adventurers whose natures approached that of fiends. Among these was Ovando, who had made slaves of the Indians, and slaughtered them at his pleasure.

Anacaona, or the Golden Flower, was the poetess of her race. She wrote the areytos, or ballads, which were sung by her nation on the national assemblies. Her grace and beauty were deemed extraordinary, even by the Spanish colonists.

When the Spanish ships first appeared, the princess, or queen, beheld them with poetic wonder and delight. She went out to visit the adventurers in one of their own boats, dressed in a manner to add the utmost lustre to her charms.

Her escort on this occasion was Don Bartholomew Columbus, the Adelantado. As the two approached the caravel, the cannon thundered across the sea.

The princess had never heard the report of a cannon before. She was overwhelmed with terror, and fell into the arms of the Adelantado.

As the boat drew still nearer, the band poured forth the martial music of Spain. The princess was charmed, or rather enchanted. She became an admirer of the Spaniards, and as long as they observed the rules of ordinary justice remained their true friend.

But the government of the gracious Don Bartholomew was transient. It was followed by the rule of men who cared for nothing but gold, power, and the gratification of their sensual appetites. The Indians were treated with less consideration than would have been due to the beasts.

Golden Flower at first welcomed Ovando. But being utterly false-hearted himself, he believed her to be the same, and determined to destroy her and her race. He caused it to be known that he was about to make her a visit of state.

"When Anacaona," says Irving, "heard of the intended visit, she summoned

288   A ZIGZAG JOURNEY IN THE SUNNY SOUTH.

all her tributary caciques and principal subjects to assemble at her chief town, that they might receive the commander of the Spaniards with becoming homage and distinction. As Ovando, at the head of his little army, approached, she went forth to meet him, according to the custom of her nation, attended by a great train of her most distinguished subjects, male and female, who, as has

THE YOUNG WOMEN WAVING PALM BRANCHES.

been before observed, were noted for superior grace and beauty. They received the Spaniards with their popular areytos, — their national songs; the young women waving palm branches, and dancing before them, in the way that had so much charmed the followers of the Adelantado on his first visit to the province.

Anacaona treated the governor with that natural graciousness and dignity for which she was celebrated. She gave him the largest house in the place for his residence, and his people were quartered in the houses adjoining. For several days the Spaniards were entertained with all the natural luxuries that the province afforded. National songs and dances and games were performed for their amusement, and there was every outward demonstration of the same hospitality, the same amity, that Anacaona had uniformly shown to white men.

"A joust was appointed to take place of a Sunday after dinner, in the public square before the house where Ovando was quartered. The cavalry and foot-soldiers had their secret instructions. The former were to parade, not merely with reeds or blunted tilting-lances, but with weapons of a more deadly character. The foot-soldiers were to come apparently as mere spectators, but likewise armed and ready for action at a concerted signal.

"At the appointed time the square was crowded with the Indians, waiting to see this military spectacle. The caciques were assembled in the house of Ovando, which looked upon the square. None were armed; an unreserved confidence prevailed among them, totally incompatible with the dark treachery of which they were accused. To prevent all suspicion, and take off all appearance of sinister design, Ovando, after dinner, was playing at quoits with some of his principal officers, when, the cavalry having arrived in the square, the caciques begged the governor to order the joust to commence. Anacaona, and her beautiful daughter, Higuenamota, with several of her female attendants, were present and joined in the request.

"Ovando left his game and came forward to a conspicuous place. When he saw that everything was disposed according to his orders, he gave the fatal signal. Some say it was by taking hold of a piece of gold which was suspended about his neck; others by laying his hand on the cross of Alcantara, which was embroidered on his habit. A trumpet was immediately sounded. The house in which Anacaona and all the principal caciques were assembled was surrounded by soldiery, commanded by Diego Velasquez and Rodrigo Mexiatrillo, and no one was permitted to escape. They entered, and seizing upon the caciques bound them to the posts which supported the roof. Anacaona was led forth a prisoner. The unhappy caciques were then put to horrible tortures, until some of them, in the extremity of anguish, were made to accuse their queen and themselves of the plot with which they were charged. When this cruel mockery of judicial form had been executed, instead of preserving them for after-examination, fire was set to the house, and all the caciques perished miserably in the flames."

The Golden Flower was loaded with chains and carried to San Domingo. Here she was hanged by Ovando in the presence of the very people whom her kindness and power had long protected and befriended. Her subjects were hunted down and murdered without mercy.

Queen Isabella, when dying, was troubled in conscience over the fate of this amiable queen. "You will recall Ovando?" she said.

It was the last touch of that womanly sympathy that makes her character shaft-like for all time.

CHAPTER XII.

COLUMBUS'S OWN STORIES OF NEW SPAIN.

ANTO DOMINGO — old Hispaniola, or Isabella — is usually reached by the Clyde Line steamers, or by those of the Atlas Line Fleet. The latter fleet, according to that company's statement, "comprises twelve iron steamships, built by the most celebrated ship-builders on the Clyde, in Scotland, to the highest class of English Lloyds. They are constructed in water-tight compartments, to insure safety, and are fitted with spacious and luxurious passenger accommodation, the saloons and staterooms being in the centre of the ship and above the main deck, thus insuring the minimum of motion." Their principal port is Jamaica, although they visit nearly all of the Windward Islands. The managers further state in their advertisement: "The company, since its formation twelve years ago, has not lost a ship or a passenger, and being largely its own insurers is the best guarantee that every care will be taken to insure the safe navigation of its vessels."

The following is a present list of the company's fleet: —

Ship.	Tons.	Ship.	Tons.
Albano	2,700	Andes	2,000
Alene	2,200	Alvena	1,800
Athos	2,200	Antillas	1,600
Alvo	2,200	Claribel	1,500
Ailsa	2,200	Arden	600
Alpes	2,000	Arran	500

SCENE IN SAN DOMINGO.

The following are two specimens of this company's excursion routes and prices,— routes which take one to the very scenes of the splendid discoveries of Columbus, which he deemed to be the earthly paradise : —

ROUTE A. — New York to Kingston, thence by branch steamer " Arden " around the island, making the complete circuit in seven days. After visiting thirteen seaports and allowing a good opportunity of seeing all places of interest, sufficient stay is made in Kingston for jaunts to the interior towns, mountains, etc., previous to embarking for New York. This tour recommends itself to those limited for time, but desiring a sea voyage, as the period between the departure and return to New York is only about twenty-four days. Cost of travelling, $100.

ROUTE E. — New York to Hayti, visiting the seven principal seaports, and remaining sufficiently long to see much of the interior; returning from Hayti *via* Jamaica. This tour occupies five weeks. Cost of travelling, about $100.

Columbus thought that Hispaniola was the Ophir of Solomon.

A paradise it seemed, a garden of the golden ocean, fit for the Great Khan. The glimmering domes of the mountains arose in an atmosphere of living light, like the fabled palaces of the gods. Everywhere was brightness; everywhere Nature was colossal and prodigal.

San Domingo is the oldest place of European origin in America. It is a walled town of some ten thousand inhabitants, and was founded by Columbus, and settled in 1494 by Bartholomew Columbus, the brother of Columbus.

1494! Almost four hundred years ago!

The Cathedral of San Domingo, though said to be modelled after a church in Rome, is unlike any other in the world. It is irregular, solemn, and imposing. Its irregularity is very picturesque. It was begun in 1512, and was some thirty years in building. Here the remains of Columbus and his brother Bartholomew rested for two hundred and fifty years.

The town was first named New Isabella (Nueva Isabella). The ruins of the old house and castle of Diego Columbus remain; all else seems to have vanished from that splendid Spain which was the dream of the old conquerors, knights, and cavaliers.

Tales of Columbus, by Columbus, occupied much of the time of the voyage between Santiago de Cuba and the old capital of New Spain, where Ferdinand and Isabella established their vice-regal court.

Columbus, as related in his narrative that we have given, left a small colony at Hispaniola on his first voyage, in a small fortress that he had built. This fortress, on account of his having been rescued from shipwreck on Christmas Day, he called Navidad (the Nativity). On returning to Hispaniola, he expected to be welcomed by his colony. One of his scribe's accounts of the fate of the colony he had left in the fortress of the Nativity is very graphic. A part of it is as follows: —

STORY OF THE SECOND VOYAGE OF COLUMBUS.

The island [Hispaniola or Santo Domingo], being large, is divided into provinces; the part which we first touched at, is called Hayti; another province adjoining it, they call Xamana; and the next province is named Bohio, where we now are. These provinces are again subdivided, for they are of great extent. Those who have seen the length of its coast state that it is two hundred leagues long, and I myself should judge it not to be less than a hundred and fifty leagues; as to its breadth, nothing is hitherto known: it is now forty days since a caravel left us with the view of circumnavigating it, and is not yet returned.

The country is very remarkable, and contains a vast number of large rivers, and extensive chains of mountains, with broad open valleys; and the mountains are very high. It does not appear that the grass is ever cut throughout the year. I do not think they have any winter in this part; for near Navidad (at Christmas) were found many bird's-nests, some containing the young birds, and others containing eggs. No four-footed animal has ever been seen in this or any of the other islands, except some dogs of various colors, as in our own country, but in shape like large house-dogs; and also some little animals, in color, size, and fur like a rabbit, with long tails, and feet like those of a rat. These animals climb up the trees; and many who have tasted them say they are very good to eat. There are not any wild beasts. There are great numbers of small snakes, and some lizards, but not many; for the Indians consider them as great a luxury as we do pheasants; they are of the same size as ours, but different in shape. In a small adjacent island (close by a harbor called Monte Cristo, where we stayed several days), our men saw an enormous kind of lizard, which they said was as large round as a calf, with a tail as long as a lance, which they often went out to kill; but bulky as it was, it got into the sea, so that they could not catch it. There are, both in this and the other islands, an infinite number of birds like those in our own country, and many others such as we had never seen. No kind of domestic fowl has been seen here, with the exception of some ducks in the houses in Zuruquia; these ducks were larger than those of Spain, though smaller than geese, — very pretty, with tufts on their heads, most of them as white as snow, but some black.

We ran along the coast of this island nearly a hundred leagues, concluding that within this range we should find the spot where the Admiral had left some of his men, and which we supposed to be about the middle of the coast. As we passed by the province called Xamana, we sent on shore one of the Indians, who had been taken in the previous voyage, clothed, and carrying some trifles, which the Admiral had ordered to be given to him. On that day died one of our sailors, a Biscayan, who had been wounded in the affray with the Caribbees, when they were captured, as I have already described, through their want of caution. As we were proceeding along the coast, an opportunity was afforded for a boat to go on shore to bury him, the boat being accompanied by two caravels to protect it. When they reached the shore, a great number of Indians came out to the boat, some of them wearing necklaces and earrings of gold, and expressed a wish to accompany the Spaniards to the ships; but our men refused to take them, because they had not received permission from the Admiral. When the Indians found that they would not take them, two of them got into a small canoe, and went up to one of the caravels that had put in to shore; they were received on board with great kindness, and taken to the Admiral's ship, where, through the medium of an interpreter, they related that a certain king had sent them to ascertain who we were, and to invite us to land, adding that they had plenty of gold, and also of provisions, to which we should be welcome. The Admiral desired that shirts and caps and other trifles should be given to each of them, and said that as he was going to the place where Guacamari dwelt, he would not stop there, but that on a future day he should have the opportunity of seeing him ; and with that they departed.

We continued our route till we came to a harbor called Monte Cristo, where we remained two days, in order to observe the position of the land ; for the Admiral had an objection to the spot where his men had been left with the view of forming a station. We went on shore, therefore, to survey the formation of the land. There was a large river of excellent water close by, but the ground was inundated, and very ill-calculated for habitation. As we went on making our observations on the river and the land, some of our men found two dead bodies by the river's side, — one with a rope round his neck, and the other with one round his foot. This was on the first day of our landing.

On the following day they found two other corpses farther on, and one of these was observed to have a great quantity of beard; this was regarded as a very suspicious circumstance by many of our people, because, as I have already said, all the Indians are beardless. This harbor is twelve leagues from the place where the Spaniards had been left under the protection of Guacamari, the king of that province, whom I suppose to be one of the chief men of the island. After two days we set sail for that spot ; but as it was late when we arrived there, and there were some shoals where the Admiral's ship had been lost, we did not venture to put in close to the shore, but remained that night at a little less than a league from the coast, waiting until the morning, when we might enter securely.

On that evening a canoe containing five or six Indians came out at a considerable distance from where we were, and approached us with great celerity. The Admiral, believing that he insured our safety by keeping the sails set, would not wait for them ; they, however, perseveringly rowed up to us within gun-shot, and then stopped to look at us; but when they saw that we did not wait for them, they put back and went away. After we had anchored that night at the spot in question, the admiral ordered two guns to be fired, to see if the Spaniards, who had remained with Guacamari, would fire in return, for they also had guns with them ; but when we received no reply, and could not perceive any fires, nor the slightest symptom of habitations on the spot, the spirits of our people became much depressed, and they began to entertain the suspicion which the circumstances were naturally calculated to excite.

While all were in this desponding mood, and when four or five hours of the night had passed away, the same canoe which we had seen in the evening came up, and the Indians with a loud voice addressed the captain of the caravel which they first approached, inquiring for the Admiral ; they were conducted to the

Admiral's vessel, but would not go on board till he had spoken to them and they had asked for a light, in order to assure themselves that it was he who conversed with them. One of them was a cousin of Guacamari, who had been sent by him once before ; it appeared that after they had turned back the previous evening, they had been charged by Guacamari with two marks of gold as a present, — one for the Admiral, the other for a captain who had accompanied him on the former voyage. They remained on board for three hours, talking with the Admiral in the presence of all of us, he showing much pleasure in their conversation, and inquiring respecting the welfare of the Spaniards whom he had left behind. Guacamari's cousin replied that those who remained were all well, but that some of them had died of disease, and others had been killed in quarrels that had arisen amongst them ; he said also that the province had been invaded by two kings named Caonabo and Mayreni, who had burned the habitations of the people ; and that Guacamari was at some distance, lying ill of a wound in his leg, which was the occasion of his not appearing, but that he would come on the next day.

The Indians then departed, saying they would return on the following day with the said Guacamari, and left us consoled for that night. On the morning of the next day, we were expecting that Guacamari would come ; and in the mean time some of our men landed by command of the Admiral, and went to the spot where the Spaniards had formerly been. They found the building which they had inhabited, and which they had in some degree fortified with a palisade, burnt, and levelled with the ground ; they found also some rags and stuffs which the Indians had brought to throw upon the house. They observed, too, that the Indians who were seen near the spot looked very shy, and dared not approach, but, on the contrary, fled from them. This appeared strange to us, for the Admiral had told us that in the former voyage, when he arrived at this place, so many came in canoes to see us that there was no keeping them off ; and as we now saw that they were suspicious of us, it gave us a very unfavorable impression. We threw trifles, such as buttons and beads, towards them, in order to conciliate them ; but only four — a relation of Guacamari's, and three others — took courage to enter the boat, and were rowed on board. When they were asked concerning the Spaniards, they replied that all of them were dead. We had been told this already by one of the Indians whom we had brought from Spain, and who had conversed with the two Indians that on the former occasion came on board with their canoe, but we had not believed it. Guacamari's kinsman was asked who had killed them. He replied that Caonabo and King Mayreni had made an attack upon them, and burnt the buildings on the spot ; that many were wounded in the affray, and among them Guacamari, who had received a wound in his thigh, and had retired to some distance. He also stated that he wished to go and fetch him; upon which some trifles were given to him, and he took his departure for the place of Guacamari's abode. All that day we remained in expectation of them; and when we saw that they did not come, many suspected that the Indians who had been on board the night before had been drowned, for they had had wine given them two or three times, and they had come in a small canoe that might be easily upset.

The next morning the Admiral went on shore, taking some of us with him. We went to the spot where the settlement had been, and found it utterly destroyed by fire, and the clothes of the Spaniards lying about upon the grass, but on that occasion we saw no dead body. There were many different opinions amongst us,— some suspecting that Guacamari himself was concerned in the betrayal and death of the Christians; others thought not, because his own residence was burnt: so that it remained a very doubtful question.

COLUMBUS'S OWN STORY OF THE EARTHLY PARADISE.

I do not find, nor have ever found, any account by the Romans or Greeks which fixes in a positive manner the site of the terrestrial paradise, neither have I seen it given in any *mappe-monde*, laid down from authentic sources. Some placed it in Ethiopia, at the sources of the Nile; but others, traversing all these countries, found neither the temperature nor the altitude of the sun correspond with their ideas respecting it; nor did it appear that the overwhelming waters of the deluge had been there. Some pagans pretended to adduce arguments to establish that it was in the Fortunate Islands, now called the Canaries, etc.

St. Isidore, Bede, Strabo, and the master of scholastic history, with St. Ambrose, and Scotus, and all the learned theologians, agree that the earthly paradise is in the East, etc.

I have already described my ideas concerning this hemisphere and its form; and I have no doubt that if I could pass below the equinoctial line, after reaching the highest point of which I have spoken, I should find a much milder temperature, and a variation in the stars and in the water: not that I suppose that elevated point to be navigable, nor even that there is water there; indeed, I believe it is impossible to ascend thither, because I am convinced that it is the spot of the earthly paradise, whither no one can go but by God's permission; but this land which your Highnesses have now sent me to explore is very

EXPLORING THE ISLANDS.

extensive, and I think there are many other countries in the south, of which the world has never had any knowledge.

I do not suppose that the earthly paradise is in the form of a rugged mountain, as the descriptions of it have made it appear, but that it is on the summit of the spot which I have described as being in the form of the stalk of a pear. The approach to it from a distance must be by a constant and gradual ascent ; but I believe that, as I have already said, no one could ever reach the top. I think, also, that the water I have described may proceed from it, though it be far off, and that, stopping at the place which I have just left, it forms this lake. There are great indications of this being the terrestrial paradise, for its site coincides with the opinion of the holy and wise theologians whom I have mentioned ; and moreover, the other evidences agree with the supposition, for I have never either read or heard of fresh water coming in so large a quantity in close conjunction with the water of the sea. The idea is also corroborated by the blandness of the temperature ; and if the water of which I speak does not proceed from the earthly paradise, it appears to be still more marvellous, for I do not believe that there is any river in the world so large or so deep.

When I left the Dragon's Mouth, which is the northernmost of the two straits which I have described, and which I so named on the day of our Lady of August, I found that the sea ran so strongly to the westward, that between the hour of Mass, when I weighed anchor, and the hour of complines, I made sixty-five leagues, of four miles each ; and not only was the wind not violent, but on the contrary very gentle, which confirmed me in the conclusion that in sailing southward there is a continuous ascent, while there is a corresponding descent towards the north.

I hold it for certain, that the waters of the sea move from east to west with the sky, and that in passing this track they hold a more rapid course, and have thus carried away large tracts of land, and that from hence has resulted this great number of islands. Indeed, these islands themselves afford an additional proof of it; for all of them, without exception, run lengthwise from west to east, and from the northwest to the southeast, which is in a directly contrary direction to the said winds. Furthermore, that these islands should possess the most costly productions is to be accounted for by the mild temperature, which comes to them from heaven, since these are the most elevated parts of the world. It is true that in some parts the waters do not appear to take this course ; but this occurs in certain spots where they are obstructed by land, and hence they appear to take different directions. Pliny writes that the sea and land together form a sphere, but that the ocean forms the greatest mass, and lies uppermost, while the earth is below and supports the ocean, and that the two afford a mutual support to each other, as the kernel of a nut is confined by its shell. The master of scholastic history, in commenting upon Genesis, says that the waters are not very extensive, and that although when they were first created they covered the earth, they were yet vaporous like a cloud, and that afterwards they became condensed, and occupied but small space; and in this notion Nicolas de Lira agrees. Aristotle says that the world is small, and the water very limited in extent, and that it is easy to pass from Spain to the Indies; and this is confirmed by Avenruyz, and by the Cardinal Pedro de Aliaco, who, in supporting this opinion, shows that it agrees with that of Seneca, and says that Aristotle had been enabled to gain information respecting the world by means of Alexander the Great, and Seneca by means of Nero, and Pliny through the Romans; all of them having expended large sums of money, and employed a vast number of people, in diligent inquiry concerning the secrets of the world, and in spreading abroad the knowledge thus obtained. The said Cardinal allows to these writers greater authority than to Ptolemy, and other Greeks and Arabs; and in confirmation of their opinion concerning the small quantity of water on the surface of the globe, and the limited amount of land covered by that water, in comparison of what had been related on the authority of Ptolemy and his disciples, he finds a passage in the third book of Esdras, where that sacred writer says that of seven parts of the world six are discovered, and the other is covered with water. The authority of the third and fourth books of Esdras is also confirmed by holy persons, such as St. Augustine, and St. Ambrose in his "Exameron," where he says, " Here my son Jesus shall first come, and here my son Christ shall die !" These holy men say that Esdras was a prophet as well as Zacharias, the father of St. John, and El Braso Simon, — authorities which are also quoted by Francis de Mairones. With respect to the dryness of the land, experience has shown that it is greater than is commonly believed; and this is no wonder, for the further one goes the more one learns. I now return to my subject of the land of Gracia, and of the river and lake found there, which latter might more properly be called a sea; for a lake is but a small expanse of water, which, when it becomes great, deserves the name of a sea, just as we speak of the Sea of Galilee and the Dead Sea; and I think that if the river mentioned does not proceed from the terrestrial paradise, it comes from an immense tract of land situated in the south, of which no knowledge has been hitherto obtained. But the more I reason on the subject, the more satisfied I become that the terrestrial paradise is situated in the spot I have described; and I ground my opinion upon the arguments and authorities already quoted. May it please the Lord to grant your Highnesses a long life, and health and peace to follow out so noble an investigation; in which I think our Lord will receive great service, Spain

SETTLING THE NEW LAND.

considerable increase of its greatness, and all Christians much consolation and pleasure, because by this means the name of our Lord will be published abroad.

In all the countries visited by your Highnesses' ships, I have caused a high cross to be fixed upon every headland, and have proclaimed to every nation that I have discovered, the lofty estate of your Highnesses, and of your court in Spain. I also tell them all I can respecting our holy faith and of the belief in the Holy Mother Church, which has its members in all the world ; and I speak to them also of the courtesy and nobleness of all Christians, and of the faith they have in the Holy Trinity. May it please the Lord to forgive those who have calumniated and still calumniate this excellent enterprise, and oppose and have opposed its advancement, without considering how much glory and greatness will accrue from it to your Highnesses throughout all the world. They cannot state anything in disparagement of it except its expense, and that I have not immediately sent back the ships loaded with gold. They speak this without considering the shortness of the time, and how many difficulties there are to contend with ; and that every year there are individuals who singly earn by their deserts out of your Majesties' own household, more revenue than would cover the whole of this expense. Nor do they remember that the princes of Spain have never gained possession of any land out of their own country, until now that your Highnesses have become the masters of another world, where our Holy Faith may become so much increased, and whence such stores of wealth may be derived ; for although we have not sent home ships laden with gold, we have nevertheless sent satisfactory samples, both of gold and of other valuable commodities, by which it may be judged that in a short time large profit may be derived. Neither do they take into consideration the noble spirit of the princes of Portugal, who so long ago carried into execution the exploration of Guinea, and still follow it up along the coast of Africa, in which one half of the population of the country has been employed, and yet the king is more determined on the enterprise than ever. The Lord grant all that I have said, and lead them to think deeply upon what I have written ; which is not the thousandth part of what might be written of the deeds of princes who have set their minds upon gaining knowledge, and upon obtaining territory and keeping it.

CHAPTER XIII.

AT THE TOMB OF COLON.—THE MISSISSIPPI.

HAT was a memorable day when, in January, 1795, the ship "San Lorenzo" moved majestically into the harbor of Havana, under the flag of Spain. The Spanish war-vessels were gay with flags. The Spanish colors on the shore were mingled with the green crowns of the palms. The wharves were thronged with people, and the squares with soldiers.

A felucca, followed by a long pageant of boats, swept out to the ship, shadowed with mourning banners, and the oars beating time to the muffled drums. A body was lowered from the ship to the felucca, or the dust of what had been a body. At the wharf the body was carried amid files of soldiers to a triumphal funeral-car, and was escorted in the greatest pomp to the cathedral. Here masses were said, and all that remained of the body of that great admiral Christopher Columbus was assigned a place of eternal rest.

Justice was done to the memory of that great man on that day, after a delay of nearly three hundred years.

As Columbus himself was a pilgrim from land to land in his life, his body was destined to make a like pilgrimage after the inspired soul that animated it had gone to its new discoveries in immaterial realms. It first found a temporary rest in Spain; then it was borne over the sea to the grand cathedral at Hispaniola (San Domingo).

At the termination of the war between France and Spain in 1795, the Spanish possessions in Hispaniola were ceded to France by treaty; but Spain asked for the body of her most illustrious son, through her naval commanders, and thus it was conveyed to Cuba.

The party made the last historic visit of their interesting tour to the faded old cathedral and the simple vault of Columbus.

CATHEDRAL OF HAVANA.

"There is the dust of one who was haunted by ideals," said Mr. Leland. "Some men are so haunted; their mission and destiny are the laws of their gravitation; they are impelled by a power mightier than they can comprehend, and they find no rest till they lie down in the silence of the grave. I will talk with you on this subject on our homeward voyage."

Out of the dusky church into the bright air again. On the same evening our tourists sailed away; the Moorish castle fading in the tropic hazes of a vermilion sunset.

The day after their departure was the Sabbath, — a Sabbath on the tropic sea. The old settle was used for a Sabbath service; and after singing and Scripture reading, Mr. Leland was asked to regard the other members of the party as a class, and to address them as he had sometimes addressed Bible schools. His topic was, —

HAUNTED BY IDEALS.

There is a poem by Keats, that is little read, that beautifully presents an allegory of life. It is founded upon the Greek myth of the fair-faced shepherd lad Endymion, who used to sleep on Mount Latmos, and who became loved of Diana. As the goddess passed nightly over the mountains in her chariot, she visited him in his dreams and inspired him, and the inspiration at last made him immortal.

The young genius of Keats in affluent imagery gives us the legend, not from the Greek point of view, but from that of the young shepherd.

Endymion one night beholds in his dreams a face of transcendent loveliness. He does not associate it with the goddess of night. Diana, when he awakes, has passed on, and is dim in the morning splendor; but he feels that he has had a vision of the face of an immortal, and the vision leaves the new inspiration in his soul. Will that face ever appear again? The question haunts him in his pastoral pursuits; he is sad and pale at the great Pan-festivals, and his life has become a quest for the unknown face that came to him in his sleep. At length the same beautiful face appears to him again; this time reflected in a fountain. He now knows that his inspiration is a reality, — that the form that has sublimated his thoughts is divine. The vision becomes fixed in his soul, and the quest goes on.. The gods love him because he has placed his affections upon an immortal. They prophesy good of him, and the goddess of beauty is made to say, —

"Endymion, one day shalt thou be blessed."

The quest is long; but the face of his young dream, the reflection in the fountain, is at last revealed to him in the form of a maiden, and the inspiration

A NEGRO FAMILY.

that he has followed lifts his thoughts into the grottos and courts of the divinities. The world loses its charm for him, —

> "What merest whim
> Seems all this poor endeavor after fame,
> To one who keeps within his steadfast aim
> A love immortal!"

The maiden changes at last into a goddess, and leads him away into the regions of eternal youth. He possessed at last his ideal.

Inspiration is the gift of heaven to the young. The world itself received it in childhood, when poets and prophets, the builders of palaces and temples, beheld the chariot of an angel or goddess in every drifting cloud. Every youth is conscious of the impulses to worthy action, as of the visit of an unknown power to him in his receptive moments, when the soul rises superior to itself. He is haunted by ideals of a better life. The chariot of Selene passes over him. The goddess of beauty prophesies, —

> "Endymion, one day shalt thou be blessed."

Every youth has his vision of the burning bush, like Moses; or of the celestial ladder, like Jacob; or of God himself, like Isaiah in the temple. Attic bees come to him as to the cradle of Pindar. The Argo was the dream of young heroes; the blossoming marbles of Greek sculpture were the conceptions of young minds. We are told that the world was thrice conquered by the genius of youth. The great benefactors of mankind have, like Endymion, been the followers of a face of some dream.

If he listens to his best inspirations, the youth will be led into the quest for the object that has inspired him, and he will meet with his divinity. The grand Hebrew poet voiced this truth more powerfully than it appears in the glowing metaphors of the Greek lyrist or of Keats: "Commit thy way unto the Lord: trust also in him, and he will bring it to pass." Count Zinzendorf dreamed of God, and he formed the Order of the Grain of Mustard Seed among his young companions before there dawned upon him the plan of the Moravian Missions that were to offer the Gospel to the outcast tribes of the world. His first inspiration was but a face in a dream.

These inspirations of youth assume a thousand forms, and come in as many different ways; but the face of a divinity is at last recognized in all. His ideals, if he attain them, will be found divine.

Let me illustrate.

It is night on the calm, moonlit ocean. The boy Nelson paces the deck of the ship under the stars. The flag of England drifts on the night wind. The boy's heart begins to glow and burn. The face of the future comes into his dream. "I will be a hero," he suddenly exclaims. It was a luminous moment. In it were born the victories of the Nile and Trafalgar. Amid the shouts of victory that fell upon his dying ears, he beheld that face again.

"Ultima Thule!" The words sound dull to your ears! It is inspiration that makes words burn and glow and live; that is the soul of words.

A young Genoese reads Seneca. The words "Ultima Thule" arrest his thoughts and bring to him the vision of a face. They haunt him day and night; they prophesy. They make his feet restless. They lead him to the Court of Spain and across unknown waters into the sunset light; he there finds his inspiring divinity to be a new world, and he plants the cross of Aragon and Castile among the palms of the Caribbean. The face of his young dream is America. "Ultima Thule!" Did you ever see the young dream of Columbus portrayed in marble in the Boston Art Museum? That dream was the inspiration of destiny. "Ultima Thule! Ultima Thule!"

The Lelands desired to return by way of the Mississippi, and to stop at New Orleans. So the old red settle was steamed, not back to St. Augustine, but towards the vast lagoons of that mysterious region where the "Father of Waters" unites with the Gulf.

The last story that was related upon it recalled the vanished French Empire of the West.

"The Spanish flag came and vanished," said Mr. Laurens, "and the Fleur-de-lis came and went. Then came the Stars and Stripes; and its appearance caused a new empire to be planted on the old, and made New Orleans the Queen City of the whole Southern territory of North America."

He then related the dramatic —

STORY OF LA SALLE.

Canada was the gateway of the exploration of the Southwest. The Mississippi Valley, once the home of a mysterious race, was opened to the wondering eyes of the European world by the heroic French Canadian pioneers. These

JESUIT MISSION.

men were pioneers of the Church as well as of political empire. They hung the lilies of France upon the cross, and bore it down the long river-ways into the wilderness. They went to the Hurons at Michilimacinac, and thence began their missionary journeys and triumphal marches. The French missionaries differed in spirit and method from the English. After proclaiming the gospel of peace they maintained it, and did not, like the English, fall upon the children of the forest with the sword. The French governor, Talon, was a man of genius and enterprise. He heard of the "Great River." He sent two missionaries, Marquette and Joliet, of immortal memory, to seek for it. He provided them with essential outfits, and anxiously awaited the results. From the outposts of the French settlements the two missionaries launched their canoes on the waters of the Wisconsin, and drifted through a region of picturesque solitude for seven days. Then they entered a new river, wide and glorious, — leading whither? It was June 17, now known as Mississippi Day. They fell upon their knees. Their joy was such as rarely comes into the experience of life.

Old men came forth to meet them, carrying pipes of peace.

"Who are you?" asked the explorers.

"We are Illinois."

Illinois! It was the first time, perhaps, that the word had been spoken in civilized ears. The 17th of June, the same date as Bunker Hill Day, deserves recognition as a local holiday in the Northwest.

The voyage of the Mississippi sent a thrill of joy and wonder through New France. Where were the borders of the land of which Quebec had become the capital?

Count Frontenac was appointed governor of New France. He came to Quebec at the time that the news of the expedition to the great river was exciting the province. He was a brilliant and ambitious man. The great river filled his fancy with dreams and schemes. Through what golden empire might it flow? What wonders might it reveal?

Marquette died. The work he had begun was taken up by another, — the Cavalier de la Salle, whose exploits are well known.

La Salle was born at Rouen, and had come to Canada about 1667. He believed that through the unexplored territories of New France might be found a way to China. He heard of the great river. Did it flow to China or the Gulf of Mexico? He became possessed of a restless desire to see the new water-course, and to follow it to the sea. He told his dreams to the brilliant Frontenac. There was an Indian trading-post where Kingston now stands. It was fortified by the French and named Fort Frontenac. La Salle was intrusted with the command of this fort. Frontenac had lost his fortune, and he wished for money and glory. His ambitions made enemies. Among these was the Abbé Fénelon, brother to the famous archbishop of French history.

It was Easter, 1674. The Abbé Fénelon was announced to preach the sermon of the festival in the church of the Hôtel Dieu in Montreal. Among the priests present was a brother of La Salle. Fénelon mounted the pulpit. He preached a sermon on the duties of the magistrates of the King. By picturing what a magistrate should be he purposely illustrated what Count Frontenac was not, and a thrill of excitement passed through the assembly. At a certain point of the sermon a tall form rose near the door. The eyes of the congregation were turned upon him. The lordly man said nothing, but he expressed in his face and by certain motions his disapproval of the words of the priest.

He was the Cavalier de la Salle.

The act was the turning-point of his life.

That frown was the means of winning the friendship of Frontenac, and the friendship of Frontenac gave him letters to the Court of France, and the Court of France placed him in command of an expedition that has thrilled time with its history. The expedition was successful. Its results are well known to history and to fame. La Salle descended the valley of the Mississippi, and followed the great river to the sea.

That was another glorious day when, on the 9th of April, 1682, La Salle proclaimed Louis XIV. the Sovereign of the West.

A few days before, he had found that the fresh water of the river was turning into brine, and the land breeze into the salt air of the sea. Soon, over the land marshes, appeared the broad waters of the Gulf of Mexico. He had solved the great question; he must celebrate the event.

A short distance above the mouth of the river, he placed a column. He erected upon it the arms of France. The Frenchmen then chanted the Te Deum.

There were volleys of musketry, and the loud voice of the Cavalier rung out on the spring air: —

"In the name of the most high, mighty, invincible, and glorious Prince Louis the Great, by the grace of God, King of France and Navarre, Fourteenth by name, in this 9th day of April, 1682, in virtue of the commission of his Majesty, which I hold in my hand, have taken and do now take possession of this country of Louisiana!"

There were shouts of "Vive le Roi!" La Salle confirmed his proclamation, bounding the new empire. Muskets were fired. Then the cross was planted

MURDER OF LA SALLE.

beside the column. But even La Salle himself did not then know what a stupendous accession the Crown of France had received. He returned to France. There he organized an expedition for the settlement of Louisiana. The expedition missed the mouth of the Mississippi. The Cavalier was killed by one of his own followers in Texas while he was seeking a way to the lost river and to the North. Few events of history are more dramatic or sad ; few more heroic.

La Salle died, but his dreams were fulfilled. The Mississippi Valley was colonized by France. Louisiana became a part of New France.

What a possession the French Crown now owned in the West ! The Atlantic, the Pacific, the Gulf of Mexico, the St. Lawrence, the Mississippi, were a part of its boundaries.

It vanished. The empire was poetic in its decline. The weakness of a corrupt court, and its vice-regal ambitions and splendors brought about its downfall.

Wolfe planted the Red Cross of England at Quebec, and the Northern Empire of France was gone. Its loss after many years caused the relinquishment of the Southern Empire. Napoleon sold Louisiana to the United States. The " Fleur-de-lis" became a ghost. A memory is all that remains of the splendid achievements of the French pioneers on the St. Lawrence and the Mississippi.

"This 9th of April, 1682," first celebrated by La Salle, is a fitting event for yearly celebration, and a most delightful day for a Southern and Southwestern holiday. It has a history that fills the poetic imagination. In fact, the two Mississippi days, June 17 and April 9, both bring to view such grand events that they might well be given places among the festivals of our national calendar. No heroes of any age ever accomplished more for mankind than the missionary pioneers of New France, or laid the foundation of more inspiring historical events and achievements.

New Orleans rose in view, — first a city of church-spires in the air; then a city of ships on calm waters; then the American-French city, with the Stars and Stripes drifting on the breezes of the Gulf, in the eternal sunshine. Here, in the largest building in the world, the Exposition Building, the Northern and Southern families pass their last day together.

They had visited together the scenes and studied the associations of the earliest settlements of America.

"I am convinced of one thing," said Mr. Leland, as the two families parted, "and this journey that we have made is the source of the conviction; and that is, that the inspiration of Columbus in its results was one of the greatest events in the history of the world."

"I hope that his work will be made more clearly to appear in the celebrations of 1892," said Mr. Leland. "Nothing to me more clearly shows the finger of God in history."

"I shall take the old red settle back to St. Augustine," said Henry, "as a souvenir of our journey."

The old red settle stands upon the veranda of the house of the Laurenses in St. Augustine. On its back is cut with a penknife the titles of the stories which were told during the journey, and which were thus recorded by Henry and Charlie as mementos of the Northern and Southern visits to the places of the old voyagers and pioneers.

www.ingramcontent.com/pod-product-compliance
Lightning Source LLC
Chambersburg PA
CBHW022047230426
43672CB00008B/1096